INTRODUCTION
TO
POLITICS

INTRODUCTION TO POLITICS

Leon Hurwitz

Nelson-Hall *nh* Chicago

Library of Congress Cataloging in Publication Data

Hurwitz, Leon.
    introduction to politics

  Bibliography: p.
  Includes index.
  1. Political science. I. Title.
JA66.H797   320   79-11293
ISBN 0-88229-321-4

Manufactured in the United States of America

10   9   8   7   6   5   4   3   2   1

Contents

List of Tables

List of Figures

*To my parents, Saul and Pauline Hurwitz,
with love and affection.*

Acknowledgments

I would like to thank several people who gave me assistance during the writing of this book. Most important, I am indebted to the countless students who graciously registered for my class "Introduction to Politics" at Cleveland State University. These students provided a sounding board, and much of the material contained in this book directly relates to their perceptive and penetrating questions. My colleagues in the Department of Political Science, The Cleveland State University, provided an atmosphere conducive to writing and the department itself provided some financial assistance. For permission to reprint charts that illustrate the text, my thanks to Prentice-Hall and John Wiley and Sons.

Ms. Jennette Kaufman of the Word Processing Center at Cleveland State University transformed my handwritten notes into finished copy and I am most grateful. I would also like to thank the editorial and production staff at Nelson-Hall for their professional assistance.

Finally, I wish to thank my wife Fran for showing infinitely more interest in, and understanding of, my writings in political science than I could ever show with her writings in biopolymers and molecular biology.

Part 1
What Is Politics?

Introduction

Any introductory textbook which at the very beginning requires pages and pages simply to define its material, even in an extremely general and loose way, is surely open to the criticism that the subject matter in question is vague, nebulous, and, therefore, not worth the time or effort needed to conduct an intelligent study of the field. The reader may even wonder whether the term *politics* or *political science* can, in fact, have a specific meaning. Most students are aware of the general content of courses in, say, mathematics or French. Mathematics is the study of numbers and quantities and the mathematics textbooks instruct the reader on how to manipulate these symbolic numerical relationships; a course in French teaches the grammar and vocabulary of the language and the textbooks explain the grammatical precepts and furnish vocabulary lists. But "politics" is not mathematics or French for it does not deal with symbolic numerical relationships or with alien word combinations. On the contrary, politics and political science are concerned with real living people and their behavior in the real world. If the definitions or descriptions of politics are hazy and sometimes conflictive with each other, it is because we as individuals and groups of individuals are nonrigorous, unpredictable, and we are not mirror images of one another. Each individual brings different values and styles to his or her behavior in the real world, and it is impossible to categorize and compartmentalize us as if we *were* verb endings or immutable numerical relationships.

Part 1, therefore, attempts to identify and describe the varying answers over time to this question of "what is politics?" The term *political science* is not dealt with in Part 1 for this latter term is a deceptively complicated name for the "scientific study of politics." What a "scientific study" of politics actually entails is discussed in Part 2 and this section deals only with the prior question of "what is politics?"

It appears that each successive generation from the pre-Christian Greeks to contemporary theorists in the United States have had their own particular (some would say peculiar) view of the nature and components of politics. But each in its own view and conception is culture-bound in the sense that they emphasize and draw attention to those aspects of "politics" which are most prevalent, important, or salient within their own individual society and culture. Thus all views are more or less limited by time and space and they have both geographical and cultural-intellectual horizons. The modern reader will examine, for example, the Greek view and, fortified by over two thousand years of hindsight and expanded intellectual horizons, will immediately be able to offer criticism and counter-argument to the Greek contribution. The student should, however, be very wary of this type of reaction for three reasons:

First, it is just not a fair or honest method of dealing with intellectual endeavors, for these people must be met on their own ground and not ours. This is to say that the Greek view, or any other attempt to define the nature of politics, must be interpreted and analyzed in terms of, in this example, Greek society and culture of 400 B.C. and not in terms of an American classroom in the 1970s.

Second, excessive criticism of past views will blind one to those aspects of the approach which *do* have relevance and credence even to a more "modern" outlook. This can be dramatically seen with the Greek view, for a full circle has almost been drawn. This point is discussed in greater detail in Part

2, and it will suffice at this point only to mention that many contemporary political scientists, this author included, are in a sense "rediscovering" the Greek conception of politics after having ignored it for some time. It is being rediscovered because many people now realize that it is directly relevant and applicable to their own views as to what actually is the content and nature of politics.

Third, although it does not so appear, even the more systematic and rigorous definitions and descriptions offered by modern-day political scientists are themselves culture-bound and only reflect the most salient components of this particular historical period and culture. Those views which might today appear as acceptable or "correct" when compared to earlier views will no doubt be reinterpreted by future critics. The point is that these descriptions are actually dealing with man and his environment and as man and the environment change, so does his conception of his behavior change.

Part 1 is divided into two chapters. Chapter 1, "A Brief Historical Overview," presents a discussion of the development of the differing general views and definitions of politics. Chapter 2, "Four Representative Conceptions," identifies specific individuals and their personal contributions and analyses. Chapter 1 includes a discussion of pre-Christian Greek thought as evidenced mostly by the writings of Plato [427?-347 B.C.] and Aristotle [384-322 B.C.]; the late nineteenth-century American view with its emphasis upon the national state and sovereignty and which even today is the dominant view in many continental European universities (as well as many American universities); and, finally, a contemporary Western view that sees politics as a "power relationship." Chapter 2 contains a formal discussion and analysis of specific individuals: Thomas Hobbes [English, 1588-1679] and "politics seen as conflict"; John Locke [English, 1632-1704] and Jean-Jacques Rousseau [Swiss-French, 1712-1778] and "politics seen as a contract"; Karl Marx [German, 1818-1883] and "politics seen as a search for just society"; and David Easton [Canadian-American, 1917-] and "politics seen as a system."

A brief concluding note to these introductory remarks appears necessary. Part 1 deals with usefulness and not with truth in the sense that the differing views and conceptions of politics are approached in terms of their utility or usefulness to describe the subject matter in question. These views are not "right" or "wrong" as if they *were* answers to a mathematical problem or verb endings. The question of rightness or truth is not relevant when one is dealing with what are essentially philosophical (some would even say theological) answers to complicated problems.

1
A Brief
Historical Overview

Pre-Christian Greek Thought:
Ethics and the Good Life

SIR ERNEST BARKER, a most respected and eminent scholarly authority on Greek political thought, once wrote that "political thought begins with the Greeks," and Andrew Hacker, another scholar, states that "Plato was the first writer to address himself to political philosophy."[1] As much as Professors Barker and Hacker are to be respected, they are probably mistaken with their praise of the Greeks. The ancient Greeks were not the first to wonder about and then attempt to provide answers to questions such as "How ought a person behave in society?" "How are we to distribute the society's resources?" "What is the selection process for the leader?" "What is the best or ideal form of community?" "What particular rules or standards of behavior should be enforced?" "What are the penalties for violating these standards of behavior? and "Who enforces these standards or rules?" It was probably the first caveperson in prehistoric times, thousands and thousands of years before the Greeks, who first thought about "politics" when he or she wondered about the cavepeople's relationships with on another,

7

and about the cave society's structures and decision-making processes. The cavepeople society generated leaders; organizational structures and decisions were made which affected the entire population.[2] This is, of course, only conjecture for the cavepeople did not leave systematic written material or treatises as did Plato and Aristotle and there is always the possibility that the cavepeople only thought about what animal was going to provide (or have) the next meal. But we do have written records from the ancient Egyptians, (Old Testament) Biblical literature, and the ancient Hindu and Chinese civilizations.[3] These people and cultures did engage in speculation about politics and they were active participants in a highly developed political process.

Even though we are thus joining the narrative in the middle, the pre-Christian Greeks provide an excellent starting point and it is here that we shall also begin. One should perhaps begin with the Greeks for it is the Greek conception of politics which, with very few exceptions, established the tone and nature of most political writing during the subsequent twenty-two hundred years. The Greek conception of politics is basically a belief that political science was the search for the ethical ideal good life and that all behavior directed at the attainment of this goal was therefore "political" behavior. The Greeks first *prescribed* what the final ethical goal should be and then *described* the ways to achieve this goal. This philosophizing, this speculation after the *ought* rather than inquiry into the *is,* became the dominant approach to politics, at least in the Western world, for centuries after the Greeks. One unnamed political scientist has even quipped, sarcastically one hopes, that all political science is only a footnote to Plato and Aristotle. It is for these reasons—the direction of the conception and its overwhelming intellectual influence—that we also begin with the Greeks.

It is, of course, a disservice to the views and specific contributions of each individual whenever such a vast range of people and ideas ("Greek thought") is forced into short summaries and the following discussion does not even pretend to present a wide-ranging analysis or treatment of all the facets of Greek political thought. Only a fraction of that segment of the writings Plato and Aristotle thought relevant to the central concern of this Chapter have been abstracted out for presentation. A very brief overview of Greek society, as well as a brief description of the life of Plato and Aristotle, are offered before discussing the essential characteristics and definitional components of the Greek conception of politics and political science.[4]

It was during the Age of Pericles (461-429 B.C.) that "democracy" in the city-state (*Polis*) of Athens could be described as reaching its highest level. It was, of course, quite undemocratic by modern-day Swedish or Swiss standards but compared to its immediate environment—the city-state of Sparta, in particular—Athens was at least more democratic than the quasi-fascist surroundings. Athens had an Assembly and a Council and the Assembly could initiate legislation of its own as well as having the power to pass on the Council's proposals. The Assembly was composed of all male citizens and the Council (known as the Council of Five Hundred) was chosen by lot from among these citizens. The Council served as the executive branch: it prepared legislation for the Assembly and administered the day-to-day operation of the city-state. Under Pericles, a Board of Ten Generals was established. This Board was also chosen by the Assembly and slowly supplanted the Council of Five Hundred and became the chief decision-making institution in the system even though the Board was theoretically still responsible to the Assembly. Pericles' exact position for more than thirty years was President of the Board of Generals—the functional equivalent of a prime minister in a parliamentary system.

The Athenian system had the structural facade of democracy but it was not a functional democracy. The very term *democracy* is from the Greek *demos*, meaning people: democracy is thus rule by the people.[5] But the pre-Christian Greek society did not have a very expansive definition of *demos*. Athens allowed only male citizens to participate in the process and *citizen* had a very limited meaning: slaves and women were excluded and only a small minority of the total population was thus seen as citizens. Athens in the time of Plato and Aristotle is probably better described as an oligarchy with very

strong and obvious overtones of racial, sexual, and class oppression along with a blatant imperialistic and colonialistic foreign policy.

This imperialism led to Athens' downfall. Athens succeeded in the Persian Wars (493-479 B.C.) and, strengthened
by the victory, began to spread its influence to other areas.
The Delian League, a military alliance among Athens and
various other independent city-states formed to fight the Per-
sians, was reduced to a condition of colonial vassalage by
Athens. The one other strong independent city-state, Sparta,
feared this increasing spread of Athenian power and war broke
out between Athens and Sparta. The Peloponnesian War (431-
404 B.C.), a war between the pseudodemocratic Athens and the
quasi-fascist Sparta, was a total disaster for Athens. The Atheni-
ans' receptivity to, and use of, brutality and degradation increased in an almost direct relationship to its military defeats.
Totally abandoned by its allies and with its food supply cut
off, Athens surrendered in 404 B.C.

Sparta then dominated the southern area of Greece (Pelo-
ponnesia) to about 370 B.C. until it was, in turn, over-
thrown by the city-state of Thebes. This continual and inces-
sant warfare drained the Greeks of all economic and military
capabilities and, in 338 B.C., Philip of Macedon easily con-
quered the area. Power then passed to Philip's son, Alexander
the Great, and Alexander extended Greek hegemony to the
vast area between the Nile River in Egypt and the Indus River
in India. But this takes us beyond the time of Plato and Aristotle and the discussion of classical Greek history stops at this
point.

Plato was born in Athens about four years after the outbreak of the Peloponnesian War. The war lasted for twenty-
seven years (the *blitzkrieg* was not invented until 1939) and
thus the first twenty-three years of Plato's life was spent in an
atmosphere of a brutal and debilitating war and the rest of his
life witnessed Athens as a tributary state of Sparta and then
the victory of Thebes. It was during this middle period, Athens
a vassal of Sparta, that Plato's former teacher Socrates was
executed by the Athenian despots. Prior to this act, Plato, who
came from a wealthy aristocratic family, entertained ideas of

entering Athenian politics. But Socrates' death turned him away from overt participation in the political process and toward a life of quiet contemplation of philosophy. Donald Kagan cites a passage from Plato which shows dismay over Socrates' fate as well as his own conception of the role that philosophy must play in the attainment of the ideal society:

> At last I came to the conclusion that all existing states are badly governed and the condition of their laws practically incurable without some miraculous remedy and the assistance of fortune; and I was forced to say, in praise of true philosophy, that from her height alone was it possible to discern what the nature of justice is either in the state or the individual, and that the ills of the human race would never end until either those who are sincerely and truly lovers of wisdom came into political power, or the rulers of our cities learn true philosophy.[6]

This quotation illustrates the core of the Greek approach to politics: it is only through philosophy, through speculation into what *ought* to be rather than hard analysis of what actually *is*, that an ideal and just political society could be created. Plato established an academy in Athens in 386 B.C. and taught (taught is not used in its modern meaning—"communed" with his fellow philosophers would be a better description of Plato's activities in the academy) until his death in 347 B.C.

Aristotle was born in 384 B.C. in the northeast part of Greece near the Macedonian border. Aristotle was thus not an Athenian although he later became one of the strongest adherents of Athenian principles. He came from a middle-class family; his father was attached to Philip of Macedon's entourage, and Aristotle came to Athens. He communed at Plato's academy from about 370 until Plato's death (347), traveled quite extensively from 347 to 335, tutored Alexander the Great for a time, and then returned to Athens to establish his own academy which he supervised until his death in 322 B.C.

The major characteristics of Greek conception of politics and political science have been alluded to above. Plato's desire that philosophers become kings or that kings become philosophers refers to the belief that it is only through wisdom that the good life could be attained. "Wisdom" is True Knowledge gained through philosophy and not practical "how to do" knowledge. Aristotle supported the view that it was only the Polis type or form of society which could provide for the Good Life. In other words, political science was this search for the good life and political behavior was behavior directed toward the achievement of this ethical goal. Aristotle's view of the Polis refers to the belief that all human behavior in the Polis ought to be directed at the attainment of this goal and thus all forms of behavior in the Polis become, by definition, political in nature. Political science was regarded as the "master science" for, due to its extremely broad-based character and all-encompassing net, it included the study of the entire range of human activity.

Politics as the master science! The very phrase is a succinct description of the Greek conception of political science. The word *politics* itself comes from the Greek *polis* and its original meaning was "life in the Polis." Politics as the master science!— there are several articulate contemporary spokesmen for the Greek claim. Herbert J. Spiro, in his book *Politics as the Master Science: From Plato to Mao,* advances the view that politics stands at the *"pinnacle* of human activities" and is the *"most important* discipline that can be a subject of systematic study."[7] Professor Spiro describes political science as the "queen of the sciences" and even places geology and medicine as being within the scope of political science.

It does not, however, serve any useful purpose to argue at length whether political science is, in fact, number one in the scheme of things or number fifty. The point is that the pre-Christian Greeks (and their modern-day counterparts) believed that political science *was* the master science and this belief is a major characteristic of the Greek answer to the question "what is politics?" What else is present in the writings of the Greeks which bear on our question? One word of caution is necessary, however, before discussing some of Plato's and Aristotle's specific ideas. Both Plato and Aristotle were not describing how society actually was organized or how society actually behaved but, rather, how they conceived how man in society ought to have behaved. Athens, as described above, bore very little resemblance to the ornate and speculative descriptions and prescriptions offered by the philosophers. Real-life politics and political behavior, what people actually said and did, in pre-Christian Greek society was as far removed from the search for the Ethical Life as what actually was said and done during the Watergate affair and it is important to keep this distinction in mind: Plato and Aristotle devoted much of their intellectual capacities into speculation into what *ought to be.* A change in conceptualization, a change from the ought to the systematic study of what actually is, did not occur until approximately twenty-two hundred years later. The Greeks and, as will be shown below, most subsequent writers on politics over the following twenty-two hundred years emphasized the prescription or the contents of the final ethical, ideal society and then they described the steps necessary to reach this goal.

A major portion of Plato's *Republic* is devoted to a discussion of his conception of the Ideal State.[8] His republic would not be a democracy and there would be no emphasis, even on the theoretical level, upon liberty or equality. Plato's republic would be so organized that, in modern terminology, he would be called an aristocratic snob with an extreme distrust and distaste for the common individual person. One could even make the case that Plato was perhaps one of the first statements of totalitarianism.[9] Plato divided people into three distinct categories, each category corresponding to his view that the soul had three functions. The soul's functions were (1) appetite—the base, crass, materialistic nature of people; (2) spirit—the will to fight and to endure deprivation and discipline; and (3) reason—the "best" function of the soul for reason was the love of wisdom. Plato's classification probably was influenced by the then current Greek conception of the physical universe and the environment. Greek thought at that time believed that the entire physical universe was divided into four distinct categories, each with separate properties or characteristics. Everything was either fire, earth, air, or water. It was but a short step from this division of nature into discreet categories to the division of individual human beings into distinct categories. Each person would be classified as appetite, spirit, or reason depending upon which function of the soul gained ascendancy within the individual. The parallels between Plato's view and the conception of the pioneering psychoanalyst Sigmund Freud are obvious at this point. Freud divided the individual's psyche into three parts: the id, the ego, and the superego. Freud attempted to explain human behavior by employing these constructs and the id is directly connected to appetite, the ego is spirit, and the superego is reason.

Thus there were to be three separate classes of people for Plato, each corresponding to the divisions of the soul. The appetitive function was represented by the lowest class in the Republic, and this class was called the workers. Constituting approximately 85 percent of the total population, these workers had only practical knowledge or information (they did not have wisdom) on how to do things and farmers, artisans, professors, lawyers, engineers, physicians, merchants, and the like comprised this class. These people were seen as being interested only in satiating the appetitive or crass materialistic function of the soul. The second or middle class, about 10 percent of the population, was called the guardian or auxiliary class and this corresponded to the spirit function of the soul. This class was brave, had the will to fight, endure discipline, and thus the police, soldiers, bureaucrats, and administrators of the Republic were the auxiliaries. The tax collectors and bus drivers (?) had one characteristic in common, however. The auxiliaries and the workers only had practical knowledge—how to do something—and they did not have wisdom.

The highest and best class, about 5 percent of the total population, corresponds to the reasoning function of the soul, and this is the intellectual aristocracy within the Republic. These few people are the philosopher-kings and it is *only* these people, disdaining the practical information and knowledge of the other classes (the is), who are seen to possess the TRUTH (the ought). The philosopher-kings would be trained from birth to seek out the GOOD LIFE, the ETHICAL IDEAL, and then to translate this prescribed goal into state public policy through the auxiliaries. This returns to Plato's statement above: philosophers must be kings (or kings must be philosophers) before the State can exist on ethical principles. The workers and the civil servants (95 percent of the population) do not know what the TRUTH is—only the philosopher-king has wisdom!

In Plato's conception, this Ideal State would be a utopia for there would be total absence of conflict, oppression, exploitation, uncouth activities, and unethical/immoral behavior. Each of the three classes would live in peace and harmony because each individual would have achieved the goal of his or her (for Plato, it was only "his") own specific self-realization or self-fulfillment: the workers are workers and they are satisfied with this level for they do not envy or resent the aristocratic philosopher-kings.

Plato's description of these social classes and his conception of who can know the TRUTH runs into severe opposition from modern liberal democrats, and it is here that Plato is open to the charge of being an aristocratic snob with latent fascist tendencies. Without entering the argument whether there is, in fact, such a thing as the soul, the modern liberal democrat simply does not believe that each individual is fated by his or her soul to one particular class or occupation as did Plato. The liberal democrat believes that all members of society must have an equal chance or opportunity to claim the range of human activities and individuals must not be forced into a particular niche or "station in life" from the time of birth. Plato would be aghast at the very thought of Equal Opportunity laws or Affirmative Action Programs of contemporary American society.

But there is more serious and telling criticism with Plato's conception of the Truth and who can know what the Truth is. For Plato, the TRUTH or WISDOM was distinct from practical knowledge or information. Knowledge is what the workers and auxiliaries had in the sense of how to collect taxes, how to build bridges, how to wage war, how to farm. Wisdom was the possession of the ethical ideal truth, and *only* the philosopher-king had wisdom in the Republic. The liberal democrat totally and completely rejects this conception of the Truth. The Truth, for the liberal democrat, is not eternal and blessed with everlasting life: it changes as the individual's conception of himself or herself changes and thus the search for the Truth is a constant process of revision, change, and adaptation. The Truth is also seen as a relative concept and thus not the private reserve of the philosopher-kings. Every individual, and not just a select few, has an equal claim to the possession of the Truth. This view is essentially the argument offered by John Stuart Mill, a nineteenth-century English political philosopher. Mill argued that each individual may only have a minute portion of the truth, but society must listen to this person, for without even this one, the wholeness of the Truth would not be complete. Even Jean-Jacques Rousseau, who was not a liberal democrat, disagrees with Plato. For Rousseau, the truth was not some eternal concept available to a few select individuals—the truth was what the *people* said it was through the operation of the society's general will and all one had to do to arrive at or discover the Truth for Rousseau was to count noses.

Plato (and Aristotle) regarded the process of majority vote to discover wisdom as an obscene perversion of the entire process. Majority vote by the people? Institute rule by the *demos* or people (democracy)? Fools would be put into office if the crass and uncouth common people had an equal share in the decision-making process along with the philosopher-kings. Such a society would not be guided by ethical precepts but, rather, by the crude materialistic rabble. It may, of course, be true that certain societies in certain historical time periods do put fools and charlatans into office—it has been rumored that the democratic approach to equal participation in the United States during the presidential elections has, at times, elected people of less than high moral standards, particularly if one wishes to approach Watergate in moralistic terms—but, on the whole, fools and charlatans do not maintain effective power for an extended time. We should not point to Watergate as an example of what would happen if Plato's views were not followed; we should point to Nazi Germany or the Soviet Union under Stalin as examples of what would happen if Plato's views were followed: a few select people who claimed possession of the Truth with very drastic and mostly fatal consequences to anyone who dared question the five percent's interpretation of the Truth. Charlatans who resign high office under charges of abuse of power and obstruction of justice might be an inherent flaw within this "perverted" form of government the Greeks called democracy but, hopefully, this is preferable to a society in which an open and honest search for the Truth is prevented. It is for these reasons that Plato could be characterized as having latent totalitarian tendencies.

Aristotle (his *Politics* and *Ethics* are most relevant for purposes of this chapter) conceived political science to be the search for the supreme good, happiness, as well as the description of the means by which people might achieve harmony within the Polis.[10] Aristotle is revelant here for two major points: the all-encompassing nature of political science and the role and function of the Polis.

The all-encompassing nature of political science was stated with a pristine clarity by Aristotle. Political science was the prescription of the final goal and a description of the ways to achieve this goal; people in the Polis were expected to devote all their behavior patterns to the achievement of this goal; political science, therefore, was the study of *all* life in the Polis! Since all behavior ought to have been directed at this final goal, all behavior was political behavior. With this type of reasoning, it is very easy to see why the pre-Christian Greeks and their contemporary supporters such as Professor Spiro could argue that political science included all other areas and was indeed the "master science."

The necessity of the Polis was also a very important point with Aristotle. In his discussion of the Ideal State/Polis, Aristotle believed that the State's end was a moral life and any social association which did not permit a person to seek this goal could not be called a true Polis. The nuclear family or a neighborhood association was not a Polis for it did not allow the achievement of this moral end. A hermit, living in an isolated cave far from Athens, could not engage in political behavior for this person would not be in a Polis. This example of a hermit is not at odds with the late nineteenth-century view of politics seen as State activity or with the more contemporary view of politics as seen as a power relationship between and among individuals. All three conceptions see political science as a "social science" and the social aspect implies that at least two people are necessary before a political relationship can exist. This hermit could engage in a whole range of activities—linguistics, agriculture, philosophy, mathematics—but all three views say the hermit cannot engage in politics. The hermit could even have a goat or two and therefore engage in additional activities (the hermit could even eat the goat for dinner) but there would be no politics with the goat.

But what of two people in this cave? It is at this point that differences are evident. The Greek approach and the nine-teenth-century approach say that these two people cannot engage in politics but for different reasons: the nineteenth-century view argues that this mini-society is not a formal sovereign state, and since the state is necessary for politics, the activities of the two people are not political. Aristotle argues that these two friends in the cave far from Athens whose total existence was directed at mere physical survival could not hope to achieve the good life—our cave is not a Polis—and thus whatever they did (and the whole range of human activities would be open to them) simply could not be political. It is the contemporary view of politics which criticizes this "nonpolitical" nature of the two people in the cave. It is entirely possible, and quite probable, that our hermits do engage in political behavior because neither the State nor the Polis is required. All that is required is at least two people interacting. The difference is one of conception for the hermits are doing the same things for all three approaches. The problem is, however, that one approach says some behavior is political, while two approaches say the identical behavior is nonpolitical. The activity cannot at the same time be both political and nonpolitical and it is exactly at this point where the unresolvable differences lie.

To summarize the pre-Christian Greek answer to the question "what is politics?": it was the *ought* and not the *is* and it included *all* behavior within the Polis. The Greek approach emphasized philosophy and ethics, the ought and not the is, and thus was basically moral philosophy. The approach was also extremely broad-based and at the same time too restrictive. To answer the question "what is politics?" one has to have some idea of what is not political, some idea of the boundaries to political behavior. The Greeks never really faced this problem of boundary identification: politics was extremely broad-based for it included *everything* in the Polis. The Master Science in-cluded what we, if it happened today, would certainly term nonpolitical behavior, such as the equivalent of robbing a gasoline station or a street mugging. Even with the one attempt at boundary identification with the necessity of the Polis, their answer was too restrictive. The two or three people in the cave would not be in a Polis and thus could not have politics. It just goes against *my* common sense to argue that three or four people on an isolated island could not have politics. These people could not have an eight-piece band or a basketball team but they most certainly could have political relationships.

The Greek conception did not die out with the classical Greeks, however. This view is still quite alive in contemporary political science although it is a minority viewpoint. Some of the best and most readable political science is being written by political philosophers and one should not denigrate the approach. And, as will be shown in Chapter 5, contemporary political science is rediscovering the benefits of this ethical approach to political science. But, as stated above, this Greek concept set the tone and nature for most political writing (inquiry into the *ought,* not into the *is*) for the subsequent twenty-two hundred-odd years with very few exceptions. It was not until the latter part of the nineteenth century that a different conceptualization and view of politics and political science became evident. The following section, "Nineteenth-Century America: The State and Sovereignty," discusses this second general view of politics.

Nineteenth-Century America:
The State and Sovereignty

The Greek conception of politics, the search for the "good" or "just" life (what *ought* to be the final goal of people and organized society?) and what these people and society must do to achieve this ethical goal, a conception which included practically all facets of human relationships and organizations, was the overriding and dominant view of politics and political science in the West from that time to approximately the late nineteenth century.

There were, of course, several notable exceptions to this dominant *Weltanschauung* (world view) between 400 B.C. and

1880 A.D. It is quite possible that these exceptions are so
notable because they *were* exceptions to the general approach
and presented such a then-radical conception. But this is only
conjecture for these writings do stand out on merit alone. Perhaps the most often cited and most widely read of these "mav-
ericks" is *The Prince* by Machiavelli (Florentine, 1469-1527).
Machiavelli wrote *The Prince* in 1513 although it was not published until five years after his death. Machiavelli has written
several other notable works, *The Art of War* and *History of
Florence* among them, but it is from *The Prince* that the adjective *Machiavellian* (connoting cynicism and deceit) came
into existence. Very briefly, *The Prince* deals with the operating
procedures for the successful ruler or prince. Machiavelli does
not speculate about things as they ought to be but, rather, as
they actually are—a classic statement of power politics. A second example can be seen in the writings of Chanakya (or
Kautilya [345 B.C.-300? B.C.], prime minister of Chandragupta
and founder of the Maurya dynasty in ancient India. The *Ar-
thasastra* by Kautilya ignores ethical or religious standards (what
ought to be) and emphasizes political realism.[11]

There were other exceptions to this general approach but
speculation on ethical goals provided the great bulk of "political"
writing and practically every writer on politics fits into this
general mold. All the major political philosophers—Hobbes,
Locke, Rousseau, Marx, Mill, Burke, the church philosophers,
just to mention a few—were all theorizing along the same basic
lines: first prescribing some final goal and then describing the
ways to attain this end. Whatever courses offered in universities
as "political science" were invariably political philosophy courses
which dealt with textual exegeses of these classical and influential writings. "Political science" courses in American universities prior to the late nineteenth century would seem quite
strange to the student today. A contemporary English political
scientist, Bernard Crick, mentions that *The Elements of Moral
Science* by Francis Wayland (published in 1835) was a widely
used textbook in the United States until about the Civil War.
Crick's review of *The Elements of Moral Science* is not very
flattering:

[I]ts sections on Civil polity contain well-worn homilies and precepts on the relation of liberty to order. It shows no critical technique at all, nor even a compulsion to advance rational evidence—except a quasi-theological proof that the accumulation of property was simply God's reward to especially deserving Christians.[12]

It was not until the late nineteenth century that a separate and distinct major view or approach became evident. This view partly grew out of an intellectual reaction to and disillusionment with the then-current conception. The philosophical [Greek] approach was burdened with scholasticism, philosophy, metaphysical and metaethical rumination, and was quite devoid of any hard facts or data. But this "new approach" was not just a reaction or protest to the past. It also grew from an honest intellectual search for alternative ways to wisdom and knowledge. The seminal and ground-breaking works for this approach are generally considered to be Woodrow Wilson's *Congressional Government*, published in 1885 (the same Woodrow Wilson who became U. S. president in 1912), and James Bryce's *American Commonwealth,* published in 1888. These books, and the approach which they advocated, aimed at realism in political science, objectivity, relevance, facts, science, and it did not speculate as to the ethical goals of people in an organized society. Research was carried out through observation, categorizing, classifying, and not through introspection or divine inspiration. The sovereign, territorial national State was seen to be the chief organizing component of this approach and political science was thus altered to be the "scientific study of the State in all its aspects."

A brief glance at some of the representative writings of the approach adds a flavor to the view which cannot be imparted by mere description. The following excerpts serve as a fascinating window into the past and a better appreciation of political science's central nature during those years can be gained by the original comments.

Raymond G. Gettell, *Political Science*, first published in 1933:

Considerable difference of opinion exists as to the best approach to the study of political science. Some prefer to begin with a description of American government, since it deals with things with which students are already somewhat familiar. Others favor a comparative study of governments of a number of the most important modern states, using this material for purposes of contrast and the deduction of certain general principles. . . . [This author] believes that the best introduction to the field consists in a study of the state as an institution, giving attention to its nature, its origin and development, its organization and its theories, its relation to the individuals that comprise it and other states.[13]

Westel W. Willoughby (a former president of the American Political Science Association), *The Fundamental Concepts of Public Law,* 1924:

The Province of Political Science. Political Science, using the term in its broadest sense, has for its purpose the ascertainment of political facts and the arrangement of them in systematic order as determined by the logical and causal relations which exist between them. These political facts, which include both objective phenomena and the subjective forces which create them or fix their functional activities, are those which relate to the State; and by a State is understood a group of human individuals viewed as an organized corporate community over which exists a ruling authority which is recognized as the source of commands legally and, in general, ethically, binding upon the individuals composing the community. The qualifying adjective, political, may, therefore, be applied to all matters which relate to the origin and history of the State, to its governmental organization, its activities, its aims, its administrative methods, its legitimate sphere of authority, and to its very right to exist.[14]

Steven Leacock, *Elements of Political Science,* first published in 1906:

. . . One may proceed to a formal definition of political science, which may best be accepted in the form offered by

> Paul Janet: "Political Science is that part of social science
> which treats of the foundations of the State, and of the
> principles of government." Besides this may be placed the
> definition of J. K. Bluntschli, which draws especial atten-
> tion to the dynamic nature of the study involved: "Political
> Science is the science which is concerned with the State,
> which endeavors to understand and comprehend the State
> in its conditions, in its essential nature, its various forms
> and manifestations, its development." . . . Political science,
> then, deals with the State; it is, in short, as it is often
> termed, the "theory of the State."[15]

This second general approach thus conceived political
science as the scientific study of the State and the definition of
"politics" was seen as State activity or, in other words, as "government." Politics no longer included the whole range of human
behavior but, rather, it was severely reduced to only those activities in which the formal national sovereign State or state's
agents participated. But this emphasis upon the state as the
defining and organizing concept forced its proponents and adherents into several tenuous and hard-to-defend positions. Although these positions were not considered to be tenuous at the
time, it is through hindsight and increased intellectual horizons
that several damaging criticisms can be directed at this approach. First of all, the emphasis upon the primacy of the sovereign national state is severely culture-bound. Anglo-American
and the European monarchies/democracies provided what was
then thought to be the most normal and usual pattern of societal
evolution. Very little attention was paid to those societies in
Africa and Asia which were not regarded as States. But this is
a hindsight criticism for the state at that time *was* a prevalent
and salient concept and did not appear as culture-bound.

But perhaps more damaging than equating politics and
political science with the State and governmental activity is the
definitional components of the state. Dozens and dozens of books
were published which examined the very meaning of the state.
Since political science was the study of the state, this approach
had to define what was meant when the term "state" was employed. The essential, required, and necessary elements of the
state—required in the sense that if any were missing, then the

state (and politics, political science, and political scientists) could not exist—were seen to be (1) population, (2) territory/ residence, (3) government/organization, and (4) sovereignty. These four definitional components of the state were described as follows:

1. *Population*: a certain number of actual human beings must be present;
2. *Territory/Residence*: a physical, readily identifiable geographical area in which the above population resides and this residence must be of a permanent nature;
3. *Government/Organization*: the institutions or structures through which the purposes of the state are created and administered; and
4. *Sovereignty*: the above government is supreme over all the people residing in the above territory and it is also free from any external control.

At first glance, the nineteenth-century approach appears to be just a restatement of the Greek *polis* for the *polis* was also characterized as a group of people residing in an identifiable geographical area with a sovereign government. But this approach is much more restrictive than the Greek approach as to the boundaries of politics and political science. Whereas the Greeks included all human activity under the rubric of political, this second general conception reduced politics to the actions of the government and did not extend the boundaries of political science to the geographical boundaries of the state. In other words, the Greek *polis* and the nineteenth-century State may be interchangeable in the sense that both concepts describe the identical social model but, and this is the crucial difference, actions which were deemed political by the Greeks (taking place in the *polis*) were not necessarily political according to this second view if the State or the State's agents did not participate.

As mentioned above, the real problem is not one of restating the Greek approach; the problem is one of equating politics and political science with the State. The logician's argument would run along these lines: the adherents of this view believe that politics and political science is the study of the State

(A is the study of B); the State (B) is defined as population, territory/residence, government/organization, and sovereignty (C); therefore, political science (A) is the study of the State's components (C). The logical conclusion and one which was explicitly accepted at that time is that if *any* of the components of the state were missing *there could be no state!* Without a State, without people *and* territory *and* government *and* sovereignty, there can be nothing for political scientists to study for there would be no politics. This latter conclusion, that there is no politics without a state, was never openly recognized at that time but intimations and hints in this direction are plentiful in the literature of the period. The point is, and some examples follow, that this view with its dependence upon the State was unable to classify and study as "political" many obvious (at least what we would today call obvious) activities that would appear to be "political." Whereas the Greek approach was too broad and included things which we would today not classify as political, this approach was too restrictive and confining for it did not include things which we would today classify as political.

The first component of the State (and politics) was seen to be people: a certain number of actual human beings must be present. It is not the quality of this component that a more "modern" view disputes for even the more modern and behavioral conceptions of politics and political science requiring living human beings to be present before political activity can take place. Any view of politics requires people. Whether political science is described as a behavioral science or as a social science is not relevant: politics is social interaction and, as such, requires people. But it is with the quantity of this component, the actual number of human beings, which meets opposition. The modern view requires at least two people before political activity can occur and these two people could very well be hermits far removed from any *polis* or state. The State approach to political science never precisely defined the number of people required before a State (and political activity) could exist. The number was certainly more than two because two people could never have had a government and their society could not be characterized as sovereign. The actual number of people required, judging from those countries which received attention, appears to be well into the millions.

The second component of the State was territory/residence: a physical, readily identifiable geographical area in which the actual people permanently resided. The State was so organized that one knew when the frontier was crossed into another state. But this emphasis upon and necessity for a fixed, recognizable, geographical territory as a defining element of the State forced the exclusion from study various phenomena which we would today call political and worthy of study by political scientists. For example, Leacock writes that ". . . without a definite territory there can be no State. The Jews, being scattered abroad and disassociated from the occupation and control of any particular territory, do not constitute a state. . . . It seems advisable to insist on the idea of land being necessary."[16] Leacock's remarks, of course, predated the establishment of the State of Israel by forty-two years but this is not the point. The crucial point is that Leacock is, in fact, saying that the international Jewish organizations such as Theodor Herzl's Zionist Organization did not engage in politics and thus was not worthy of study by a political scientist. Leacock is arguing that such organizations are not states because a definite territory is not present. But Herzl and his organization were certainly engaged in some type of behavior and, if it were not political, one is then hard put to say what they were doing. Most people would probably agree that "political" behavior was a prime part of the international Zionist movement.

The insistence upon the actual people having a permanent residence within this fixed territory is an additional stumbling block for this view. Raymond Gettell comments on this necessity of permanent residence:

> Although history shows nomadic peoples, in the hunting or fishing or pastoral stages of development, living under a tribal form of organization in which the idea of definite and permanent territory played little part, it is doubtful whether the term "State" [and politics] is properly applied to such a condition. Such peoples may have rulers and may

be subject to discipline and law. They are often a state in
the making. . . . The State, as the etymology of the word
shows, is associated with a fixed place. . . . The possession
of territory is a necessary basis. . . .[17]

What is not stated but which is so implicit with this view
is that nomadic tribes or *any* territoryless group just do not engage in politics for there is no State.[18] What is one to say, for
example, about the Black September movement and all the other
Palestine liberation groups? The concept of the State with people
having a permanent residence in a defined geographical area is
most definitely lacking with the Black September movement but
is not this group engaged in "political" behavior? What is one
to do with the now-defunct National Liberation Front of South
Vietnam (Viet Cong)? Again, there is no "State" in its formal
sense, but is there also no politics? The Viet Cong was, and the
Black September movement is, doing some type of behavior
and if all of it is not political, one is again very hard put to say
what they actually were doing. The point is that insistence upon
a readily identifiable physical territory and permanent residence,
even if rulers and laws are present, leads to some awkward and
quite indefensible positions.

The third component of the State was government or organization: the institutions of structures through which the purposes of the State are created and administered. The insistence
upon the existence of government/organization before the State
(and politics) can exist also leads to some (now) strange-sounding statements. Leacock again comments:

Even granting that we have a territory and population dis-
connected from the rest of the world, and thus in a sense a
unit, we have not yet a State. Imagine, for example, that a
"numerous assemblage of human beings" . . . were deposited upon some uninhabited island not owned or controlled by any existing government. Here we should have
land and population and unity, but the inhabitants, having
as yet no cohesion or connection, would not form a state.[19]

The next statement is, of course, that these people would
also have no politics or political behavior due to this lack of an

organized government to administer State will and decisions. But, as was the case with the Viet Cong and the Black September movement, most people today would probably admit that political activity would begin the moment these people first put a foot on this isolated island. One could even make a plausible argument that these people engaged in politics on the boat en route to this "uninhabited island not owned or controlled by any existing governmental." Formal governmental structures and organizations may be a sufficient cause of political activity (when government exists, politics can exist) but formal governmental structures and organizations are not a necessary cause of politics (political behavior can exist without a government). The concept of the state as an organizing principle of politics is just too restrictive and confining and cannot include within its boundaries all facets of politics.

The final component of the State was sovereignty. Sovereignty here means that the government is supreme over all the people residing in the territory, it is free from any outside control, and it is recognized as such by other governments/States. The insistence upon sovereignty, internal supremacy and external independence, also leads to some (now) strange-sounding positions. Colonies are not "sovereign"; the League of Nations did not, and the United Nations does not, meet this requirement of sovereignty. Is one forced to conclude that the people in colonies did not engage in political behavior or that these international organizations do not participate in politics? The Indian National Movement, the Congress Party under Gandhi and Nehru, certainly engaged in political activity against the British colonial power. This criticism may be an overstatement in regard to international organizations, however. This approach saw such international groups as a collection of sovereign nation-states, international *governmental* organizations, and as such, included them under the heading of politics and thus worthy of study by political scientists.

But a more serious criticism to be made against the requirement of "sovereignty" concerns all those international organizations which are not comprised of sovereign territorial states but, rather, comprised of private individuals and groups. An interesting example can be found with the International

Olympic Committtee (IOC). The IOC is not sovereign and it does not have a fixed readily identifiable territory; it does have people and organization. The IOC is thus not a State for two of the four requirements are missing. We are not attempting to make the IOC into a State—that is not the problem—but we are attempting to demonstrate that institutions such as the IOC, although not a State, can and frequently do engage in political behavior. The IOC's late president, Avery Brundage, had been accused of many things during his long tenure in office but no one ever accused Brundage of being "nonpolitical." The decisions to ban Southern Rhodesia from the 1972 Summer Games and to allow East Germany to participate as a team separate from West Germany were without doubt political decisions by the IOC. The IOC is also involved in the "two Chinas" controversy: invitations to participate in the Games have been sent to both the Republic of China (Taiwan) and the People's Republic of China. But each will not participate unless the IOC withdraws the invitation from the other. These examples can be multiplied time and time again on the national level. Organizations such as the American Medical Association (AMA), American Bar Association (ABA), National Rifle Association (NRA), National Collegiate Athletic Association, (NCAA), and even Peter Rozelle and his National Football League sometimes engage in political behavior which could be analyzed by political scientists. These associations are not "States" but that does not prevent them from participating in the political process.

The central point to this discussion of the State's attributes is to demonstrate that the concept of the State is just too narrow, legal, restrictive, and formal for present-day conceptions of politics and political science. It might have been, and quite probably was, an excellent organizing concept for the period in which it developed but it proved to be too static and could not cope with the changing environment. David B. Truman, a well-known contemporary political scientist and a former president of the American Political Science Association, has characterized this general approach to political science as having six basic features:
1. an unconcern with political systems as such, including the American system, which amounted in most cases to taking their properties and requirements for granted;

2. an unexamined and mostly implicit conception of political change and development that was blandly optimistic and unreflectively reformist;

3. an almost total neglect of theory in any meaningful sense of the term;

4. a consequent enthusiasm for a conception of "science" that rarely went beyond raw empiricism;

5. a strongly parochial preoccupation with things American that stunted the development of an effective comparative method; and

6. the establishment of a confining commitment to concrete description.[20]

Professor Truman continues and writes that an unconcern with systems (1) meant that this approach emphasized the institutions, the concrete and the practical, and thus was unable to deal with the "system" as a functioning interrelated and interdependent whole. The optimistic and unreflectively reformist conception of political change (2) meant the inevitable progression to democracy even though the hard facts and reality of political life outside the borders of the United States did not corroborate this view. The neglect of theory (3) led to the increasing isolation of each subfield in political science for without theory, there were no common ties. Science (4) meant just the collection of raw facts and data, often just for their own sake, without any real attempt to interpret them. Truman writes that this view assumed that the facts spoke for themselves. The lack of an effective comparative focus and method (5) meant a preoccupation with the "minutiae of American phenomena" and comparative politics really meant the study of the governmental structures of the major European countries (Great Britain, France, and Germany). The narrowness of this view is evidenced by (6) the emphasis on and commitment to pure description.

A deeper understanding and knowledge of this view can be gained by an analysis of the view as it was manifested in one of the subfields of political science—comparative politics—but, at that time, it was not comparative "politics" but, rather, comparative "government." Comparative government was the study of foreign governments carried on in historical and legalistic manner. It was also quite parochial with emphasis upon Anglo-America and Western Europe. Roy Macridis has presented an excellent summary of what is now termed the "traditional" approach in the study of comparative politics and government.[21]

Comparative politics was limited to the Western world, representative democracies, and very little consideration was given to nondemocratic Western areas or to non-Western cultures and societies. Anglo-America and Western Europe were the universe and the rest of the world simply did not exist. Whatever research was done was purely descriptive in nature and thus, in Macridis's terms, the research was "comparative in name only." Finally, this traditional or institutional approach did not engage in the generation or validation of hypotheses and thus very little intersocial comparisons could be made.

It should be obvious that Truman's remarks on the general characteristics of the approach and Macridis's comments on traditional comparative government, and the above discussion of the State, were presented as criticism of the approach and not just a mere recapitulation of its components. But these very same remarks can also be taken as laudatory and flattering for it really depends in which direction the individual is pointed. In relation to "modern" political science, this approach is severely chastised for the above-described characteristics and components. But this is using hindsight and increased intellectual horizons to denigrate the approach (the Black September movement and the Viet Cong did not exist in the late nineteenth century and the early twentieth century, not even in someone's imagination). It is much more honest and beneficial to meet this approach on its own ground, in its own time, and take the same direction it took, i.e., looking backward to the then dominant speculative and philosophical approach to and view of political science. If we view this approach as a reaction to the older one and compare it to the older one, we will see that it attempted to get away from pure philosophical speculation and move into realism, relevance, facts—how things actually were and not how they ought to have been. If this is done, the conclusion is that this approach, political science as the study of the State, represents a break with past tradition and outlooks that was as great as, if not greater than, the break that "behavioralism" had with the State. It is this characteristic of the approach which should receive emphasis rather than placing emphasis upon the now obsolete components of the view.

But the approach is not that obsolete, for a substantial segment of the political science profession still ascribes, more or less, to this view and places emphasis upon the description of state/governmental activity. This reincarnation, as it were, of the traditional approach exhibits very few of the restraining and restrictive elements of the approach during the 1880-1930 period. This is to say, the modern adherents of the State no longer claim that political science is the study of the state, pure and simple, and they do not maintain that only the State/Government or its agents participate in political behavior. This new version recognizes that there is a lot more to "politics" than just "government" but they have opted to place their particular expertise and interest upon this one facet of political science. This is entirely different than the exaggerated view presented above. An excellent example of this "modern-traditional" approach can be seen in the writings of Alexander P. d'Entrèves particularly in *The Notion of the State: An Introduction to Political Theory*.[22] D'Entrèves does deal with the basic notion of the State but approaches it on three different levels: force/might, power, and authority. These concepts represent a totally different conception of the State than the one illustrated above by the writings of Leacock, Gettell, and Willoughby; and d'Entrèves rather than the others should now be used as representative of this view of politics and political science.

A Modern View:
Politics as a Power Relationship

A third general approach to and conception of politics and political science is a more contemporary and behavioral answer to the question "what is politics?" This view says that politics is "power" or, more specifically, "political" activity (activity which political scientists should study) is a relationship between at least two individuals which involves the presence of this abstract concept of "power." Stated briefly and without embellishment, this view defines politics as a power relationship between

or among individuals and/or groups of individuals. This conception changes the entire focus or emphasis of political science:
whereas the philosophical approach of the Greeks emphasized
society in general (the *Polis*) and the institutional approach of
the Statists emphasizes the State's organizations and behavior,
the contemporary conception directs attention to and emphasizes
the individual or groups of individuals and the nature of the
relationships between these individuals or groups. The root is
now the individual and not some philosophical *Polis* or an an-
thropomorphic state.

Compared to the Statist conception, this view is more inclusive because more categories of behavior and activity can
now be termed "political." It is more inclusive because politics
is now much more than *just* laws, constitutions, organizations,
and the activity of the sovereign national State. One no longer
requires, as the nineteenth-century conception required, the
Sovereign State or its agents to be an active participant before
a "political" situation could exist. As mentioned above, there
were and still are several societies which do not have anything
resembling our Western and, therefore, culture-bound conception of the State. But with the view that politics is a power relationship between or among people, it should then become obvious that Stateless or sovereignless societies and individuals can
and certainly do engage in political behavior. It must be pointed
out, however, that this view does not denigrate the State or reduce the State to a meaningless position. Now the State as a
formal entity is only a sufficient cause of political behavior
(whenever the State acts a power relationship and politics are
present) but the State is no longer a necessary cause (power
relationships and politics can exist without the participation of
the State).

With this view of politics, the *Polis* is no longer required before
political activity can take place: *two* people alone on a desert
island or eking out a subsistence-level existence hidden away in
some cave in the middle of the Sahara can now engage in power
relationships and political behavior. All three conceptions—the
philosophical, the institutional, and the behavioral—all agree,
however, that *one* person in this cave or on the island *cannot*
engage in politics although this agreement is based upon totally

different criteria. All three approaches say that our hermit in the cave may have or do a lot of things (linguistics, philosophy, religion, mathematics, etc.) but not politics. The philosophical Greek approach argues that a *Polis* is not present and, therefore, the hermit cannot attain the Good Life; the Statist argues that the cave is not a State; the behaviorist argues that there is no one else upon whom the hermit can exert "power."

It is at this point that students usually pose a question with a ramification which goes far beyond its seemingly simple content: "I agree with the basic premise—politics is a power relationship—but why cannot this hermit have political activity by exerting 'power' over the goat who also lives in the cave?" The naive response is, of course, that since politics is a power relation between at least two individuals and since this goat is not a person, *political* behavior and activities simply cannot be present by definition. The hermit may have all sorts of power relationships with the goat, the goat may even provide the hermit's dinner, but relationships between and among *people* are not present and no matter how much power this hermit has over the goat, it is not a political relationship.

Compared to the Greek view, politics as a power relationship is seen as more restrictive. Every activity within the society is not now regarded as being directed at the attainment of some vague undefined ethical goal and now there are vast areas of human activity which, if lacking this concept of power, are not political. Political science is, with this conception, absolutely not the "master science" and political science does not lay claim to the whole range of human activities. But this point leads into a very difficult and confusing area as to what actually constitutes the boundary line between political and nonpolitical or quasi-political acts. The problem can be stated along these lines: let us assume that there is no disagreement with the basic premise that power is required before an activity can be termed political; but, and this is the nub of the problem, are *all* power relationships between or among individuals political? If the answer to this question is "yes," then an enormous number of tenuous positions would have to be defended: behavior such as robbing a bank, disciplining a child, pushing to the front of a line, a street mugging, and the use of bribes would become "political" activity (power is most certainly present) and thus worthy of study by the political scientist. This situation is just the obverse of the nineteenth-century view: the earlier approach says that what is obviously a political activity is not political and the contemporary position says that certain activities which are obviously nonpolitical are now political.

This question has been extensively dealt with by several people, most notably Harold Lasswell and David Easton. Professor Lasswell ascribes to the expanded, all-inclusive position that *all* power relationships *are* political and thus a valid area of study for the political scientist. Professor Easton takes a more limited and restrictive view. He says, after a fashion, "I agree with Lasswell that power is required before an act can be said to be political but all power relationships are not political. Acts such as those mentioned above (muggings, nasty behavior) are not political but parapolitical."[23] Easton employs the term "authoritative allocation of value" as the boundary line between political and quasi-political or nonpolitical acts: the specific act must be binding upon the whole society in question before it can be political. This "authoritative allocation" is not present in the above examples and thus a bank robbery or a street crime is not political.[24]

It might appear that Easton's reliance upon this authoritative allocation of value is just a restatement, albeit in modern terminology, of the nineteenth-century view and its emphasis upon State activity. What category of activity could possibly be binding upon the *whole* society if the State or its agents do not participate? This very point is what sets the State apart from other groups in the society. The bank robber's activity is short-lived and binds only his hapless victim, but the policeman's response is not transitory and it does, in a sense, bind the whole society. Easton, however, is not a nineteenth-century thinker. To him, the term *society* can refer to whatever unit of analysis happens to be under study. These units could be the family, school, trade union, church group, or business association as well as the State. These subsocieties or subsystems engage in all sorts of activities and if what expires within them involves power and is binding upon all members of the group, we can then talk of activities such as campus politics, union politics, church politics, corporation politics, and the political scientist can study these manifestations of political behavior.

The above remarks concerned only the linkage or connection between politics and power and completely avoided any mention of the meaning of this term *power*. The problem is that this concept of power is almost as elusive and vague as the term *politics*. The term *power* frequently means all things as various individuals attempt to define and measure the kind or "amount" of power present in their particular universe and the following remarks seek to delineate and expand the meaning of the term. First, it is probably necessary to say what power is not. *Power* in a political context does not refer to any of the definitions given to the term by other fields of study:

1. Biology—a mental or physical function or attribute (the *power* of speech, the *power* of smell);
2. Law—an instrument authorizing one to act as the agent of another (the *power* of attorney);
3. Mathematics—the product obtained by multiplying a quantity by itself one or more times (2 to the fifth *power* = 2^5 = 32);
4. Mechanics—energy or force available for application to work;
5. Optics—the magnifying capacity of a microscope or telescope;
6. Physics—work done, or energy transferred, per unit of time; and
7. Theology—an order of angels.

The above conceptions of the term must be reserved for their own particular uses and should not be borrowed for a political context. To borrow a current expression, the term *power,* when used in relation to politics, has suffered a "bad press." Although it is actually a neutral and abstract term, *power* is frequently employed as a pejorative term. Expressions such as *power play, power seeker,* or *power politics* (this last expression is really a tautology for politics is power) conjure up all sorts of emotive images and responses, most of which are not laudatory or flattering. A brief listing of some of the synonyms employed for *power* gives some idea of this pejoration: *control, command, domination, dominion, force, jurisdiction, manipulation, rule, strength,* and *sway.*

Although there is disagreement in most of the literature as to the precise meaning of the term *power* and although there is a lack of consensus regarding the operationalization of whatever definitions are employed, there are strands of common agreement as to the basic broad meaning of the term and the following excerpts will serve as examples:

> HANS MORGENTHAU: When we speak of power . . . we have in mind not man's power over nature, or over an artistic medium such as language, speech, sound, or color, or over himself in the sense of self-control. When we speak of power, we mean man's control over the minds and actions of other men. By political power we refer to the mutual relations of control among the holders of public authority and between the latter and the people at large.[25]

> KARL DEUTSCH: . . . *Power* is the ability to make things happen that would not have happened otherwise. In this sense, it is akin to causality, that is, to the production of a change in the probability distribution of events in the world. And since the world is changing already, power deals with the change of change—or second-order change. Thus power involves our ability to change the changes that are already underway and would continue without our intervention.[26]

> MAURICE DUVERGER: By "authority [power] relationship" we mean any unequal relationship in which one or several individuals dominate the others and bend them, more or less, to their will.[27]

> HOWARD LASSWELL and ABRAHAM KAPLAN: *Power* is participation in making of decisions: G has power over H with respect to the values K if G participates in the making of decisions affecting the K-policies of H. . . . The definition of power in terms of decision-making adds an important element to "the production of intended effects on other persons"—namely, the availability of sanctions when the intended effects are not forthcoming. It is the threat of sanctions which differentiates power from influ-

ence in general. Power is a special case of the exercise of
influence: it is the process of affecting policies of others
with the help of (actual or threatened) severe deprivations
for nonconformity with the policies intended.[28]

L. S. SHAPLEY and MARTIN SHUBIK: Our definition of the
power of an individual member depends on the chance he
has of being critical to the success of a winning coalition [participation in majority votes].[29]

A particular view of power that I am partial to—not because it is "correct" for truthfulness or falseness is not relevant
here but because it is relatively straightforward, at least in its
outward appearances— is the one offered by Robert Dahl: ". . . A
has power over B to the extent that he can get B to do something that B would not otherwise do."[30] The obvious addition
or corollary to Dahl's statement would be that A also has power
over B to the extent that he can prevent B from doing something
that B would otherwise want to do. This seemingly straightforward and precise view is, however, not that simple, especially
when one attempts to operationalize or measure the actual
amount or degree of A's power over B. But this problem of
measuring power is discussed in a later section.

The statement "A can 'get' B . . ." should not be confused
with "A 'causes' B . . ." for, as Dahl mentions, causation and
causal relationships of inferences to this effect must be avoided.
"A gets B . . ." means that there is a higher probability that B
will (or will not) do some activity after A tells B to do (or not
do) it than exists if A does not interact with B. Dahl approaches
the entire concept as an exercise in probabilities: if the probability of B voting for one specific candidate is, say, 50 percent
without A's interference, but after A tells B to vote for this
candidate, the probability of B doing so is 75 percent, one can
than say that A's interaction with B increased the probabilities
of the desired outcome (75 > 50) and thus A influenced B.
But if the probability remains the same, 50 percent before *and*
after A's intercession, then A does not have influence/power
over B. Even with an increase to 75 percent, one cannot validly
say A "caused" B to vote the way B did. This is why the term
influence is more meaningful because this term does not carry

or evoke a causal relationship: "A influences B . . ." or "A gets B . . ." is preferable to "A makes or causes B. . . ."

Thus, for our purposes *power* (*influence* can be used interchangeably with *power*) means person A has the ability to get B to do act X ($A \to B \to X$) and/or person A has the ability to get person B not to do act X ($A \to B \nrightarrow X$). But this view of power is not that neat or precise to be limited to the simple statement ($A \to B \to X$). There are a large number of explanatory points to be made concerning the differing kinds, sources, and consequences of power. Table 1.1, "Power (or Influence)," breaks the general concept of *power* into its component parts or types. There are three basic types of power: authority, force (or coercion), and manipulation.

Authority is *legitimate* power or a power relationship in which person B or the B's grant to A the right to influence them. This voluntary submission is based upon one or more of three grounds. The sources of authority are (1) tradition, (2) charisma, and (3) legal-rational. The second type of power, force or coercion, is just the opposite of authority. A force relationship exists when B or the B's do *not* grant to A the right to influence them. With force, B either resists or there is involuntary submission to A's directives. The third type of power is termed manipulation and this occurs when B or the B's are *unaware* that A is applying a power relationship over them with the goal X known only to A. Once B becomes aware of A's interaction *and* intentions, such a power relationship changes from manipulation into authority or force, depending upon B's perception of the relationship. These three types of power—authority, force, and manipulation—are discussed in greater detail below.

Authority

Authority or legitimate power occurs when person B or the B's grant to A the right to exert influence or have power over them: in other words, voluntary submission of B to A's directives. This voluntary submission can be based upon one or more of three different conceptions that B has regarding his status or relationship to A. These sources or bases of authority have been identified by Max Weber [German, 1864-1920], a

Table 1.1

Power (or Influence)

Authority (legitimate power)	Force/Coercion (illegitimate power)	Manipulation

A ----→ B ----→ X

A ----→ B ---/→ X

Authority: The B's grant to A the right to influence or exert a power relationship over them (voluntary submission) and this submission is based on one or more of the following sources:
  A. Traditional Authority
  B. Charismatic Authority
  C. Legal-Rational Authority

Force/Coercion: The B's do *not* grant A the right to influence or exert a power relationship over them (resistance or involuntary submission); sanctions are present with force relationships.

Manipulation: The B's are *unaware* that A is applying influence or exerting a power relationship directed at a specific act known only to A.

very influential political sociologist, to be "legal-rational," "traditional," and "charismatic." Weber describes these terms in the following manner:

> Rational Grounds—resting on a belief in the "legality" of patterns of normative rules and the right of those elevated to authority under such rules to issue commands (legal authority);
>
> Traditional grounds—resting on an established belief in the sanctity of immemorial traditions and the legitimacy of the status of those exercising authority under them (traditional authority); or finally
>
> Charismatic Grounds—resting on devotion to the specific and exceptional sanctity, heroism, or exemplary character of an individual person, and of the normative patterns or order revealed or ordained by him (charismatic authority).[31]

Weber continues and writes that:

> In the case of legal authority, obedience is owed to the legally established impersonal order. It extends to the persons exercising the authority of office under it only by virtue of the formal legality of their commands and only within the scope of authority of the office. ... [with] traditional authority, obedience is owed to the *person* of the chief who occupies the traditionally sanctioned position of authority and who is (within its sphere) bound by tradition. But here the obligation of obedience is not based on the impersonal order, but is a matter of personal loyalty within the area of accustomed obligations. ... [with] charismatic authority, it is the charismatically qualifed leader as such who is obeyed by virtue of personal trust in him and his revelation, his heroism or his exemplary qualities so far as they fall within the scope of the individual's belief in his charisma. ...[32]

Some specific examples of these types of legitimate power or authority would probably be more beneficial than more definitions or descriptions although it will be seen that the three types

frequently overlap and there are elements of all three in practically every authority relationship. Some examples of the first
category (legal-rational) would be the United States president
(although some presidents such as Franklin Roosevelt, Dwight
Eisenhower, and John Kennedy were fortunate enough to also
have some charismatic authority), European prime ministers,
practically all elected officials, the judge in the court, the law
enforcement officer on the street corner. The law enforcement
officer on the street corner is an excellent example of legal-
rational authority. Most people *do* grant to the State and its
agents, the police, the right to regulate traffic flow and thus such
a relationship—the police and the motorist—is legitimate power.
But why does the individual obey the directives of the traffic
officer? There is probably not more than one person in a million
who obeys on charismatic grounds. People do not stop or slow
down when asked (told?) on account of the officer's exemplary
character. It is the office and not the person which demands and
receives submission from B; a different officer could be on the
job the next day and B would continue to obey.

Examples of traditional authority would be a contemporary
monarch (Queen Elizabeth of Great Britain), the pope (although
there are elements of legal-rational authority with the pope and
some popes have also enjoyed a vast amount of charismatic
authority), and tribal or village chiefs. Charismatic authority
has been enjoyed by Jesus, Hitler, Gandhi, Nasser, and for some
contemporary charismatic authority relationships, one can point
to Raquel Welch or Joe Namath.

Some further examples reinforce the difficulty of finding
a pure case of just one of the three categories: it has been
rumored that there are some professors (A) who can get their
students (B) to do the required reading (X) or not to cut class
(Y) solely on the basis of the professor's charismatic, endearing,
drawing personality but it is probably just a rumor. It is more
likely and probable that the professor's power is partly legal-
rational (the State and university have in a sense elevated him to
this office) and thus his directives flow from assumed obedience
to the position and partly traditional authority—the professor-
ship as a position/office to which obedience is due harks back

to the Middle Ages and its ancient and quaint customs. But what is more important is B's attitude because it is B's perception of his relationship to A (the professor) which really determines what category of power is present. Unscientific and nonrigorous classroom surveys performed by this authority has found that charismatic authority is totally lacking, only ten percent of the students submit on traditional grounds, whereas the other ninety percent submit to the directives on legal-rational grounds. One is then forced to conclude that any person could assume this position (professor) and the students would submit because submission is directed at the office, not the person.

Another example can be found within the power relationships between the child and the parents: legal, traditional, or charismatic? From the parents' (A) point of view, the power relationship is probably legal-rational: the State has given the authority to exert power, within limits, over the children. There are also strands of traditional authority present: parents have from time immemorial been sanctioned by society to demand submission from their children. But from the child's (B) point of view, it is probably charismatic authority until at least the child reaches adolescence. Charismatic for the 2-3 year old because he or she is not aware that the parents have either the legal or traditional right to influence, and the child is aware only of the parents' exemplary and endearing personalities. This relationship between the child and parent probably changes into legal-rational authority during adolescence and the teen-age years. To the rebellious child, the parents are no longer perceived as exemplary personalities but, rather, only as people who have been sanctioned by the State to exert influence over the child. Once the child becomes an adult, however, there is no longer any legal-rational authority present. The parent has no claim to legal authority, the parent probably has very little charismatic authority over the grown child, and now the relationship is one of traditional authority if there is, in fact, any authority at all.

These three types of legitimate power or authority can also be employed to aid in the explanation of the levels of stability/ instability in certain regimes and societies. Those societies which operate under legal-rational authority experience very little instability or dislocation when, say, the decision-maker (A) dies because the office devolves on another person and the process is maintained. The change in the United States from John Kennedy to Lyndon Johnson in 1963 is a case in point. Voluntary submission or obedience is directed at the office, not the individual, and when the individuals change, there is not a resultant instability. The change from Nixon to Ford is another excellent example of the stabilizing character of legal-rational authority patterns. American society and the political process might have been immobilized during the summer of 1974, but Mr. Ford, immediately upon accession to the presidency, had legitimate power because the B's, Americans, grant power to the Office of the Presidency and not to the particular person holding the office.

There is also relatively little dislocation with a society under traditional authority. The traditional leader and his successor are determined by the mores and customs of the culture—the eldest son, the strongest warrior, the oldest person. It is within societies whose power is based upon charismatic leadership which experience dislocations and upheavals when the leader (A) is no longer on the scene. Unless the society can replace the former charismatic leader with another similar personality, the society will be in a state of flux until the new decision-maker builds up an aura about him. This may not happen, however, if the former leader had been able to change the system from one based purely on charisma to one which has at least the beginnings of a legal-rational basis. President Tito of Yugoslavia may be a case in point. The death of Mr. Tito in the late 1940s would have presented a very difficult situation for the continuance of a viable Yugoslav state but after approximately thirty years in power, Tito has been able to construct some legal-rational basis to the regime. Perhaps the death of Martin Luther King better illustrates the consequences of charismatic authority: the civil rights movement in the United States has simply not been as unified or effective after Dr. King's death. The entire authority pattern was one based upon Dr. King's charisma, and as able as Jesse Jackson, Ralph Abernathy, and Dick Gregory are, the successors to Dr. King cannot maintain his relationships.

Force

The second type of power is termed "force" or "coercion" and this is "illegitimate" power: the B's do not grant to A the right to influence or exert a power relationship over them. With force, B will resist or there will be involuntary submission to A's directives. Force is always accompanied by sanctions (rewards and punishments) for it is only with sanctions that person A can get B to do or not to do act X when B does not willingly submit. But violence is not necessary for violence is only one type of sanction.

Sanctions are rewards or punishments (if B does X or refrains from doing X, he will receive a positive or negative return). Sanctions can be one or a combination of three types. First are physical rewards and punishments—overt physical payoffs if B does (or does not) submit to A's directives. These overt physical payoffs can take various forms. Rewards for compliance could be food, shelter, or protection; physical punishments for noncompliance take the form of violent retribution such as forty lashes, the electric chair, a slap for the child, and all the various forms of torture. The second type of sanction is nonphysical: fines (bribes), imprisonment (pardon), loss of a special privilege (granting a special privilege), or a failing (passing) mark in the course. These are nonphysical because the individual's person is not involved. The third type of sanction is psychological-emotional-metaphysical: A will reward B with respect, honor, or love if B complies or A will punish B with the loss of such attributes if B does not comply with A's directives. The metaphysical sanction (rewards *and* punishments) of the promise of life after death in Heaven or the threat of life after death in Hell or the punishment of excommunication was a very effective sanction, particularly during the Middle Ages. Metaphysical sanctions have frequently been, in fact, more effective in inducing B to comply than mere physical or nonphysical punishments. The martyrs who were burned at the stake because they refused to "recant" or admit heresy perceived the metaphysical sanction as more salient than the overt physical punishment.

Positive sanction (rewards) most often entail concrete returns—do this and you will receive ten dollars, or if you refrain from doing that you can have this present, or if you come to class every day and take good notes, you will receive at least a C in the course. But, and this may be a difficult point to grasp, the avoidance of a negative sanction (punishment) can be regarded as a reward. Submission to A's directive *in order to avoid* a fine or to avoid being put into jail (perhaps the relationship between the traffic officer and motorist is not one of legal-rational authority but a force relationship) can in a real sense be regarded as a reward: B could have been fined but was not; B could have been put into jail but was not; B could have been executed but was not. The attitudes, perceptions, and expectations of B determine the category (reward or punishment) of the applied sanction. If a student does not come to class and does not do the required reading, the student, let us assume, has convinced himself that he is about to fail the course. But the magnanimous professor assigns a D—. From the professor's point of view, the D— is seen as a negative sanction (a punishment): a D— is not a very good grade and will lower the student's average. But, and this is the crucial point, the student received a reward—the student *avoided* the punishment of the F and thus the D— is a reward from the student's perspective.

The use of sanctions, both positive and negative but particularly negative sanctions, is, however, not as straightforward as it might appear. Negative sanctions involve the use of threats: A promises B that if B does (or does not) perform a certain activity, A will apply some horrible punishment upon B. But there is a difference here between rewards and punishments: to be successful in getting B to comply when rewards are promised, A must deliver on the promise. The ten dollars must be paid, the love must be given, the grade of A+ must be assigned. If A does not deliver, B will no longer comply and the promises of rewards become meaningless. With threats and negative sanctions (punishments), however, just the opposite conditions are present. A successful threat is one that *does not have to be applied*. That is to say, A wants B to do X and, since it is a force relationship A accompanies the directive with a threat: ". . . and if you do not do X, I will. . . ." The successful threat is one that will get

B to do X without having to apply the contents of the threat. The goal of the interaction is A → B → X and it is not the application of the threat; if the goal *were* the threat, A would not need the interaction A → B → X. All A would have to do would be to apply the punishment. But a successful threat, a threat which does not have to be actually applied, must meet several criteria or requirements.

First of all, and probably most obvious, A must communicate the nature of the threat to B and B must be able to receive this communication in legible or understandable terms. If A tells B to do act X within two minutes or A will—and all of a sudden A begins to mumble so that B cannot hear (and A knows that B cannot hear, and B knows that A knows . . .), the threat is meaningless and B need not do X. But for this situation to develop, both A and B need to be aware that the threat had not been received in understandable terms and that both A and B know that the other knows. If A thinks the threat *was* received by B, person B is then in the unfortunate position of being forced to choose between X and the (unknown) threat. Since there is a high probability of B preferring an unknown outcome to X, the threat would have to be applied and then it would thus not be a successful one (remember that A's goal was X, not the punishment of B).

Another necessary component for the successful threat is that the content or nature of the threat must "hurt" B more than it does A. The child who promises to stamp his feet and yell until he gets his way will soon learn that he must think of alternative sanctions to employ against his parents for, if carried out, the child's activities will not harm B. The country who threatens to block a certain trade deal but, if they do, will have a substantial increase of domestic unemployment, and both sides are aware of this, will not get much political mileage from the threat (B will simply ignore it, knowing full well that A will not carry out the threat). The politician who threatens to resign if his particular bill is not passed receives very few additional votes from his fellow legislators because the resignation of the politician will harm A more than B.

But these remarks are predicated on the assumption that the person making the threat is a rational person in that he realizes that he will be harmed and therefore does not carry out the threat. There is no adequate way to deal with people who are not rational when it comes to threats: the kidnapping and killing of the Israeli athletes in Munich during the 1972 Summer Olympic Games is a case in point. The terrorists threatened that they would kill their hostages if they (A) were not given unhindered exit from the country. But everyone knew that they would not carry out the threat for if they did, they themselves would then be killed and this would harm them more than it would harm the B's. But, and this is what was so tragic, the terrorists could not convince the German police (the Israeli government was probably convinced, however) that they would actually carry out the threat even though it meant their own death. One side acted as if the threat was meaningless, the other acted in an irrational manner (irrational for our discussion only, the activities of the terrorists were terribly rational from their own point of view).

A further component to the successful threat, and one that is perhaps most important, is that the threat has to be believable or creditable. B must believe that whatever A threatens is true and that A has the manpower, technology, or courage to carry out the threat. The professor who threatens his students that they will fail the course if they miss one and only one class meeting is really mouthing a nonbelievable threat because the aware student should realize that the professor does not have the ability to carry out this particular threat. It is simply noncreditable and cannot be employed as a bargaining tool by the professor. Another example of this can be seen with the decision by the United States to use the atomic bomb against Japan. Much has been written on this particular episode in U.S.-Japanese relations, particularly on the moral/ethical aspects of the actual use of the bomb and on whether or not the United States should have done something else to get the Japanese to surrender. But for our purposes, the use of the first A-bomb over Hiroshima can serve as an example of a threat by the United States (A) which simply was not believed by Japan (B) for Japan thought that the United States did not have the ability to carry out the threat.

There was much debate in American political and military circles on what to do about warning Japan of the impending devastation. The United States could have invited a group of Japanese politicians and generals to a testing ground for a preview of the bomb; one could have been exploded offshore in the Pacific; the nature of the bomb could have been communicated to the Japanese. The first two alternatives were discarded for if the United States had given a nonlethal preview it was quite possible that the bomb might not have exploded. This was in 1945, just at the beginning of nuclear technology and if this happened, the Japanese would have been convinced that the threat was only a poorly played bluff. There was also the problem of the United States not having that many operational bombs at that time. There might not have been an operational bomb left for the real thing if the Japanese knew of the limited stockpile and requested a few demonstrations and complimentary instant replays! To refuse a replay would have convinced the Japanese that no bombs were left and then they would be free to ignore the threat.

The United States opted for a more limited approach: it informed the Japanese government that a brand-new, totally devastating and destructive bomb would be dropped and, to avoid this hideous situation, Japan was to surrender. Unfortunately, the Japanese regarded this as propaganda. *They* had no evidence that such a bomb actually existed for the United States had maintained stringent secrecy over the Manhattan Project. Very few people knew about the bomb, Harry Truman did not become aware of it until he became president (he was kept in the dark while he was vice-president), and the Japanese dismissed it out of hand for it was simply not creditable or believable, and the resulting tragic consequences followed.

The point is, to make threats believable and creditable, to threaten a country with the Doomsday Machine, the country being threatened must know or have some idea that it actually exists. If a country keeps a secret weapon so secret that its adversaries know nothing about it, the weapon is totally useless to use as a bargaining tool or as a threat (it is, of course, not useless if the country just decides to set it off). This can help

to explain why there are constant quasi-official "leaks" of information from one side to the other. The Soviet Union's May
Day parade with its emphasis upon newly developed sophisticated military equipment is a case in point; let the Americans
see these weapons so they can then be used for other purposes
than actual use (the threat of a missile rather than the use of
the missile itself).[33]

The successful use of threats and sanctions is thus not that
simple. The threat must be communicated, received, be rational,
and be believable. If any one of these components is missing,
the threat cannot achieve its goal: $A \rightarrow B \rightarrow X$ without the
threat being applied.

Leaving aside the question of sanctions for the time being,
one can see that there is a severe problem for societies in which
the A's and B's do not agree as to the type of power being exer-
cised. This is most prevalent in situations where A believes, and
acts upon that belief, that he is exercising some form of legitimate power or authority but the B's regard his activity as force.
It is tragic because each side believes in their own righteousness
and very seldom can there be an accommodation between the
A's and B's. The draft resistance movement in the United States
in the late 1960s and, also, the military deserters are a case in
point. These people have not granted the government (A) the
right to exert power over them (the draft, soldier status) and
refuse compliance whereas the government is relying upon legal/
rational authority to enforce its will. Other examples of this
dislocation of perceptions about the nature of power can be
found in the United States with the Blacks' drive for equality
and nondiscrimination and the termination of the enforcement
of the separate-but-equal doctrine. Gandhi, Nehru, and the
Indian National Congress in preindependent India were simply
at loggerheads with the British imperialists: the British believed
and acted on the basis of legal/rational authority, the Indians
on the basis of "force" (the Indians did not grant the British the
right to exert power over them).

One of the more idealistic responses to this situation is nonviolent passive resistance on the part of the B's. Nonviolent
passive resistance is based on the belief that the government (or

the A's) do not have the right to demand obedience and submission from the people (the B's) and thus the people do not comply with the government's directives. The more successful examples of such resistance to force can be seen with Martin Luther King's Southern Christian Leadership Conference in the United States and the Indian response against the British colonial government. The more prevalent form of resistance against force, however, is revolt and revolution. The government demands obedience but the population no longer perceives A's activities as legitimate power or authority. The people resist, usually through violence.

Manipulation

The third type of power is termed manipulation and this occurs when B or the B's are *unaware* that A is applying influence or exerting a power relationship directed at a specific act known only to A. Manipulation, when approached from B's viewpoint, can take two forms. The first type of manipulation can be described as $A \rightarrow B \rightarrow X$ but B is unaware of the linkage between A, B, and X. This type of manipulation is, however, not very frequent for there are very few times that B is not cognizant of the A, B, and X linkage.

The second type of manipulation is more frequent and here B is aware of the $A \rightarrow B$ linkage but may not be aware of A's intention or B may be aware of the $A \rightarrow B$ relation but mistaken as to A's intentions ($A \rightarrow B \rightarrow X$ when in reality A wants B to do Y and X is only a subterfuge). The child can be manipulated quite easily; consumers are inflicted with the subtle messages usually delivered by pretty girls, nations are subjected to propaganda. But whatever the particular form of the manipulative relationship, B just does not know that A wants a specific activity accomplished. Once B becomes aware of the $A \rightarrow B \rightarrow X$ linkage, the power relationship changes into either authority or force, depending upon A's and B's perception of the relationship. Manipulative relationships usually, but not always, are transformed into force/coercive situations. Person A usually resorts to manipulation in the first place because he does not perceive

himself to have legitimate power or authority; person B usually
resents and opposes A when manipulation becomes observable—
manipulation is usually a substitute for force.

Some Additional Types of Power

A few points should be mentioned with this concept of
power: there is also (1) indirect power, (2) negative power, and
(3) circular power. A symbolic representation of these types
would be as follows: $A \to B \to C \to X$ (indirect); $A \to B \to X$
but $B \to Y$ (negative); and $A \to B \to C \to A$ (circular). Such
situations and relationships are not that uncommon and some
examples follow.

Indirect Power

A influences B so that B will influence C to do or not do X
and this final result is A's original intention. These relationships
$(A \to B, B \to C)$ may be manipulative but not necessarily. The
once-removed relationship $(A \to C)$ is most likely of the three
to be manipulation although the example of indirect power
which follows is probably not manipulation (but, once again, this
depends upon B's and C's awareness and perceptions): (A) the
president gets (B_1) and (B_2), members of his cabinet, to influence (C_1) and (C_2) and (C_n) to act X—vote for the president.
There is no direct relationship between the president (A) and
the voters (C_n) and thus this is a form of indirect power. The
entire Watergate affair was dominated by indirect power with
very strong overtones of manipulation. The president (A) constantly employed his subordinates (B_n) to influence the activities
of lesser personalities (C_n).

Negative Power

Person A attempts to influence B to do X and this act (X)
is A's original intention and desire. But by the very fact of
$A \to B \to X$ leads B to resist and not only does B not do X, he
perhaps does Y, which is the total opposite of A's desire. If Y
were the original intention of A, this would be a classic case of

manipulation: A → B → X when A's original intention is Y and B, upon hearing that A wants him to perform X, therefore resists and does Y. An example of negative (nonmanipulative) power can be seen in the following case: the Soviet Union (A) wants the United States (B) to remove its troops from Western Europe (X). The Soviet Union attempts to accomplish this by threatening the United States with an increase in its (A's) own forces if X is not done. The United States reacts, not by doing X, or not by doing nothing—the United States does Y and Y is the complete opposite of the Soviet Union's original intention. The United States increases its own troop strength to meet this alleged new threat to the balance of power. This result actually entails negative power for the Soviet Union.

Circular Power

A has power over B who has power over C who has power over A. It is quite difficult to actually identify the person who has the most power in the situation for this is no longer a two-person relationship. An example of circular power might be that a professor (A) has power over a student (B) who has power over her father (C), and the father happens to be president of the university, who in turn has power over the professor. Each two-person relationship (A → B, B → C, C → A) is recognizable and may be able to be measured but problems arise when more than two people are present.

Can Power Be Measured?

Basic to the behavioral approach to politics and political science is the belief that the substance of politics can be measured, compared, quantified, or counted. And since "Politics as a power relationship" is, in essence, a behavioral answer to the question "What is politics?" the task at hand is to construct a measuring device in order to quantify the degree or amount of power present in the relationships between and among individuals. This measuring scale must be able to note, first, the absolute amount of power A has over B and, second, the relative amount of power A_1 has compared to A_2. There have been several admirable quantification schemes presented in the literature but these specific comments and contributions need not be reproduced here. Rather, the remarks which follow attempt only to identify some of the basic problems one must overcome before any meaningful measuring device can be employed to note the amount of power A has over B or to compare A_1's power to A_2's power.

Perhaps the most important component or variable to be considered is the pre-existing attitude of B toward whatever act A is demanding at the time. To have any sort of meaningful power relationship between A and B, B must be adverse or negative toward the actual act or accomplishment of the act. If B is neutral (it does not make any difference to him whether he does the act or refuses to do it) or if B is positive (he wants to do the directed activity), the additional fact of A telling him to do it has no meaning. The person (A) who tells person B to jump from the window ledge on the tenth floor and B does it may or may not have power. If B were about to commit suicide (i.e., his pre-existing attitude toward the act was positive), then A did not exercise any power over him. But if B wanted to commit suicide and A told him "not to jump" and then B followed A's directives by climbing down from the ledge, then one could reasonably say that A does have power over B. If I attempted to encourage Julie Nixon Eisenhower to vote for her father rather than for George McGovern, and she did, it would be obvious that I had no power over Mrs. Eisenhower because her pre-existing attitude toward the act was such that any additional encouragement from me could not change the probability of her voting for her father.

A problem is encountered, however, in the identification of the direction and degree of B's pre-existing attitude toward X. Quite frequently B does not publicize or make available pre-existing attitudes to the same extent as Mrs. Eisenhower did during the 1972 elections. Senators often refuse to publicize their stance on an upcoming bill and it really is not valid to employ someone's actual vote as the pre-existing attitude. One simply does not encounter in real-life situations too many situations where: (1) B announces his pre-existing attitude toward X; (2) $A \rightarrow B \rightarrow X$; (3) $B \rightarrow X$; and (4) calculating the resulting change in probabilities. But if this variable is lacking, it is then quite difficult to measure power.

Another factor to be considered is A's intention or attitude. A must have the conscious desire to change B's behavior patterns before one can say that A has power over B. An inadvertent and completely chance encounter between A and B which leads to a decision by B to change his behavior cannot in truth be employed as evidence that A has power over B. Person A must consciously desire and also attempt to influence B although B is not required to be aware of the fact. If he is not aware, it is manipulation; if he is aware of A's activities, it is then authority or force. This question of A's attitude spills over into the problem of actual (what was just discussed) power versus potential power (some sort of power reserve that A could perhaps employ but is not currently utilizing). Potential power is impossible to deal with until and unless it becomes manifest as actual behavior. The potential or latent power of an individual remains only as an abstract attribute until A decides to make use of his resources.

A third important factor or variable to be considered in measuring power deals with the time span between A's communication to B of the desired activity and the actual accomplishment of the act. All other variables being equal, A_1 has more power than A_2 if B does the act in less time for A_1 than for A_2. An important difference to note is that the above statement (A_1 and $A_2 \rightarrow B \rightarrow X$) is entirely different than ($A_1 \rightarrow B_1 \rightarrow X$ and $A_2 \rightarrow B_2 \rightarrow X$). The first statement refers to the same person being acted upon by two different A's and being told to do some identical act. The second statement refers to four people: A_1 and B_1, A_2 and B_2. The time delay as a measuring device for power is only valid in the first statement for here the same person is being acted upon for the same act: the time B takes to do the act for each of the A's can be used to measure A_1's and A_2's power over B. But to use the time delay to compare A_1 and A_2 when there is also B_1 and B_2 is just too arbitrary because B_1 may be slower to react than B_2 for physical reasons, his attitude toward the act may be different and A_1 might have more to overcome than A_2. A longer/shorter time span between the directive and the act may not necessarily mean more or less power.

The central point is that all the other variables cannot be kept equal or constant for we are dealing with attitudes, intentions, and other variables discussed below (the nature of the act, the frequency of the act, and the type of B being acted upon). The time delay usually has to be relatively immediate: if I were to tell my students to read the required texts but if they wait until after the final examination before even purchasing them, I may have some influence over them but a lot less than if they had rushed out of the classroom immediately and deluged the bookstore with money in hand. The longer the time between the communication of the desired behavior and the actual accomplishment of the act allows for countless other variables and stimuli to enter the statement $(A \rightarrow B \rightarrow X)$. A's power is effectively reduced, if not eliminated, when there is too much delay on B's part. Of course, the time delay is in part determined by the nature of the act being requested for some activities may require months or years before completion. One last example will suffice (an example of a situation where there is a long time delay but also where one is on safe ground) to say that A does or did have power over B: the mother constantly tells her son that he must, when he grows up, marry a nice ———— (the reader is free to supply any descriptive adjective desired) girl and, fifteen or twenty years later, the dutiful son heeds his mother's wishes! There is a definite power relationship here, even though the actual accomplishment of the act required several years.

An additional factor which must be taken into account in measuring power concerns the nature or content of the act that A is demanding of B. Some sort of relative scale must be devised and each specific behavior pattern must be located along this continuum before one can say that A_1 has more power than A_2. Who has more power: A_1 who can get B to change his vote or A_2 who can get B to commit a crime for political ends? Who has more power: A_1 who can get B to jump out of a window or A_2 who can get B to pass out campaign literature? The content or nature of the act is a very important component to be considered whenever comparisons of power are being made but, even if a continuum of acts exits, the pre-existing attitude of B may alter the power relationship (B may very well be totally negative about passing out campaign literature and be favorably disposed to jumping out the window).

An additional pair of variables must also be considered and these concern the relative weights or values between the number of B's that are influenced and the number of times that the act is performed. This can be symbolically represented as: who has more power, $A_1 \rightarrow B_1 + B_2 + B_3 \rightarrow X$ or $A_2 \rightarrow B_1 \rightarrow 3X$? One is probably forced to conclude that both A_1 and A_2 in this particular example have the same amount of power, all other variables being equal. But, and this is an important caveat, it is entirely rational for A_1 to have more power than A_2. This situation is based upon Dahl's discussion of probabilities: A_1 has to overcome three (B_1, B_2, and B_3) different sets of attitudes and these attitudes may all be highly negative. A_2 has to overcome only one set of attitudes (B_1) and it is very likely that B_1 will be less negative toward the act once he did it for the first time and even less negative the third time around. A_2 has, on the average, less resistance to overcome than A_1. But if all the other factors can remain constant, that person who can influence more people to do the same act will have more power than another person (A_2) who can influence fewer people; and A_1 will have more power than A_2 if A_1 can get B to perform act X three times whereas A_2 can get B to do it only once. But all variables do not remain constant and this is a very serious problem to overcome.

One final variable has to be mentioned and this relates to the type of person B actually is. Who has more power: A_1 who can convince a United States senator (B_1) to change his vote on a crucial bill in Congress or A_2 who can convince his wife (B_2) to change her attitude toward the same bill? Who has more power: A_1 who can convince the president (B_1) not to follow a certain policy or A_2 who can convince his cousin (B_2) not to do the same? One way of getting around this problem of the nature or type of B is to first calculate how much power B has: those people (A_1) who have power over powerful people (the president [B_1]) can be said to have more power over those (A_2) who have power over less powerful people (someone's cousin [B_2]). But of course this does not solve the problem: it only makes one start again for now the B's are transformed into A's, the C's into B's, the D's into C's, and *this* is an endless and fruitless procedure.

The above variables must all be considered together and not singly for the measurement of power is a multivariate process. These variables, in summary, are A's intentions, B's pre-existing attitude toward the act, the time span between the communication of the act and the actual accomplishment of the desired behavior, the nature or content of the act, the frequency of the act, the number of B's who can be influenced, and the type (how powerful) of person B actually is. A symbolic representation of these variables would take the following form: who has more power, $A_1 \rightarrow B_1 \rightarrow X$ in W time or $A_2 \rightarrow B_2 + B_3 \rightarrow Y$ in Z time? The identification of these variables appears to be an insurmountable barrier to any neat or precise measuring scheme of "power" and thus "politics as power" is not as neat or precise as is desired. When attention turns to the question on the vital operational level (who has how much power over whom?) there are simply too many implications, ramifications, and variables to overcome and these prevent "power" from being employed as the sole organizing concept of political science.

But this conceptual approach to political science does represent a distinctly different viewpoint. The Greek approach is philosophical, very broadly based (politics as the master science!), ethical, and it emphasizes the prescription of some final goal for man in society as well as a description of how to attain this posited goal. The late-nineteenth-century approach, politics as state behavior, may have removed many of the disadvantages of the philosophical approach from political science but the State conception itself had several disadvantages. This traditional approach is legalistic, formalistic, emphasis is upon institutions and inanimate objects, and, although it severely reduced the boundaries of political science compared to the Greek philosophical approach, the concept of the State proved to be too limited and static to adapt to a changing environment. The view of politics and political activity as a power relationship between at least two individuals completely shifts the focus: the emphasis is now upon the individual and his or her behavior, ethics and morality do not enter the relationship, final goals and the "oughts" of society are not really relevant, and politics as a power relationship neither unduly restricts the scope of political science nor offers the claim that all forms of human activity are political.

2
Four Representative Conceptions

Politics as Conflict
Thomas Hobbes (English, 1588-1679)

Thomas Hobbes, in his major and most famous writing, *Leviathan* (1651), presents the first important philosophical analysis of politics published in the English language.[1] Firmly entrenched in the Greek approach to politics—the philosophical description of what "ought" to be—Hobbes can be classified as conceiving politics as conflict. The formal organized State is created to manage or limit this conflict and, for Hobbes, if the State were ever to disappear, the conflictive and violent nature of man would reassert itself and life would again be characterized as brutal, nasty conflict.

Hobbes lived and wrote during a very turbulent period of English social and political history. Elizabeth I (the second of Henry VIII's three children) died in 1603 without any direct heirs and the Crown passed to a cousin, James of Scotland. James I (1603-1625) was a firm believer in the "divine right of kings" theory: *rex gratia dei* or king by the grace of God. The divine right of kings theory posits that the king receives his power to rule from God and not from the people, and the people thus could not complain about the king's actions or revolt against the king for this would be revolt against God. The king, with this view, is subject to no power on earth but is, however, subject to God's law. During the Middle Ages and throughout the feudal system, it was the pope who exerted a tempering influence upon the king's behavior. Europe was Catholic and even though the kings received their authority from God, the pope, as interpreter of God's will on earth, was able to maintain some semblance of ethical behavior on the part of the sovereigns. It was the Protestant Reformation which freed many sovereigns from the pope's control and, in several countries, *rex gratia dei* did not then have the tempering and civilizing input of the pope.[2]

Be that as it may, James I believed, and acted upon the belief, that he was indeed king by the grace of God. He ruled for several years with the embryonic Parliament dissolved and he also alienated both Catholics and the various forms of Protestantism with his policies. James I was an intolerant Protestant and various sects were severely discriminated against. One should note here that it was during James I's reign that one such sect, the Puritans, left England aboard the Mayflower and landed at Plymouth in 1620. James I was succeeded by Charles I (1625-1649) and Charles I had the same notions about the divine right of kings as did his predecessor. Charles I was continually at odds with Parliament (*rex gratia dei* does not admit input into the decision-making process by the people) but Parliament retaliated in 1628. One of the most famous and enduring components of English constitutional documents and behavior patterns was voted by Parliament in 1628 and this document was directed specifically at Charles I. This document, the Petition of Right, stated, in part, that all taxes not debated, voted on, and approved by Parliament were illegal, null, and void. Accepted by Charles I, the Petition of Right gave effective control of the purse and all public revenue bills to Parliament. But Parliament was soon dissolved by Charles I and the king continued to disregard Parliament until 1642 when war credits and funding, a military appropriation bill, were needed for a military campaign in Scotland. Called into session after a long absence, Parliament reacted against Charles I by not only refusing to vote the money but also by passing a law forbidding the king to dissolve Parliament again. The lines were drawn and a civil war ensued between the forces loyal to the king (the Royalist Cavaliers) and the Parliamentary forces (the Roundheads).

The civil war was bitterly fought, although intermittently, from 1642 to 1649 and this seven-year period witnessed the effective erosion of legitimate state authority. In a sense, the state had disappeared and the violent conflictive nature of man became dominant during the civil war. The Parliamentary side was victorious and Charles I was publicly beheaded in 1649. This beheading was a massive and bloody blow struck against *rex gratia dei* but it did not entirely remove the concept from England. However, Charles I's execution was a major watershed in the transformation from *rex gratia dei* to *rex gratia populi* (king by the grace of the people).

The following decade, 1649-1659, was also a turbulent period. Oliver Cromwell, head of the victorious Parliamentary army, abolished both the House of Lords and the Monarch, and Cromwell ruled as Protector of the Commonwealth. Cromwell died in 1659 and his son, Richard, attempted to succeed his father as Protector but was unable to maintain himself in office. This failure of Richard Cromwell is an excellent example of the point noted above in Chapter 1 regarding the dysfunctional and unstable ramifications when authority is based upon charisma and the charismatic personality dies. There is no question that Oliver Cromwell enjoyed legitimate power/authority but this authority was largely based upon charisma. The B's did not automatically cede to his son the right to influence them for Richard simply was not perceived as having an exemplary or heroic character. The office of Protector disappeared, the Commonwealth system disintegrated, and Parliament returned to traditional authority after the charismatic interlude.

In 1659, Parliament invited (another blow to *rex gratia dei*) Charles II to rule as king and the House of Lords was organized anew. Charles II ruled from 1660 to 1685 and he was very aware that it was Parliament and not God who invited him to rule. But in 1685, James II followed his father and it appears that James II either was unaware of the past 80 years or chose to disregard the changes. James II was an avowed Roman

Catholic in a predominantly Protestant England and he saw nothing wrong with the divine right of kings. Fearful of an extension of royal power and a re-emergence of Catholicism, the Protestant Parliament demanded that James II abdicate and Parliament then invited William and Mary of Orange (the Netherlands) to accept the title and office of king and queen and to rule jointly.

This invitation issued to William and Mary of Orange (William III and Mary II) in late 1688—early 1689 is known as the Glorious Revolution. This event may not have appeared very glorious to James II and his supporters but this was a bloodless, nonviolent palace coup d'état in which James II left for France (James II probably realized that he might have suffered the same fate as Charles I had he resisted the order to abdicate) and William became king upon the request of Parliament. The Glorious Revolution of 1688-1689 finally put an end to the divine right of kings theory in Great Britain and no monarch since William and Mary dared resurrect the view that the monarch was chosen by, and responsible to, God and not the people. Great Britain was thus in the forefront of giving power to the people. France had to endure exactly one hundred more years of *rex gratia dei* until the guillotine struck another massive blow in 1789; Russia endured until 1917 with the tsars but Nicholas too went to his death proclaiming God's authority. Hobbes' *Leviathan* was published in 1651, two years after Charles I was beheaded and during the second year of Cromwell's Protectorate although the book was written before 1651, most likely during the Civil War of 1642-1649.

Hobbes studied at Oxford and "graduated" in 1609 when he was twenty-one years old. He came from a well-to-do family; traveled widely, especially in France; and had a comfortable existence in the aristocratic circles of England and France. He was a royalist and spent several years in self-imposed exile in France over fears to his safety from the Parliamentary forces. But he returned to England in 1651 because his religious views (he was an outspoken atheist) ran into severe opposition from the French Church. He "recanted" his past associations with the Royalists, accommodated himself to Cromwell's Protectorate as well as to the restoration of the Stuart kings with Charles II in 1660. Hobbes was thus writing during a very turbulent and violent period and even though his ideas were probably formed independent of his environment, one can always wonder about the extent to which the external environment influenced his attitudes. Perhaps Hobbes peered out of his window, witnessed a violent clash between the opposing sides in the civil war, and then returned to his desk and generalized from what he had just witnessed. But Hobbes was not that empirical: his writings are philosophical answers to philosophical questions and thus he is firmly within the Greek approach to politics.

Hobbes, as will be shown below with Locke, Rousseau, and Marx, begins with a description of the *state of nature* and *man's nature*. This state of nature refers to the time, eons and eons ago (perhaps with Ms. Welch and *One Million Years B.C.*), when there were no such things as governments, states, organizations, kings, structures, parliaments, or codified laws. The only things that existed in the state of nature were people and the natural environment. For Hobbes, man is neither good nor evil in this state of nature; on the contrary, man is an amoral person whose major preoccupation is survival and the avoidance of death. Each man is equal to every other man in this state of nature, both physically and mentally, and it is this point which leads Hobbes to his very pessimistic view of the state of nature. Since all men are equal, they therefore seek the same things but due to the rising population and the increasing scarcity of resources, there is not enough to go around and this leads to violent clashes between these amoral men in order to obtain the same goals (food, land, tools, possessions).

Hobbes' state of nature is thus one of constant violent conflict among each participant. Each person wants his neighbor's possessions and is afraid of turning his back to anyone for everyone is an enemy. People in this state of nature are in a constant and perpetual state of war where brutality becomes an advantage. Hobbes writes that it is "every man against every man" and there is no place for any of the pursuits of "civilized" society such as agriculture, industry, literature, music, art. Life is a literal struggle for survival and this struggle is not due to the external environment, but, rather, it is due to man's nature. The following is perhaps Hobbes' most famous and often-cited phrase describing his life in the state of nature: ". . . there is a continual fear and danger of violent death; and the life of man is solitary, poor, nasty, brutish, and short."

This solitary, poor, nasty, brutish, short, violent, and affectionless existence is in essence Hobbes' description of man in the state of nature. It should be noted, however, that Hobbes presented the state of nature as a philosophical state—one which he divined to have (or could have) existed rather than as an historical state (one which actually did exist). Since the remainder of Hobbes' argument depends upon and follows from this assertion, the nasty nature of man and the brutish qualities of the state of nature, it appears necessary to examine his contention in greater depth. It will be immediately apparent, especially when one reads Locke and Rousseau (and even Karl Marx), that there are conflicting ideas as to the state of nature and man's activity within it. Unfortunately, there is at present no answer to this question for it is essentially a philosophical and speculative question and each person could respond according to his own particular conception and view of his fellow men. What is man's nature and behavior pattern and what are the society's characteristics when all forms and traces of organizations, government and authority are removed? Is man this nasty beast portrayed by Hobbes or is man basically good and solicitous of his fellow human beings? What compounds the problem, of course, is that anthropological evidence can be cited to support both the optimistic and pessimistic view. Two diametrically opposed examples follow on contemporary life in what perhaps comes closest to a state of nature in the twentieth century.

The more optimistic view, that man is good and the state of nature is a cooperative one, can be evidenced by the recently (1969) "discovered" Tasaday tribe in a remote area of the Philippines.[3] This tribe of approximately twenty-six people were for all intents and purposes living in a state of nature. There was no government, no centralized authority, no leaders, no organizations. All that existed were these twenty-six people and a few square miles of rain forest. This society was "untouched" by the more modern Filipino culture and has been isolated. The group calls itself and the forest Tasaday and it had no conception whatsoever about what might has been beyond the perimeter of its circumscribed geographical area. The Tasadays are food gatherers (berries, roots, flowers) and do not hunt game or cultivate crops. The tribe was organized along closely knit family units and their homes were caves. Most of the important anthropological questions about the Tasadays have yet to be answered because a combination of factors has prevented researchers from spending sufficient time in the Mindanao rain forest. Their origin is unknown and even the Tasadays themselves cannot adequately explain the lack of adventure and curiosity about the outside world.

But the Tasaday society appears as a utopian state of nature. This society was seen to be cooperative and peaceful and all interpersonal relations were optimized to provide for the entire group. Each Tasaday was solicitous of the other and no one ever raised a hand in anger against another, not even against an erring child. The Tasaday language itself reflects this peaceful, loving, tender, innocent environment because concepts (and thus verbal descriptions) such as war, hate, revenge, enemy, or deception were totally lacking in their realm of perception. The worst behavior the Tasadays could conceive of from people were "loud voices and sharp looks."[4] The Tasaday society does, in a sense, present evidence that perhaps the state of nature is not as Hobbes describes it with the "continual fear and danger of violent death; and the life of man is solitary, poor, nasty, brutish, and short."

But there is also some evidence to support the pessimistic or Hobbesian view of the state of nature and man's nature. In a book by Colin M. Turnbull, *The Mountain People,* there is a description of the life-style of the Ik tribe of Northern Uganda and it *is* a chilling Hobbesian existence.[5] There are about two thousand or so Iks and they reside in the mountainous area where Uganda, the Sudan, and Kenya intersect. Previously, the Iks were a nomadic, hunting, and food gathering society with a life-style congruent with such a society. But their hunting area was transformed into a national park, and, forced into a limited and nonproductive area, these former hunters were deprived of their source of food and life-style. Turnbull lived among the Iks for two years and remarks that the people no longer exhibit any kindness, affection, generosity, love, or cooperation. Their "reservation" and climate do not provide enough food and Turnbull writes that this constant starvation brings out their particular behavior patterns: lying, stealing, insensitivity, callousness, non-cooperation, and a total lack of concern for the young, aged, and sick.

Turnbull presents vignette after vignette attesting to the Ik's total lack of humanity and social concern. Two examples will suffice for our purposes:

> ... Men would watch a child with eager anticipation as it crawled toward the fire, then burst into gay and happy laughter as it plunged a skinny hand into the coals. Such times were a few times when parental affection showed itself: a mother would glow with pleasure to hear such joy occasioned by her offspring. ...

* * * * *

> This [an animal carrying off a child] happened once ... and the mother was delighted. She was rid of the child and no longer had to carry it about and feed it, and still further this meant that a leopard was in the vicinity and would be sleeping the child off and thus be an easy kill. The men set off and found the leopard, which had consumed all of the child except part of the skull; they killed the leopard and cooked it and ate it, child and all. That is Icien economy, and it makes sense in its own way. It does not, however, endear children to their parents or parents to their children.[6]

The Icien society is a Hobbesian society: there is constant conflict and each is afraid of turning his back to anyone for everyone is an enemy. Life for the Iks is a literal struggle for survival and there *is* the continual fear and danger of death; and the life of man is "solitary, poor, nasty, brutish, and short."

But let us grant Hobbes' contention that man is nasty and life in the state of nature is a perpetual condition of warfare and examine Hobbes' description of how man can rise above this violent and nasty and brutish existence and form an organized society. The way out of this morass is seen to be man's fear of the violent death awaiting him and it is this fear which separates man from animal in the state of nature. Man realizes this brutal competition will eventually eliminate everyone, and it is his death that he wants to avoid. Thus man begins to see the need for a government with enough power and authority to protect each man from doing the other people harm. This is, for Hobbes, the origin and reason of governments and political institutions: these violent nasty people came together one day and decide that they simply cannot continue to live (and die) the way they have been for generations and some authoritative agreement is set up with enough power to prevent the constant violence. Government is set up to manage conflict and it is only the existence of this government which prevents the return to the more anarchial and violent state of nature. Thus it is the people who create a government to protect themselves from violent death.

The mechanism of this establishment is Hobbes' *social contract/the contractual foundation of government*. The people, acting together, transfer or cede all power to an individual and this individual, who does not sign the contract, but is its creation, is then expected to protect the people. The people, in other words, become subjects and create the sovereign and then the sovereign exercises legitimate power (the legal-rational type) over the subjects. This is basic to the contract theory of government but Hobbes' contract is a bit different than is Locke's or Rousseau's. Since Hobbes' sovereign does not "sign" the contract, he is thus not bound by any obligations except one: protect the people from conflict. Beyond this, the sovereign has no *obligations* whatsoever, he has *rights*. The subjects willing and voluntarily give up their own individual rights to be sovereign and now the people have all the obligations (follow the directives of the sovereign). The sovereign cannot act illegally for he alone is the source of all laws and it is he who determines what is legal. Thus the people-turned-subjects cannot complain that the sovereign has acted illegally or outside the bounds of the contract.

This is, of course, only one variation on the contract theory of government for both Locke and Rousseau also have their own particular notion of the social contract. But what is common to all three is the significance of this contract theory of government. Government is created by a voluntary agreement among people and the sovereign is created by this action of the people. In a direct and immediate sense, the contract theory denies the divine right of kings theory and, in its place, says *rex gratia populi*— king by the grace of the people. Now the sovereign and the people are more or less on an equal footing rather than having one claim such an exalted heritage. The logical extension of this (even Hobbes recognizes it although for very limited cases) is the conclusion that what the people create can also be destroyed by the people. In other words, the contract theory of government justifies revolution. If Hobbes' sovereign does not protect the subjects from violent death the people can then abrogate the contract and seek out a new sovereign. Periodic general elections are symptomatic of this concept: the sovereign, whether a president, congressperson, senator, judge, or mayor, must have his/her contract renewed by the subjects and it is only through the people that legitimate power accrues to the sovereign.

This ceding of all rights by the subjects to the sovereign brought Hobbes to a third major and, for that time, quite radical view. This concerns the legality and/or injustice of the sovereign's acts. Hobbes writes that the sovereign cannot act in an illegal manner for it is he who creates the laws and his very actions are by definition legal. This point is not too difficult to accept: "legality" in any society is only that which is permitted. There are no other connotations or inferences (i.e., what is legal may bear no relationship to what is right). But Hobbes goes much further than mere legality for he also says that his sovereign cannot act "unjustly" and this is an entirely different point than legality. It is with Hobbes' rejection of *natural law* that leads him to believe that there cannot be any such thing as an unjust law. In fact, Hobbes rejects practically all values and ethics and believes that value judgments are only statements of personal preferences without any real ethical components.

Some discussion of the differing types of law appears necessary before commenting further on Hobbes. There are two basic types of law: man-made law, also called positive law (this determines what is legal and what is illegal) and natural law. Natural law is not created by man but only discovered by man. Natural law has two basic sources: (1) man's reason—if members of a free and equal and rational mankind employed their reasoning powers, then common standards of behavior would result (each person would "discover" the natural law); and (2) from God—the ethical precepts derived from religion.[7] The belief in the presence of natural law (God's variety, that is, the rational variety did not come into existence until about one hundred years later with the American and French Revolutions) probably had a tempering influence upon Western civilization for, even under the divine right of kings, the king was subject to God's law. The positive or man-made law was seen to be subordinate to natural law and it is at this point that the concept of justice/injustice enters. Legality is the man-made law, illegal activity is the contravention of this type of law; justice is the natural law, injustice is the contravention of this type of law. Problems arise, however, for there are many situations where the positive man-made law is in opposition to the natural law and the individual is forced to choose between legal but immoral activity or moral but illegal activity. The whole question of draft resisters in the United States is an excellent example of this antagonism: draft resistance was "illegal" (contravened man-made law) but might have been in agreement with the natural law.[8]

Hobbes would not have even entered the above discussion for he believed there were no such things as ethics, value judgments, or natural law based upon reason or God's will. The only law that existed for Hobbes was man-made positive law for he completely denied the existence of values and ethics (these were nothing more than statements of personal preference and there were no universally valid values). Thus Hobbes' sovereign *could not act unjustly* and there are no higher standards with which to compare the sovereign's law. Whatever law exists is the law the sovereign creates (man-made) and the content of these standards of behavior cannot be measured against some ethical standard found in natural law. Law is what the sovereign says it is and the people cannot appeal to any higher authority. The concept of justice is totally lacking, and this is part of the explanation of why Hobbes' writings have had such an impact for he was, in essence, the first major figure to deny the existence of natural law. This fact, the denial of God's will, and his outspoken atheistic views of religion did not endear him to the French Church and provides the major reason for his return to

England in 1651 (he probably thought his chances of survival were greater with Cromwell's Protectorate than with the French clergy).

When Hobbes' writings are reviewed as a whole, especially *Leviathan,* it is safe to conclude that Hobbes is one of the theoretical founders of the doctrine of the authoritarian state.[9] His writings contain strong support for the tenets and principles of authoritarianism but Hobbes cannot be interpreted as a founder or supporter of the absolute totalitarian state (communist or fascist). Hobbes is not a "democrat" but neither is he a "fascist." There are several reasons for this important distinction:

1. *Origin of the State/Government.* Hobbes, it should be remembered, writes that government is established through the contract theory/social contract: the people, willingly and rationally and voluntarily, come together and cede (in this particular view of the nature of the contract) all power and authority is given to this newly created sovereign. Totalitarian doctrine, on the other hand, does not ascribe to this contractual foundation of government, and fascism, especially the Nazi variety, posits that the state's origins evolve from the irrational mystical spirit of the people and not from conscious creation. The communist variety also denies deliberate agreement and the state is created from oppression and violence.

2. *Role of the State/Boundaries to State Action.* Hobbes' sovereign has a very limited and mundane mandate: to maintain law and order and insist upon obedience only within the public political sphere. Hobbes' sovereign does not "penetrate" into all the other subsystems in the society. Private associations such as the school, family, church, professional societies, and trade unions (if they had existed in Hobbes' day) were all free to conduct their own affairs without much interference from the sovereign. Hobbes also believed in *laissez faire* as an economic doctrine—the government does not intervene in the economy and private property/profit motive would be the organizing concept for the economic system. Totalitarian systems, on the other hand, have erased the boundaries between the political and social systems and the totalitarian state has penetrated into practically all the

subsystems: the schools, churches, and other societies are all seen as additional methods to socialize the population into the current required ideology. Economic *laissez faire* is, of course, unacceptable to totalitarianism. Both the fascist and communist types penetrate the economic system, although the latter variety is on a much grander scale than fascism.

3. *Nature of the Sovereign.* Although Hobbes believes the sovereign should, on grounds of usefulness and not ethics, consist of one person because this one person could then act more quickly and decisively, he did recognize that the sovereign could, under certain circumstances, be composed of an assembly or, in other words, a representative parliament. Hobbes' view of the sovereign was one of "supreme administrator and lawgiver" but not a propagandist. The one-individual leadership cult (Hitler, Mussolini, Stalin) has been basic to totalitarian practice.

4. *Necessity of Conflict/War.* Hobbes' state was created for the very purpose of limiting conflict, this was its *raison d'être,* and although Hobbes recognized the unfortunate necessity of the state engaging in *defensive* wars, there is no glorification of warfare and no calls for aggressive, expanionist, or imperialist wars. The fascist brand of totalitarianism, however, views war as desirable and welcomed and it is something to be actively sought.[10] Although believing that international warfare will be eliminated once all countries enter the sixth stage of history (the Communist stage), communist theory nonetheless emphasizes the inevitability of internal conflict and class oppression until the last stage is reached.

5. *Official Ideology.* One of the characteristics of any totalitarian system is its insistence that it possesses the Truth and that this Truth can only be found within the one official recognized ideology. Conformity in thought patterns as well as outward obedience are required in totalitarian systems. Deviation in thought patterns frequently entails as severe penalties as does deviation from the law. The 1970 film by Costa-Gravas, *The Confession,* and the book, *A Question of Madness,* by the Russians Zhores and Roy Medvedev,

provide chilling examples of how some societies punish non-belief in the law almost as severely (if not as severely) as nonobservance of the law. *The Confession* is a thinly veiled fictional account of the political purge trials (Slansky *et al*) in Czechoslovakia around 1948, and *A Question of Madness* is a true account of one man's experience with the Soviet Union's practice of incarcerating political dissenters in insane asylums.[11] Hobbes, on the other hand, sees no need for thought control and only outward conformity to the law is required. Hobbes is concerned with law and order, not with the Truth, and the subjects need only obey the law, not believe it.

6. *Relationship of the Individual to the State.* The utter lack of any individual existence outside the State in Hitler's Germany and Stalin's Russia need not be recited here except to note that human life was not held to be all-important. Hobbes did feel that individual life was all-important—it was for this very reason that the social contract was signed and the State created—and Hobbes allows the individual to resist any attempt by the State to take his life. The very purpose of the State was this maintenance of peace and order, and the individual was inalienable in his own self, and if the State did not accomplish this task, then the population could resist. Hobbes himself makes this point quite clear:

> The obligation of subjects to the sovereign is understood to last as long, and no longer, than the power lasts by which he is able to protect them. For the right men have by nature to protect themselves when none else can protect them, can by no covenant be relinquished.[12]

There is much that could be said as criticism with Hobbes but most of the criticism would not add to a better understanding of the concepts Hobbes presents. This is so because, in essence, Hobbes' presentation is a philosophical discussion and what one finds acceptable in Hobbes, another will find repugnant. The point is that to counter one philosophical and nonempirical argument with another similar argument does not bring one closer to what actually exists in reality. One major point must be made, however: Hobbes' total theory on the origin of, and necessity for, an organized government rests upon his description of man in the state of nature: the life of man is poor, nasty, violent, brutish, and short. If this premise is not accepted, then the rest of Hobbes' argument become untenable. And even if this premise *were* true, Hobbes never does quite answer or explain why these nasty people come together all of a sudden and begin to cooperate. If people in the state of nature *were* that nasty and brutal, cooperation and consultation would never have been employed (as they are not employed with the Iks). Be that as it may, the salient points to note with Hobbes, salient because they are in direct opposition to Locke and Rousseau (even Karl Marx opposes Hobbes on several points), are his descriptions of man (a nasty amoral brute), the state of nature (a perpetual condition of guerilla warfare), the contract (a device to manage conflict signed by the subjects with all the rights given to the sovereign), legality and justice (natural law does not exist and the only law is positive law), and the type of system which would result from a practical application of his views (an authoritarian political system).

Politics as a Contract
John Locke/Jean Jacques Rousseau

Both John Locke and Jean Jacques Rousseau are classified (these classifications are not hard and fast divisions but only analytical conveniences) as regarding politics as a *contract*. This contract is a voluntary agreement among good, free, and equal men in order to extend the benefits and advantages of society. Hobbes also had the contract but he approached it as a means to manage conflict. Conflict was the salient issue for Hobbes and it was the prime basis of social interaction. Violence and nasty behavior are not absent in Locke and Rousseau but their emphasis is upon the contract. Yet, all three—Hobbes, Locke, and Rousseau—are within the Greek approach to politics: politics as it *ought* to be, not what it actually *is*.

John Locke (English, 1632-1704)

John Locke was a contemporary of Hobbes and thus lived and wrote during the same turbulent period of English political and social upheaval described above. Locke studied at Oxford, later taught there, and his academic interests were philosophy, science, and medicine. Except for a four-year period, 1679-1683, Locke spent from 1675-1689 in political exile, first in France, then in the Netherlands. Locke returned to England soon after James II abdicated and William of Orange became king. Locke then had practical experience as a civil servant for he served in a variety of government posts from 1689 until his death in 1704. It is, of course, far-fetched, but still possible, that perhaps Locke peered out *his* window, witnessed the same violent clash between the Roundheads and Cavaliers as did Hobbes, returned to his desk, but then concluded the complete opposite as did Hobbes. Locke's major work is *Two Treatises of Government*,[13] published in 1690 but written before the 1689 Glorious Revolution, and his major ideas can be approached along the same general lines as Hobbes': man's nature and the state of nature, the contract, natural law, and the type of system resulting from the contract.

Locke begins at the same point as Hobbes and provides his conception of man in the state of nature (the pre-ancient time when there were just people and no such things as governments or sovereigns). But Locke is much more optimistic than Hobbes regarding man. Whereas Hobbes pictured man as a nasty amoral brute living in a state of constant warfare (the war of all against all), Locke, on the other hand, conceived man to be good, reasonable, just, and living in relative peace and harmony. Locke could not see man living in Hobbes' anarchial jungle and he believed some sort of "law and order" was present, government or no government. This "law and order" in the state of nature results from man's reason and the presence of recognizable common law which, for Locke, arises from nature itself. Common law is neither "natural" nor "positive" but, rather, law which has evolved over the centuries with usage; it may be argued that common law is man-made law but it is not created by decision or by fiat—it slowly develops over time. This law and order without political institutions (government) can exist because most of the inhabitants of Locke's state of nature are aware of the prime law and structure their activities in light of it. This prime law is simply that all people have certain inalienable rights—life, liberty, and property—and that these rights cannot be taken away. Locke comments:

> The state of nature has a law of nature to govern it, which obliges everyone, and reason, which is the law, teaches all mankind, who will but consult it, that being all equal and independent, no one ought to harm another in his life, health, liberty, or possessions: for man being all the workmanship of one omnipotent, and infinitely wise master; all servants of one sovereign master, sent into the world by his order, and about his business; they are his property, whose workmanship they are, made to last during his, and not another's pleasure: and being furnished with like faculties, sharing all in one community of nature, there cannot be supposed any such subordination among us, that may authorize us to destroy one another, as if we were made for one another's uses, as the inferior ranks of creatures are for ours.[14]

But the state of nature is not as idyllic or utopian as one would imagine. Although these standards of behavior exist from natural law, Locke concedes that not *everyone* in the state of nature can "see" or "find" the law and thus there are frequent transgressions of the natural law (life, liberty, and property *were* violated in the state of nature). But Locke claims that most of the violations were punished in the state of nature; not by the government because there is no governmental apparatus, but by the injured party. Locke is, in a sense, describing a primitive or traditional society without a separate and distinct law enforcement and law adjudication structure: a violation of the law occurs and the injured individual, family, clan, or tribe takes vindictive action. This retribution is, in essence, not "revenge" but "punishment" based upon authority (traditional authority), and the injured party has both the right and obligation to seek redress. These transgressions are small in number compared to the behavior patterns in Hobbes' state of nature but Locke recognized that the injured party frequently may not have been able to actually accomplish what he was entitled to do and thus certain unjust actions go unpunished in Locke's state of nature. It is with this point, unpunished violations of the law, that Locke describes his view of the contract theory of government.

For Locke, governments are established to achieve two goals: (1) to make the content of the natural law clear to every member of the society and (2) to ensure that violations of the law do not remain unpunished. Locke, as is Hobbes, is a firm supporter of the contractual foundation of government and the people, willingly and voluntarily, come together and agree to establish an organized society with a government and a sovereign. But what is significant here, however, is the difference between Hobbes and Locke: Hobbes sets up the contract because of the constant violence and only the Government and the Sovereign can prevent a return to the nasty state of nature; Locke, on the other hand, sets up the contract in order to improve upon an already good, rational, and beneficial society. One may even argue, moreover, that the level of conflict and violence might be greater in Hobbes' post-state of nature government with the sovereign than in Locke's pre-contract state of nature. Locke seems to define the level of conflict in his state of nature as less severe and frequent than Hobbes does in his organized society. It is for this reason that Hobbes is classified as seeing politics as conflict management and Locke is classified as seeing politics as the contract and as consensus formation.

Locke's contract is the complete opposite of Hobbes'. Whereas Hobbes' contract was signed by only the people and these people gave up all their rights to the sovereign (they in a sense said "rule us and we will submit"), Locke approaches it quite differently. Locke's contract is a *trust* arrangement and the sovereign exists only to carry out the will of the people. The sovereign has to perform what the people decide and if he refuses to abide by the population's mandate, the people can remove the sovereign from office. The change from James II to William III of Orange in 1688-1689 can be regarded simply as a situation where the people removed the sovereign because he did not follow the terms of the contract. The trust arrangement is organized similar to any modern trust agreement with a *trustor,* a *trustee,* and a *beneficiary.* Perhaps an analogy with a contemporary financial trust agreement can illustrate Locke's views. A father (the trustor) takes his after-tax lottery winnings to a local bank and hires someone (the trustee) to manage the money for the best interests of the trustor's children (the beneficiary). The banker as trustee signs the contract and this contract contains all the clauses and stipulations of the agreement. The children as beneficiary receive the benefits of the agreement and it is the trustor and *not* the trustee who defines what the beneficiary's "best interests" are. The trustee may have the liberty to choose methods to achieve the best interests but the banker as trustee *cannot* define the ultimate goals.

Locke's contract is the same as the example above except for a change in roles. For Locke, the people are the trustor, the Government and Sovereign are the trustee, and the people are also the beneficiary. The sovereign as trustee is created by the people/trustor through the contract and thus the sovereign must sign the agreement containing all the clauses and stipulations. Moreover, with this particular view of the contract, it is the people and not the sovereign who determine what the people's best interests are. The people as trustor create the contract, decide upon its terms and content, decide how the "goods" or resources are to be used, and then the people as trustor hire the trustee-sovereign to do the everyday and mundane work of administering the agreement. The sovereign as trustee has absolutely no claims to the resources (just as the banker has no claim to the money in the trust fund) but the trustee does receive a salary for his work. The sovereign must abide by the terms of the contract or be fired (voted out of office, exiled, beheaded). With Locke, the sovereign has the obligations, the people have the rights. Hobbes' sovereign, on the other hand, had the rights and the people had the obligations.

The bitter conflict between former President Nixon and his supporters, on the one side, and the press, Congress, the special prosecutors, and even the Supreme Court (*U.S.* v. *Richard Nixon*), on the other side, throughout the Watergate affair can be approached through Hobbes' and Locke's discussion of the nature of the contract and of the sovereign's powers. Mr. Nixon was arguing the Hobbesian stand: the president as sovereign had the sole right to determine what the best interests of the people and society were and the surrender of the subpoenaed tapes was not in "the best interests" of society. Special Prosecutors Cox and Jaworski, on the other hand, argued the Lockean approach: the president is only a hired hand (the trustee) and it is for the people and the people's representatives to determine their own best interests (surrender the tapes). The votes on the Articles of Impeachment by the House Judiciary Committee (obstruction of justice, abuse of power, and, especially, contempt of Congress) reduced Hobbes' argument to mere philosophy. The Lockean conception that the sovereign is a hired hand who has no claims to the nation's resources, no special insights to the people's best interest, and who can be fired at will was given practical application during those weeks in July and August 1974.

Another striking contrast between Hobbes and Locke is found with their views about natural law. Whereas Hobbes believed that there were no such things as justice, morality, ethics, or natural law (there is only positive or sovereign-made law), Locke again takes the opposite view. Locke believes that justice *does* exist and "justice" is that which is in agreement with the natural law. For Locke, the sources of natural law are God and nature itself and the basic components of the law are each *individual* person's inalienable right to life, liberty, and property. Locke's view of the natural law should be immediately apparent in relation to the American experience. *The Declaration of Independence* (1776), written primarily by Thomas Jefferson, emphasizes the contract nature of society, the sovereign as a hired trustee, and the existence of natural law. The second paragraph of *The Declaration of Independence* reads, in part:

> We hold these Truths to be self-evident, that all Men are created equal, that they are endowed by their Creator with certain inalienable rights, that among these are Life, Liberty, and the Pursuit of Happiness—That to secure these Rights, Governments are instituted among Men, deriving their just Powers from the Consent of the Governed, that whenever any Form of Government becomes destructive of these Ends, it is the Right of the People to alter or abolish it, and to institute new Government. . . .[15]

Locke's sovereign, created trustee by the contract, does not make or create the law as does Hobbes' sovereign, but only "finds" or "discovers" the natural law and makes it known and visible to the population. Locke's sovereign can act in an unjust manner (against natural law) and thus there are definite limits to the sovereign's power.

Locke and Hobbes also differ in their views as to the type of system which would (ought) result from their contracts. Hobbes was a supporter of the Royalist faction during the civil war and his system, described above, is partial to a powerful monarch and is strongly authoritarian. Locke supported the Parliamentary faction and his system is a statement of a classical representative parliamentary democracy with periodic renewals of the contract. Locke interpreted the Glorious Revolution of 1688-1689 as a situation where the trustor (people) believed the trustee (James II) was no longer honoring the terms of the contract (not operating in the best interests of the people) and thus one trustee was fired and another hired (William and Mary of Orange). Locke's *Treatises* provided, along with the actual events of 1688-1689, the final blow to the divine right of kings theory for Anglo-America although the European continent had to wait another one hundred years until 1789 and the French Revolution. Hobbes and Locke lived and wrote during the same historical time period but their views are as far apart as is possible. Table 2.1 contains a summarized presentation of the major points of divergence between Hobbes and Locke but these two English writers and political philosophers concurred on one vital aspect: the Sovereign and the Government are not created by God but by the people and it is the people to whom the sovereign is ultimately accountable.

Jean-Jacques Rousseau (Swiss-French, 1712-1778)

Jean-Jacques Rousseau is also classified as regarding politics as a contract although his contract is quite different than Hobbes' or Locke's social contract. Rousseau was born in Calvinist Geneva, his mother died when he was an infant, his father was not a very successful clockmaker, and Rousseau experienced what, were it the latter part of the twentieth century, would be termed an underprivileged and deprived childhood. Rousseau left Geneva

Table 2.1
A Comparison of Hobbes and Locke

	Hobbes	*Locke*
Man's Nature	nasty/amoral	good/reasonable
State of Nature	a violent jungle, constant warfare	law and order but with some problems
The Contract	a one-way flow; the Sovereign has the rights, the people have the obligations	a trust arrangement; the people have the rights, the Sovereign have the obligations
Natural Law	no such thing; no justice; the Sovereign makes the law	does exist (life, liberty, property); justice also exists; the Sovereign finds the law
Type of System	authoritarian	liberal, representative parliamentary democracy

at sixteen and was for quite a while a wandering beatnik (beat-nik in Jack Kerouac's meaning as contained in his *On the Road;* Rousseau was not an eighteenth-century Yippie) without any real profession or any visible means of legitimate support. He traveled extensively in Europe and, while some of the travel was in response to his wanderlust, most was in response to having been asked (required) to leave a specific locality by the authorities. Most of his time was spent in France, particularly in Paris, and he was able to ingratiate himself with a succession of rich aristo-cratic women, and thus Rousseau managed to have at least a place to sleep and food to eat. Rousseau's major writings include *A Discourse on the Moral Effects of the Arts and Sciences* (1751), *Émile* (1752), *Discourse on the Origin of Inequality* (1755), and his most famous work, *The Social Contract* (1762).

Rousseau created and built a doctrine of revolution and was probably the first to anticipate the modern slogan of "all power to the people." Rousseau symbolized the cry for change and revolution in Europe and particularly in France of the Ancien Régime. France under the Bourbon dynasty had as a

major societal characteristic the conspicuous and blatantly osten-
tatious consumption by the King and Court at Versailles, a
parasitic aristocracy, and a church establishment not known for
its piety or poverty. The gulf between the upper class in France
and the rest of the population widened as the upper class continued its political, economic, and cultural oppression. Very
briefly, Rousseau believed that man was essentially good but
that the contemporary society of France under the Bourbons
ruined him. Thus Rousseau argued that the old society had to
be destroyed prior to creating a new society. Rousseau even
thought it was man's duty or obligation under God to destroy
these ungodly institutions (the Monarchy, Government, Aristocracy, and the Church). Rousseau can be interpreted as one
of the intellectual or doctrinal fathers of the 1789 French Revolution, another tremendous blow at the divine right of kings
theory.

Rousseau, like Hobbes and Locke before him, has his own
particular conception of man's nature and the state of nature.
Rousseau's concept of man in the state of nature is summed up
in one of his most famous quips: Man is a "noble savage"—
noble because he was compassionate and humane; savage because he was led by his instincts and desires. Even with humanity
and compassion, the savage element or side to man's nature was
just as strong and influential as his goodness or nobility. Rousseau is thus a combination of Hobbes and Locke: from Hobbes
he takes the external environment and some of man's activities;
from Locke he asserts that man is essentially good, free, equal,
and compassionate (Hobbes thought man was a nasty brute).
But for reasons that Rousseau never makes entirely clear—he
alludes to the rising population and the resulting scarcity of
resources—a civil society or government is established in which
some become rich and powerful and prevent most of the people
from existing as free and equal souls. Rousseau looked around
Europe of the 1750s, especially in France, and saw an untold
number of unnatural institutions and practices (unnatural in
the sense that such institutions and practices did not exist in
his view of the state of nature). In other words, Rousseau believed European civilization and society of the 1700s was ruining
man for it did not allow him to be free and equal as he was in

the original state of nature. Another famous comment by Rousseau points this out: "Man is born free, and everywhere he is in chains."

Rousseau thus called for the violent overthrow of all existing institutions and the re-creation, through the social contract's mechanism, of a new civil society in which man could "return" to the state of nature and be free and equal. Rousseau's contract is perhaps the first statement of the slogan "all power to the people." Hobbes did not give power to the *people* because people gave up their rights and it was the *sovereign* who held the power. Locke did not give power to the sovereign; nor did he give it to the people. The people had some power but this was limited by natural law and there were some things the people as an entity could not do to the individual. The final locus of power for Locke was the *individual*. But with Rousseau's conception of the social contract, it was the people and not the sovereign or individual who held ultimate power. The people, after destroying the evil and ungodly institutions, would willingly and voluntarily come together and set up the contract. The terms of the contract would be organized by a very important concept in Rousseau's thinking—the *general will*.

Each individual for Rousseau had his (and *his* means *his*; Rousseau did not ascribe to the doctrine of women's liberation and women did not have much equality or freedom) own particular *individual will*. When the people met together, each would express his own individual will and the resulting combination of all the individual wills is termed the general will. It is this general will which would organize the society, choose the sovereign, decide upon the sovereign's continuance in office, and determine what policies would be pursued. In other words, the general will defines the contract's content and form.

Rousseau's general will is by definition (Rousseau's definition) greater and more valid than just the sum total of all the isolated individual wills because it represents the will of society, the general will. An analogy would perhaps be an automobile: one has two-thousand-odd parts scattered about the room but when they are added together in the right manner and sequence, the result—an integrated functioning automobile—is more than just the sum total of all the individual parts. A symphony orchestra is perhaps another analogy of this characteristic of the general will: the 106 or so separate pieces in the orchestra each has its own individual will but the resulting combination of the isolated notes produces a finished product which is more "valid" than the separate notes. For Rousseau, the individual will is equivalent to one automobile part, or to one violin; the general will is the equivalent of a Rolls-Royce or a Beethoven symphony. The general will is greater than any individual will and it is greater than even the sum total of all the individual wills.

But Rousseau went one step further with his concept of the general will and it is here that a serious criticism can be offered. Rousseau also equated the general will with the Truth and the Right. Since Rousseau believed man was good, free, and equal, once this good and free human being was afforded the opportunity to articulate his will, then this individual will (and the resulting general will) would be by definition Good and True and Right. This is the concept of *vox populi—vox dei,* the voice of the people is the voice of God, and the *people* cannot be wrong. And, of course, *vox populi—vox dei* is also in opposition to *rex gratia dei.* But by giving all power to the people and equating the people's voice with that of Truth and Reason can lead to unfortunate results. Rousseau could not conceive of a 50-50 or 51-49 split in individual wills (free and equal people would not have such disparate wills) but he did discuss the situation of having a 99-1 or 98-2 split in individual wills. What happens to the one or two individuals who have wills the complete opposite or wills not in agreement with the general will? Rousseau remarks in another famous statement that these people would be "forced to be free." "Forced to be free" was not seen as a contradiction by Rousseau: the dissenting minority will be required to adhere to the general will for it is only within the general will, and not with the individual will, that an individual can find true happiness, freedom, and equality. This is a simple but classic statement of majority rule! The poor misguided minority will be shown the errors of their ways and be forced to be free!

What Rousseau believes here, Locke does not. Locke believed that the *people* were not the most important but, rather, it was the *individual* with his inalienable rights to life, liberty, and property (or Jefferson's life, liberty, and the pursuit of happiness). According to Locke, God gave these rights to the *individual* and these innate rights could not be taken away by society, the people, or by the general will. John Stuart Mill, a nineteenth-century English political philosopher, held the same basic view as Locke and Jefferson except, instead of God-given, Mill based the individual's rights on rational utilitarian arguments. Both Locke and Mill argued that in the situation of having one million (the people) against one individual, it is the one individual who *must* be protected by society for this one individual may have the Truth and the Right and not the people or society. Locke and Mill feared the people—the mob—and attempted to place certain activities beyond society's reach. Rousseau, on the other hand, in his attempt to give all power to the people, says the one individual must submit to society. The *people* cannot be wrong and it is the one or two individuals who are misguided and they must be led back to the Truth. There are thus no minority rights with Rousseau. "Forced to be free" is conformity to the general will but Rousseau, in his desire to bring down the oppressive and parasitic Ancien Régime, did not foresee the dangers inherent in the proposition.

Rousseau believed *vox populi-vox dei* but it is so easy and tempting to substitute *vox populi—vox diaboli* (the voice of the people is the voice of the devil). History is full of examples of the "general will" being a hideous distortion of the Truth or the voice of God. What Rousseau did, in effect, was to substitute the mob for Hobbes' sovereign and each was given the same amount of authoritative decision-making power. Moreover, and this is what is especially dangerous with both Hobbes and Rousseau, these philosophers ascribed the same degree of truth and righteousness to the content of these decisions.

A brief summary of Rousseau's conception and views has him defining the social contract as the general will in operation. The contract, a voluntary agreement among free and equal men, contains elements from both Hobbes and Locke but with some major modifications (it is not Hobbes' sovereign or Locke's individual who has the power but Rousseau's people). The most telling criticism of Rousseau is perhaps his description of the people's voice with that of God, Truth, and Reason. It is entirely possible that *vox populi—vox diaboli* and the individual being "forced to be free" would not be free at all but be completely stripped of his status as an individual and stand exposed to society's whims. If this criticism is valid, it is Rousseau and not Hobbes who is closest to totalitarianism and fascism.

Politics as a Search for a Just Society
Karl Marx (German, 1818-1883)

A third representative conception of politics and a third answer to the question of "what is politics?" can be found in the writings of Karl Marx. Marx's views represent a third conception in terms of content and not in terms of a completely distinct theoretical approach. Marx, like the Greeks, Hobbes, Locke, and Rousseau before him, in essence first prescribed what the final goal of man and society should be, what the "good life" ought to include, and then described the step-by-step procedure necessary to attain this posited ethical goal. Marx was, in certain areas of his writings, more "empirical" or "scientific" than were Hobbes, Locke, or Rousseau because these latter three divined what the good life ought to be whereas Marx based some of his analyses upon empirical data. Marx thus does not immediately appear as a moral philosopher; nonetheless, his final goal of "communism" was not just the best of all possible worlds but, rather, it was the only possible world to which all people everywhere must seek to attain. Marx is firmly within the Greek approach to politics with his conception of the good life and the description of what was necessary to attain this goal.

Some discussion is necessary, however, about this categorization of Marx regarding politics as "a search for a just society" or "utopia." This is a difficult point to hold for Marx's writings are filled with virulent polemics, character assassination, *ad hominem* arguments, and calls for violence, bloodshed, conflict, and revolution. But this conceptualization and categorization of Marx is based upon his final goal—the stage of communism—and although violent conflict may have been the most likely method of achieving this goal, once this goal was attained, there would then be a utopian society. Violence might have been the most likely or prevalent way to Utopia for Marx but such violence was not always necessary. Marx, after living in London with the British parliamentary system for some time, wrote in his later years that it was not totally and absolutely necessary for violence to be employed to reach the goal of communism. It could be possible to attain the desired end through peaceful parliamentary procedures in certain societies and under certain conditions.

Marx's goal can be briefly described as a humane society where there is peace, no internal violence or international warfare, justice would administer itself for the individual's innate goodness and would be able to develop and flower, the oppressive state would disappear, there would be no class conflict for society would be classless, no private property for there would be enough for all, and all social and interpersonal relationships would be based upon Marx's maxim of "from each according to his ability, to each according to his needs."

Marx does not ascribe to the contract theory of government as did Hobbes, Locke, and Rousseau. Governments and States are created (and then destroyed!) for Marx, not with or by any voluntary agreement among the population but, rather, by the operation of some inevitable laws of history. Another immediate difference between Marx and the other philosophers discussed in this chapter is with the need and function of an organized state. For Hobbes, the State was an absolute necessity and it was only the State which prevented a return to the anarchial state of nature. For Locke, the State enabled society to improve upon an already good system and Locke's State was beneficial. For Rousseau, the State served as the transmission belt for the free and equal general will. Marx, on the other hand, saw the State as an oppressive organization and there would be no State whatsoever in the final stage of communism. Marx's view of the need and function of the State is discussed in greater detail below.

Eric Fromm has presented an excellent defense of Marx as a humanist.[16] Fromm writes that the usual view of Marx— that he is anti-individual and espouses uniformity and subordination of the masses to an elite—is not quite true. Marx wished to emancipate man from both spiritual alienation and materialist need which then would enable him and his society to exist in harmony and peace with each other and with the environment. Professor Fromm comments:

> I shall try to demonstrate that this interpretation of Marx [materialism] is completely false; that his theory does not assume that the main motive of man is one of material gain; that, furthermore, the very aim of Marx is to liberate man from the pressure of economic needs, so that he can be fully human: that Marx is primarily concerned with the emancipation of man as an individual, the overcoming of alienation, the restoration of his capacity to relate himself fully to man and to nature: that Marx's philosophy constitutes a spiritual existentialism in secular language and because of this spiritual quality is opposed to the materialistic philosophy of our age. Marx's aim, socialism, based on his theory of man, is essentially prophetic Messianism in the language of the nineteenth century.[17]

The difficulty of accepting Marx as a liberal humanist, to use Fromm's term, lies not only in the nasty nature of his writings but, also, in the vast misconceptions and stereotyped reactions that most people have regarding the man and his ideas. Karl Marx has been misinterpreted, misunderstood, and reinterpreted as perhaps no other man, including Charles Darwin and Sigmund Freud. The Soviets and Chinese have distorted and misapplied his views; the Western world is either ignorant of classical Marxism and simply employs contemporary Soviet practice as evidence of the evil nature of Marx or it simply refuses to meet Marx on his own ground and time.[18] Marx was writing in the mid-nineteenth century and witnessed the urban proletariat being oppressed by both the State and the upper classes. The reader should note that common practices such as trade unions and minimum wage-hour laws were prohibited by the British Government when Marx was writing. Marx was not writing in a social welfare state such as Norway or Sweden in the 1970s; he was writing during the heyday of capitalist exploitation of the masses and it is the environment of his time which must be kept in mind. The following discussion of Marx and his ideas is presented as I see them and I also approach

Marx as does Eric Fromm: Marx as a moral philosopher and a liberal humanist who sought the just society in order to liberate and emancipate the individual and to bring harmony among men and between man and his environment.

Karl Marx is of such stature and influence that some information on his life should be presented.[19] Marx was born in the German Rhineland town of Trier and experienced a rather uneventful and normal childhood and adolescence. His father was a middle-class lawyer and Marx, to once again use a current phrase, did not experience a deprived childhood. Both of Marx's grandfathers, as well as his paternal great-grandfather, were orthodox Jewish rabbis but his father converted to Lutheranism a short time before Marx's birth. Marx was not brought up as a Jew although it was impossible for him to deny his religious background. Several writers have employed this fact—the Jewish cultural background and the conversion to Protestantism—to help explain, at least in part, why Marx wrote what he did. Isaiah Berlin intimates that Marx's later hostility to all things religious, and particularly Judaism, may have been due to the overcompensation of his ambiguous religious position.[20] Sidney Hook draws a very interesting analogy between Marx's writings and Old Testament literature, and Hook's comments bear citing:

> Despite his refusal to appeal to ethical principles, Marx had a passionate sense of social injustice which burns fiercely in everything he wrote. He would have scoffed at the idea that he was in line with the Hebrew prophets, but he sometimes spoke of the laws of History as if they were the decrees of Jehovah punishing a wicked society, and of the socialist revolution as if it were the catastrophic prelude to a new dispensation.[21]

Marx attended the University of Bonn and then Berlin and received a doctorate in philosophy from Berlin. He was editor of the *Rheinische Zeitung* for a brief time but the journal was suppressed by the Prussian authorities for its too liberal views. Married, Marx went to Paris and met Friedrich Engels. Engels was from a wealthy manufacturing family and became Marx's collaborator on most of the published writings. Engels also supported the Marx family and probably kept them from starvation. The 1848 revolutions in Europe found Marx traveling between Paris-Brussels-Germany but each country or city decided that they did not want what they considered to be a rabble-rouser within their geographical boundaries. Marx finally found asylum in London in 1849 and lived in London until his death in 1883. The time spent in London was devoted to painstaking research in the British Museum, writing, and propagandizing his views. He was able to eke out a subsistence level of existence by furnishing dispatches to the *New York Tribune*. But this did not last and he was forced to exist on Engels' generosity and loans from pawnbrokers. His family suffered hardship and deprivation; three of his six children died, probably from causes connected with malnutrition.

Very few people outside his immediate circle were aware of his work and growing stature at the time of his death in London. It has been only after his death that his writings found a large and appreciative audience and that his ideas influenced the real world. His major writings, most in collaboration with Engels, include *Economic and Philosophic Manuscripts of 1844, The German Ideology* (1845), *The Poverty of Philosophy* (1847), *Communist Manifesto* (1848), and *Das Kapital* (1867-1894). Until Marx's death in 1883, the basic doctrines were formulated by close collaboration between Marx and Engels and the latter continued to write until his own death in 1895. Marx and Engels termed their theories "scientific socialism" in order to distinguish them from the earlier and more idealistic socialism of the Utopian Socialists such as Robert Owen, Charles Fourrière, and Claude Saint-Simon. The following comments present a very brief discussion of the major ideas of Marx. As noted above, Marx is firmly within the Greek approach, as were Hobbes, Locke, and Rousseau although, unlike these latter three, Marx does not adhere to the contract theory of government.

The State of Nature/Nature of Man

It is reasonable to state that Marx and Engels began in almost the same fashion as did Hobbes, Locke, and Rousseau:

an analysis of man's nature and a description of the state of nature as they existed before all the evil and corrupting organizations and structures appeared. Marx and Engels regarded this state of nature as a historical state, one that actually existed and whose existence could be documented, rather than as a philosophical state whose existence could only be assumed. Marx believed in the innate goodness and worth and importance of the individual. Marx's man is not afflicted with original sin or with crass materialistic motives and he is perfectable, even though he may appear to be far from perfect in specific historical milieux. It is the environmental pressures of society and the ways the means of production are organized which alienates and oppresses the individual and leads him astray from his potential goodness and righteousness. Thus, very briefly, if the environment can be altered, if one method of organizing the means of production could be replaced by another (and Marx believes that such could be done) then man would be liberated and free. If the "correct" means of production are present man would in a sense be returned to the state of nature in which there would be no class conflict, no oppressive state, no private property, and the individual would be freed from material needs for the society would then provide each according to his needs and each would contribute to society according to his ability.

Historical Materialism / The Stages of History

This is Marx's materialist conception of history and this concept posits that all history and societal institutions and arrangements, as well as the content of all modes of thought (philosophy, religion, art, etc.), are *determined* by the basic economic arrangement of who owns the means of production. This is to say that the "superstructure" of society—its government, literature, social relations—are determined by the way goods are produced and when ownership of the means of production changes, so then will all other aspects of society correspondingly change. Economics is at the foundation of societies and determines the nature of political institutions and intellectual life.

This economic interpretation of history can be seen in Marx's analysis of the stages of history. Marx conceptualized six major historical stages: three were in the past, he was writing during the fourth stage, and the last two stages were for the future. Each stage is determined by the organization of the means of production and when this organization changes, society moves into the next stage. The six stages are:

1. *Pastoral.* This is Marx's state of nature; the very beginning of man in society. Perhaps the closest contemporary parallel would be the recently "discovered" Tasadays for here, as well as in Marx's pastoral stage, there is no personal private property except for personal use items which cannot oppress another person, there is no class conflict for there is only one class, there is no State or Government or political parties to oppress the workers, each receives his share and each contributes according to his ability, the means of production are "owned" in common by the whole society, and there is no surplus value—the worker receives the value of his labor.

2. *Slavery.* Here we have the beginnings of man's downfall because, for various reasons, some people have become stronger than others and have appropriated the means of production, established a State, and then employed the State to oppress those who produce (the slaves). There are now class differences with the inevitable class antagonisms and the worker receives a miniscule share of the value that his labor produces (the slave-owner class receives the profits of the slaves' labor).

3. *Feudalism.* This stage is quite equivalent to the Slave stage except that now the oppressed class is not the slave but the serfs tied to the land. Marx comments that the feudal ideology, personal obligations between vassals and lords and the sovereign national state resting upon the divine right of kings, was due to this particular mode of production. As freedmen established towns and cities, and as the bourgeois became more and more insistent upon political power, this system fell with a resounding crash into the fourth stage.

4. *Capitalism.* This is the stage in which Marx lived and wrote.

Now the means of production are owned by the bourgeois and the workers, or proletariat, supply the bourgeois with profits. The workers are paid only a small fraction of the value of the goods their labor produces and the bourgeois class controls the State and employs the State's apparatus to oppress the proletariat. Friedrich Engels, with his *The Condition of the Working Class in England* (1845), wrote a brilliant and honest treatise on the condition of the working class: no minimum wage laws, no regulation of hours, child labor, very poor and unsafe working conditions, no paid holidays or sick leave, no pensions, very low salaries, trade unions were outlawed, the right to vote severely limited. It was not just that these characteristics were present; they were present because the bourgeois class, who controlled the State, employed the State's power to legally prohibit the institution of many of these programs. This was evidence for Marx and Engels that class conflict was inevitable for the stronger class in any society would oppress the weaker class. Once again, the reader is reminded that the bourgeois, *laissez-faire,* capitalist State of the 1840s and 1850s was Marx's universe, not the profit-sharing and strong trade union activity of the 1970s. The urban proletariat would get poorer and poorer and the parasitic bourgeois would get richer and richer until the proletariat would rise up in violent armed revolution, eliminate the bourgeoisie, and institute the fifth stage.

5. *Socialism.* This stage was a transitional stage between Capitalism and the final stage of Communism. The socialist stage would begin with private property but Socialism would eliminate private property and have the means of production owned by society as a whole; there would still be different classes and thus class conflict (but now the proletariat would oppress the bourgeois) although Socialism would eliminate class distinctions and its conflict. The State would still exist and the workers would employ the State's machinery to eliminate the bourgeois; once this was accomplished, the State would simply wither away to oblivion. This stage would also have the end of surplus value for

now the worker would receive the full value of his labors. When all these tasks were accomplished, the society could then move into the sixth and final stage.

6. *Communism.* This is Marx's just and ideal society: there are no political parties or State to oppress the people; class conflict does not exist for there is only one class; there is public ownership of the means of production and private property is limited to those goods which are nonoppressive; the worker receives a fair return for his labor. The individual human being would be liberated and emancipated from crass materialistic motives, alienation would disappear, and each person would contribute all that he or she was able to contribute and each person would receive all that was necessary. Such a society would not be based upon a monetary value system (how much money are people or things worth?) but, rather, its value system and emphasis would be upon aesthetics and the usefulness of things. This last stage of Communism was Marx's utopian society and it is with this goal for man that Marx is classified as a moral philosopher and a liberal humanist.

Marx and Engels believed these six stages of history were an inevitable progression arising from mechanistic laws of history. The six developmental stages were bound to take place; man could perhaps speed or delay the arrival of one stage for a period of time but human intervention could not prevent the stages. Moreover, the stages had to follow in order and, therefore, stages could not be completely skipped nor could a society move backward. Once a stage was reached, the society was locked in until the subsequent stage. Marx and Engels presented these stages of history as a linear development. Stage 1 and 2 to . . . 6 and then this progression would stop. But Marx's description of the first and last stages appears to make the progression a circular development rather than a linear development. In other words, Marx's descriptions of Stage 1 (Pastoral) and Stage 6 (Communism) are quite similar: no private property, no class conflict for there are no class distinctions, no state or political parties, no surplus value. But Marx recognized the cyclical nature of the stages and argued against such an interpretation. The final stage of Communism may be similar to Stage 1 except for two vital areas and these prevent a circular progression. The last stage of Communism has inherited the industrial base of Capitalism and Socialism and thus it is *not* a Pastoral Stage 1 society and the last stage also has the advantage of knowing the previous five stages and their attendant evils.

Dialectical Materialism

This is the Marxian theory of social change or the nature of the forces which change one historical stage into another. The "dialectic" aspect of this was adapted from German philosopher Georg W. F. Hegel's triad regarding the development of ideas. For Hegel, the triad was composed of an idea or Thesis, the very existence of this Thesis created an opposite idea or Antithesis, and from the clash of these two, a third and higher idea or Synthesis was formed. This Synthesis was then recycled back to form a new Thesis, a new Antithesis was formed, and so on until the final Synthesis of the strong national Prussian state was reached for Hegel. This Synthesis is quite similar to Rousseau's concept of the general will: it is more true and valid than either the Thesis or Antithesis for it includes only those segments of the two inferior ideas that are valid and deletes those segments which are not valid. It is an example, as in Rousseau's general will, of synercism: the whole is greater than the sum of the parts. The analogy of the automobile discussed above is also relevant here. A fully assembled, functioning automobile has more "validity" than just the two-thousand-odd parts strewn about the room even though the final product contains the same number of parts. This triad of the Thesis/Antithesis/Synthesis is the dialectic.

The materialist aspect enters through Marx's use of the Triad. Each stage of history (Thesis) contains in itself the seeds of its own destruction (Antithesis) and these seeds are the materialist organization of who owns and who profits from the means of production and class conflict. The resulting Synthesis is the subsequent stage of history and the process is repeated and repeated until the final Synthesis (Communism) is reached. For example, Capitalism is the Thesis (private property, surplus value, class conflict, oppressive State); the rising misery and the rising politicalization and radicalization of the working class are the Antithesis, and these two combine in a violent clash with the resulting Synthesis being the Socialist stage. Then Socialism becomes the Thesis, the Antithesis is the eventual elimination of class, property, and surplus value, and the resulting Synthesis is the last stage of Communism.

The above ideas and concepts—man's nature, the stages of history, and dialectical materialism—are the major and most crucial elements of Marxian thought. There are, however, several other areas alluded to above and the following remarks present a brief discussion of the theory of surplus value/labor theory of value, the inevitability of class conflict, the dictatorship of the proletariat, the withering away of the State, and public ownership of the means of production/no private property.

Theory of Surplus Value/Labor Theory of Value

This concept of Marx entails the belief that (a) labor is the only creator and measure of value; (b) the salary the worker receives represents only a fraction of the amount for which the capitalist sells the product; and (c) the difference between the value received by the worker and the value the capitalist receives in the marketplace is the surplus value stolen by the bourgeois from the worker. By stealing this value, the parasitic capitalist class exploits and oppresses the proletariat. Marx writes that this is one of the prime reasons for the eventual downfall of Stages 2, 3 and 4 (Slavery, Feudalism, Capitalism). The proletariat would receive less and less of his labor's value until the working class would rise up in armed revolution. In the fifth stage, Socialism, surplus value would be reduced, the worker would receive a larger and larger share of his labor, and when surplus value is totally eliminated, the society would then be able to move into the sixth and final stage of Communism.

Theory of the Class Struggle / Inevitability of Class Conflict

Marx believed that class conflict was inevitable in any society that had class differentials. One class would seize the machinery of the State and perpetuate the economic system in order to exploit and oppress the other class(es): the slave-owners employed the State to oppress the slaves; the aristocracy employed the State to oppress the serfs; and the bourgeois capitalists employed the State to oppress the proletariat. For Marx, what was significant was that the capitalist class controlled the English Parliament and used the machinery of the State to exploit the workers: it was *illegal* to engage in union activities, it was *illegal* to limit the working day to ten hours; the proletariat was *not* given the right to vote. There still would be class conflict during Socialism for now the proletariat would employ the machinery of the State to oppress the bourgeoisie into oblivion. When the bourgeoisie disappeared, the society could then move into the sixth and final stage.

Dictatorship of the Proletariat

A small group of workers, the vanguard of the proletariat, would engineer the shift from capitalism on through socialism to communism. This vanguard of the working class would seize power from the bourgeois and then institute the dictatorship of the proletariat over the remaining exploiters (landlords, creditors, capitalists). The State would continue to exist under the firm control of this small group of workers until the exploiting class was totally eliminated. Then and only then would the State disappear and the society could move into the sixth stage of Communism.

Withering Away of the State

According to Marxian analysis, the State exists only as the agent of the ruling class to oppress another class within each particular society. Once the society attained the communist

stage—once there were no class differences—there would therefore be no one left to oppress and the State would simply wither
away into oblivion. Justice and the distribution of the various
goods and services would administer themselves in the communist stage. Such self-administration was believed possible by
Marx for, now that the Communist stage had been attained,
man was liberated, emancipated, humane, and perfected. Marx
has, after a fashion, solidly allied himself with John Locke
against Thomas Hobbes regarding the existence of natural law.
Marx did not write that natural law from God exists but it would
be some sort of natural law which would organize and direct
the individual's behavior in his final stage of communism. There
can be no positive law because the State has withered away.

Public Ownership of the Means of Production/No Private Property

This concept of Marx does not imply or include the total
elimination of all private property as so many of Marx's critics
have intimated. Items for personal use and personal possession
(a house, an automobile, a chair, a table, consumer goods,
etc.) are all reserved to the individual in the sixth and final
stage. It would only be the means of production which could
be employed to oppress other people that are to be taken from
the bourgeois. Such means of production are to be held and
operated in common by society at large for the public interest
and not for the private profit of some small groups of share-
holders. State ownership/control of the major means of production have become commonplace and countries such as France
have instituted large-scale and wide-ranging programs. The
French people, through their elected representatives in Parliament and through the administrative bureaucracy controlled by
a cabinet minister, "own" and "operate" for the public interest
(this means that the profit motive is not the only consideration) a wide area of goods and services. Electricity, gas, coal
mines, the merchant marine, Air France, the railroad network,
aircraft construction, city transportation, and a good portion
of medical, insurance, financial, and credit services are only

a partial list of goods and services France has transferred to public ownership.

Marxian ideology has been deified by millions of people but this reverence by post-Marx Communists has shown two points: (1) the extent to which Soviet ideologues attempt to justify Soviet practice by Marxian precepts; and (2) the extent to which Soviet practice denies Marxian ideology. Some examples of these points are discussed below.

The insistence by Marx that the six historical stages must be followed in order and that a stage could not be skipped was taken quite literally, at least on the public level, by Leon Trotsky. Trotsky, who played a crucial role along with Lenin in the Russian Revolution, had to justify having the Russian state move into Stage 5 (Socialism) from what most observers believed to have been Stage 3 (the feudal Tsarist regime). What was to be done with Stage 4 (Capitalism)?—Marx wrote that it could not be skipped! There were several people who argued for delaying the Socialist revolution in order to permit the society to fully develop its capitalist and industrial characteristics, including the seeds of its own destruction, before moving into Socialism. This was quite logical according to Marx for an oppressive capitalist class was necessary before the proletariat could destroy it. But Trotsky very neatly "solved" this problem by arguing that Russia did not, in fact, skip the fourth stage, but only telescoped it into ten months! The change from Feudalism to Capitalism took place in February 1917 under the leadership of Alexander Kerensky and the Social Democrats. Tsar Nicholas was forced to abdicate and an embryonic capitalist system was observable. But the Capitalist stage lasted only until November 1917 when the Bolsheviks engineered the coup which moved the Russian society into the fifth stage of Socialism. Such ideological acrobatics only underline the stature of Marxian ideology.

In 1935, the Soviet Union under Stalin published a new Constitution. This Constitution contained many liberal democratic procedures and clauses respecting civil liberties and human rights but most people in the West could not see any similarity between the contents of the document and the then-current Soviet practices. A Western journalist asked Stalin a question along these lines: The Constitution states that each citizen has complete freedom of choice but only one party— the Communist Party—is allowed to operate. How can these two facts be reconciled? Stalin's answer employed Marxian ideology to describe Soviet practice even though the two had very little in common. Stalin's response went somewhat along these lines: Marx wrote that political parties are only the agents of one class to oppress the other classes in the Society. Since our society now has only one class, we only require one political party. It is the multiparty systems of the West who are undemocratic, and not the Soviet Union, for multiparties mean multiclasses. Multiclasses mean class conflict and oppression by that one class and party who can capture the organs and the machinery of the State.

Nikita Khrushchev was visiting the United States for an appearance at the U.N. and an American journalist asked him a very nasty question somewhat along these lines: Marx wrote that the State should wither away during the Communist stage. It has now been approximately 40 years since the Soviet Union moved into Socialism. But the State is not withering away; it is becoming larger and stronger. How can you reconcile this Soviet practice with Marxian ideology? Mr. Khrushchev's legerdemand response, in a paraphrase: It is true that we have moved into Communism and thus there is no need for the State to exist *within* the Soviet Union. But there still is class conflict among nations because some nations remain mired in the Capitalist stage. Until there are no longer any capitalist countries, the Soviet Union will require a strong State to protect itself from the international bourgeois! What Khrushchev did here was to transfer Marxian internal precepts into external requirements. No longer can the State wither away in one country, even if it does have only one class, as long as there are capitalist countries beyond the frontier. Marx wrote, in effect, that when the last capitalist is eliminated from the society, then that society can enter Communism; what Khrushchev said, in effect, is that when the last capitalist is eliminated from the face of the earth can socialist countries move into the sixth stage and dismantle the State.

Marxian thought has had an enormous influence and impact upon later generations. There was some immediate action in the 1860s and 1870s resulting from Marx's and Engels' theorizing and propaganda. Marx's influence on the socialist movement was seen by his activities in the "International Association of Workingmen" (the First International) which had its inaugural meeting in 1864. The First International attempted to serve as a clearinghouse and central actor for the working class of several countries and their goal of transforming the existing capitalist society. These meetings gave support to the creation of socialist political parties and the first such party, the German Social Democratic Party under Ferdinand Lassalle, was established in the 1870s. The Franco-Prussian War in 1870 and the subsequent decimation of the Paris Commune in May of 1871 contributed to the First International's disintegration. The Second International, established at Brussels in 1889, lasted until 1917 and this organization was a very loose collection of national Socialist parties and movements. It was throughout this period (1864 to 1917) that the split between what is now termed "Socialist" and "Communist" ideologies took place.

The Socialists and Communists both believed themselves to be the true followers of Marx but, as events in the Internationals transpired, the Socialists became known as "revisionists" and the Communists became known as the "orthodox" Marxists. The Socialist ideology also was termed "parliamentary" or "evolutionary" Marxism while the Communists were termed the "revolutionary" Marxists. The following discussion presents some of the major points of convergence and divergence between these two wings of thought as existed until approximately the early 1960s on the European continent.

Both the evolutionary parliamentary Socialists and the Communists agree with Marx (and each other) that capitalism is bad for it exploits the worker and alienates the individual. Both also agree with Marx in the materialist conception of history (economic determinism) and the inevitability of the class struggle. But Socialists differ from Communists because the former do not advocate the complete elimination of the Capitalist system as do the Communists. Socialists advocate less drastic aims for they wish to modify and not destroy capitalism. Communism advocates the total elimination of private property but Socialism, with its less drastic aims, advocates only the nationalization of certain key, select industries and not the entire economy. The parliamentary Socialists also, in general, advocate that its methods in the transformation of society are to be peaceful: political parties, candidates, ballots, elections, bargaining, and constitutionalism are all tactics employed by the Socialists. The "orthodox" Marxists or the Communists, on the other hand, advocated the violent overthrow of the Capitalist society and the dictatorship of the proletariat. The final major difference concerns the scope or area of the two viewpoints' goals. The Socialists concentrate and emphasize their aims on the national level and the Communists emphasize the internationalism of the orthdox approach and believe in the unity of all Communist parties.

But the 1960s saw a fundamental change in European socialist parties and the 1970s are witnessing a reciprocal change within some European Communist parties, particularly the French and Italian Communist parties. In a sense, these two "orthodox" Marxist parties are now acting as the Socialists did in the 1950s and the Socialists now are renouncing many of their previous central principles. The tenets which have characterized European parliamentary Socialism since 1870 have changed in Great Britain, the Netherlands, and Germany. At the 1959 Annual Meeting of both the British Labor Party and the Trades Union Congress, the tenet of nationalization was de-emphasized. The Socialist Party and the TUC stressed increasing the scope of social services to the population and they supported the retention of the private enterprise system but liable to governmental regulation. The Labor Party thus became very similar to the Conservatives and Liberals in their support for a social welfare state. The 1960 annual meeting of the Dutch Socialist Party turned in the same direction: for the Dutch Socialists, it was not who *owns* the means of production which was important but, rather, how people lived. The German Social Democrats, also in 1960, published their "New Socialist Manifesto" and this was the first major revision of German Socialist thought since World War I. The "New Socialist Manifesto" repudiated the main components of Marxian thought and, as did the British and the Dutch, supported the retention of the free enterprise system, the expansion of social services, and governmental regulation in place of governmental ownership.

As the European Socialists are becoming "less" Socialist as compared to the period 1864-1914, the French and Italian Communists are becoming "more" socialist. The French and Italian parties now can be described as "evolutionary" parliamentary parties whose tactics include constitutionalism, elections, parliamentary bargaining, and the ballot box. Their methods are peaceful—the French Communist Party did *not* support the student uprising in the late 1960s—and their aims emphasize the national level. There are, of course, splinter Communist parties, especially in France, who oppose the parent party and accuse it of being "revisionist." The Trotskyite and Maoist groups in France consider themselves to be the true inheritors of Marx but such groups have very little strength compared to the dominant Communist Party. But Marxian thought, or at least segments of his ideology, continues to influence and guide these Communist parties.

To conclude, Karl Marx's greatest contribution to his time was perhaps his entirely different and then-radical way of interpreting history and the development of societies. Marx presented a compelling analysis of the first four stages of history (pastoral, slave, feudal, and capitalist) and his description of the abject poverty and misery of the working class under the bourgeois exploiters was an immense indictment of the capitalist system as it then existed. One should read Engels' *The Condition of the Working Class in England* for the factual information about mid-nineteenth-century capitalism and how it degraded, alienated, and emasculated the worker and his family. But Marx's real problem came when he attempted to peer into the future—to describe his utopia and what people ought to do with the end of capitalism and the stages of socialism and communism. Marx was just unable to predict that "capitalism" would take on new meanings and new characteristics. Even in the United States, much more capitalistic than the socialist European countries, trade union activity, profit sharing, minimum wage-hour laws, and all the other paraphernalia of a modern industrialized society have given the average proletarian a standard of living that Marx simply could not foresee. Marx's analysis is culture-bound for it is too much tied up with mid-nineteenth-century capitalism. But this cannot be taken as an honest criticism because Marx cannot be blamed for not knowing the future. His time and universe *was* the period of the most blatant abuses of the workers by the oppressive capitalist system and it is against this background, not the background of satiated unionism in the 1970s, that Marx should be interpreted.

Politics as a System
David Easton (Canadian-American, 1917-   )

The final (final only for this chapter, not for political science) conception of politics is categorized as Politics as a System and its major and most influential proponent is David Easton. Professor Easton is the exception among the group of people reviewed in this chapter: he is not a vagabond as was Rousseau, he is not an international revolutionary as was Marx, and he has not been required to flee any country in fear of his life as were Hobbes and Locke. David Easton is a political science professor with a life-style congruent with contemporary academic life. Born in Canada and educated at the University of Toronto and at Harvard, Easton has taught at several major universities, including Harvard and Chicago. He has written extensively on many aspects of politics and political science, particularly in the field of systematic political theory, and his writings most relevant to this chapter are *The Political System* (1953), *A Framework for Political Analysis* (1965), and *A Systems Analysis of Political Life* (1965).

Easton differs from the above discussed individuals in two respects: one is, of course, in content for Easton is talking about different things, but a more important difference is the fundamental and basic approach to and conception of politics and political science. Easton does not, as did Hobbes, Locke, Rousseau, and Marx, first prescribe the ideal society and then describe the best procedures for attaining this goal. He is not interested as a professional political scientist, although as a private individual he most surely is, in the *oughts* of politics; he is concerned with the *whats, hows,* and *whys* based upon observable and verifiable knowledge, that is, what people and political systems actually *do*, not what they ethically or morally should do.[22] And politics is not just the study of the State: politics, and this is the central categorizing issue for Easton, is the study of a "political system." The sovereign national territorial State is most certainly a political system, and thus can be examined from Easton's approach, but there are many entities other than territorial States which also qualify as "political systems." Some examples of such systems qualifying as "political" systems but which are not States would be the AFL-CIO, the American Olympic Committee, the National Rifle Association, Americans for Democratic Action, a university, and the family unit.

Easton writes that the distinguishing element of "political" interactions or political behavior compared to other types of social interaction is that the political variety are "predominantly oriented toward the authoritative allocation of values for a society."[23] Political science is thus the study and analysis of that system of interactions in a society "through which binding or authoritative allocations are made and implemented." This authoritative allocation of values is for Easton what identifies the boundaries of the political system from other systems in the society. Easton comments:

> Briefly, authoritative allocations distribute valued things among persons or groups in one or more three possible ways. An allocation may deprive a person of a valued thing already possessed; it may obstruct the attainment of values which would otherwise have been attained; or it may give some persons access to values and deny them to others.
>
> An allocation is authoritative when the persons oriented to it consider that they are bound by it.... But regardless of the particular grounds [legal, traditional, charismatic], it is the fact of considering the allocations as binding that distinguishes political from other types of allocations....[24]

This authoritative or binding allocation of values is thus what sets off the political from the nonpolitical or, in Easton's words, it sets off the political from the "parapolitical." Easton recognizes that his description of the system in which members feel obligated to submit to the decisions can also be employed for a whole category of systems which are, in a sense, subordinate or subservient to the "political system"; e.g., a fraternal organization such as the Elks, churches, universities, families. This entire area gets back to the discussion above on the boundary identification problem between Lasswell and Easton: Lasswell believes politics is all power relationships; Easton says that only those power relationships binding upon the whole society are political and the other power relationships are parapolitical. There is, of course, a fundamental difference between these two points but it is in truth not that important for, basically, it is an individual and arbitrary boundary location and each can be employed for its own purposes.

Easton devotes a great deal of space in his *A Framework for Political Analysis* to the differences between political and parapolitical systems: the parapolitical systems are subsystems in the larger social system and the governing body of a parapolitical system cannot speak or act in the name of society. These governing bodies of the sub- or parapolitical systems may be able to successfully allocate values *within* their specific area but this power does not travel beyond the borders of their special area of activity. The "political system," on the other hand, can authoritatively allocate values which are binding upon the whole and entire system, including all the smaller subsystems. But if one leans toward Lasswell's approach—that *political* behavior and not *sub-* or *parapolitical* behavior does take place even within Easton's parapolitical units—Easton's framework and systems analysis is still an excellent conceptual and methodological approach with which to study political behavior. In other words, Easton's framework can be employed to analyze the family, church, trade union, or university. Easton employs the *system* as the organizing concept and his delineation of the system's characteristics and components can thus be employed, whatever one's particular definition of the system happens to be.

Figure 2.1 is adapted from Easton's description of the system's characteristics and components. It should be noted that Easton is referring to the "political system" and not to the sub- or parapolitical systems but, as mentioned above, the diagram can also be used in reference to the subsystems (the family, university, professional society, trade union, fraternal

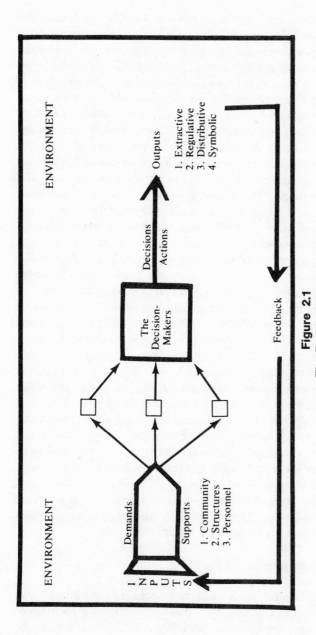

Figure 2.1
The Political System

From David Easton, *A Framework for Political Analysis*, Copyright © 1965, p. 112. Adapted by permission of Prentice-Hall, Inc., Englewood Cliffs, New Jersey.

organization). This system analysis is based upon inputs and outputs and it has several advantages as an organizing concept for politics and political science. First, it does not appear to be culture-bound (later generations will probably find differently) as were previous conceptions and approaches. It really does not describe or relate to any one particular society and it is not limited by time or geographical location. Contemporary U.S. society as well as contemporary Russian society can be approached with the diagram; the aborigine culture of Australia as well as the ancient Greeks can also be studied. Perhaps its major advantage can be seen if we compare it to the study of a foreign language: the study of French grammar and vocabulary will give the student no knowledge of French literature but it will give the tools, the techniques, the ability to read Proust or Sartre and, hopefully, understand the contents of these writings. It is the same with Easton's systems analysis: the understanding of his systems approach will give the student no knowledge whatsoever about specific systems or societies but, rather, it will enable the student to have the tools or ability to approach different systems and begin a reasoned and careful analysis and comparison. This very abstractness of Easton's contribution is one of its merits. Marx's contribution, for example, is too much tied up with mid-nineteenth-century *laissez-faire* capitalism. Another use of this input/output analysis is with the whole area of system maintenance or system stability-instability. Why do some political systems or some subsystems have the ability to adapt to a changing environment and thus remain viable while others are unable to handle the stress or strain and lapse into instability or eventually disappear? Again, Easton's framework will not provide the answers, but it will provide a neat and precise way of looking for the answers (assuming there are such answers). The following discussion presents the most important features of Easton's systems approach.

The Environment

There are two types of environments: (1) the *intrasocietal* and (2) the *extrasocietal*. By intrasocietal, Easton is referring to that part of the social and physical world which is outside the political system but within (intra) the same society. The intrasocietal environment is itself composed of different subsystems such as the ecological system, the biological system, the personality systems, and the social system. These social systems are, in turn, the cultural norms, social structures, the economic system, demographic system, religious and education systems. This intrasocietal environment affects, and is in its turn affected by, the political system.

The second type of environment is termed extrasocietal for this environment is not within the same society as the political system but external (extra) to it. In other words, this second type is the international societal characteristics composed of the international ecological system, the international social systems (international cultural norms, international social structures, international economics and demographics), and the international political system (the individual political systems of each society and the international structures and organizations such as the United Nations, NATO, OPEC, the European Common Market, etc.). The relationship between the intra (internal) environment and the political system is direct, immediate, and almost impossible to avoid. An analogy would be a fish (the political system) swimming in the ocean (the intrasocietal environment). But the relationship and linkage between the political system and the extrasocietal environment may be less direct, less immediate, less numerous, and, perhaps, even nonexistent. Our fish (the political system) can possibly isolate itself from the worm (the extrasocietal environment) attached to a random fishing pole as a country can attempt to isolate itself from external influences. The Great Wall of China or, more recently, the Berlin Wall, can be regarded as attempts to protect the political system from extrasocietal influence or pressure. But both environments, while not a part of the political system, interact with the political system and help shape its structure, activities, and policies.

Demands and Supports

These are the basic raw input into the political system fed into the decision-makers, but demands and supports have different natures. *Demands* are "articulated statements, directed toward the authorities, proposing that some kind of authoritative allocation ought to be undertaken."[25] In other words, a demand is a statement that something should or should not be done. It is here that the merits of the analysis as an analytic concept begin to show because all political systems have demands and they can be stated or expressed or articulated in various ways. Voting, writing a letter or a telegram to a Congressperson, petitioning—all are "demands" in a democratic society. Walking up to the village elder in an aborigine society and informing him that the tribe should go hunting instead of fishing is only, to use the jargon, an expression that a certain authoritative allocation of value be or not be done and this serves the exact same function as the demands expressed in other societies. The content may differ and the volume of the demands may differ but they are all demands nonetheless. Demands present an excellent area with which to compare different political systems. Easton's analysis will not tell us about any one specific political system but his conceptual approach is, in a sense, transparent and it can thus be superimposed over different systems. What kinds of demands are made in these political systems? What groups are voicing these demands? Can the volume and frequency of demands be compared? One may discover, for example, that there might be very little difference, except for language, of course, between the frequency and content of demands expressed by the American Joint Chiefs of Staff and its Soviet equivalent. Easton's analysis will not tell us about these demands but it will point the way for cross-national comparison.

A *support* refers to the inputs to the political system which are favorably oriented to the system or to the components of the system and they can be both overt behavior or states of mind (attitudes or latent support). Supportive inputs are buttresses or sustaining inputs: not "I want" (demands) but "I agree" (supports). This description is not that precise but it will serve the purpose. Easton isolates and identifies three different levels on which support is solicited and directed: (1) the political community, (2) the governmental structures, and (3) personnel and policies.

Support for level (1), the political community, is support for the analytical concept of the system itself—not support for the United States but support for the concept of "America." This is the concept or level of national unity: unity under some common structural form and unity with common practices, feelings of sameness and commonality, and the expectation that disputes and the decision-making process will be carried out through peaceful methods. This level of support is basic to the continuance of any political system. Easton comments:

> No political system can continue to operate unless its members are willing to support the existence of a group that seeks to settle differences or promote decisions through peaceful action in common. The point is so obvious—being dealt with usually under the heading of the growth of national unity—that it may well be overlooked; and yet it is a premise upon which the continuation of any political system depends. To refer to this phenomenon we can speak of the political community. At this level of support we are not concerned with whether a government exists or whether there is loyalty to a constitutional order. For the moment we only ask whether the members of the group that we are examining are sufficiently oriented toward each other to want to contribute their collective energies toward pacific settlement of the varying demands.[26]

Without support on this level, the political system cannot be created or, if already in existence, it cannot be maintained. The current problems in Northern Ireland, the recent civil war in Nigeria, the antagonisms between the French and English in Quebec, between the Scots and English in Great Britain, and between the Flemings and Walloons in Belgium are all examples of where support for the political community does (did) not exist to a high enough degree to maintain the existence of the system. Examples of overt behavior supportive of the political community in the United States would be the singing of the National Anthem or the Pledge of Allegiance to the Flag. These acts are not tied to the constitutional order or to the individual decision-makers, but, rather, it is support directed to the community itself.

Support for level (2), the governmental structures or con-

stitutional order/rules of the game, refers to support directed
at the specific structures and organization of the system or what
Easton terms the *regime*. The regime

> ... consists of all those arrangements that regulate the
> way in which the demands put into the system are settled
> and the way in which decisions are put into effect. They are
> the so-called rules of the game, in the light of which actions
> by members of the system are legitimated and accepted by
> the bulk of the members as authoritative. Unless there is
> a minimum convergence of attitudes in support of these
> fundamental rules—the constitutional principles, as we
> call them in Western society—there would be insufficient
> harmony in the actions of the members of a system to meet
> the problems generated by their support of a political com-
> munity. The fact of trying to settle demands in common
> means that there must be known principles governing the
> way in which resolutions of differences of claims are to
> take place.[27]

Support on this level is support for the United States with
its federal structure, fifty states, a president elected every four
years, a Congress, a Supreme Court. Or, in Great Britain, it is
support for the parliamentary system or organization with the
prime minister and Parliament, the House of Lords, the queen.
There is little overt nonsupport in the United States on this
level. Perhaps the Republic of Black Africa (this movement
desires to establish a separate Black Republic in the southern
part of the United States) can serve as an example but it is a
rare and infrequent example. Democrats, Republicans, and
American Independents all support the constitutional structure
and operating procedures. Historical examples of nonsupport
on this level can be found with the Russian émigrés after the
1917 Revolution: this group gave support to level (1), the
political community or the concept of "Russia," but they did
not give support to that particular organization or constitutional structures which were in operation after 1917. Other
examples would be the various separatist groups in Europe:
the Welsh Nationalists, Scottish Nationalists, Fleming Nationalists, or the Basque Separatists.

Support for level (3), the personnel who are the decision-makers and their output or policies, is directed at the specific individuals who populate the authoritative positions and at the specific policies which filter out of the decision-making process. Support or nonsupport on this level is usually much lower than support for the other two levels, especially in pluralistic democratic societies. Support means support for the president (not the office of the president but the individual himself) and the current Administration's policies, support for the actual Justices sitting on the Supreme Court and the content of their decisions rather than support for the Supreme Court as an institution. A shorthand method of identifying support at this level in the 1972 presidential election would be that support is measured by the number of people who voted for Mr. Nixon and nonsupport is measured by the number of people who voted for Mr. McGovern or Mr. Schmitz. This latter group shows nonsupport by definition because it voted against the individual and his policies. The Democrats and the American Independents *did* support the Community (level 1) and the Constitutional Order (level 2), but, and this is the crucial element, they simply did not exhibit support for level 3 (personnel and policies). Nonsupport for level 3 does *not* necessarily entail nonsupport for the first two levels.

One of the tragedies of political life, but especially American political life, is the inability of the leadership (the decision-makers) to perceive the conceptual difference among these three levels of support. Time and time again those people who do not give support to the specific individuals and policies of whatever administration happens to be in office, Democrat or Republican, are invariably characterized as working against the best interests of the society (nonsupport for levels 1 and 2) or, less frequently but more dangerously, as traitors or subversives. In the United States, this can be seen most dramatically with the opposition to the war in Vietnam under both Presidents Johnson and Nixon, as well as with the opposition to Mr. Nixon during the Watergate affair. Opponents to the war in Vietnam were constantly accused of nonsupport on level 1 and Mr. Nixon consistently depicted his opponents vis-à-vis his role in Watergate as wanting to destroy the office of the presidency (level 2).

Some societies have, however, been able to perceive these conceptual differences and have organized their structures so as to split level 3 away from levels 1 and 2. Most constitutional monarchies fall into this category and Great Britain is an excellent example. The prime minister and his Cabinet are personnel and policies; the monarch (Queen Elizabeth) is the symbol and recipient of support for the Community and the Contutional Order. Britons can demonstrate and oppose certain governmental officials and their policies without being accused of also opposing the concept of the community or the rules of the game. The monarch represents the nation and system; the prime minister represents the Government. The United States does not have a differentiated structure such as Great Britain (the president also represents the nation), and the confusion over support levels results. The crisis in India during the summer of 1975 also illustrates the inability of the decision-makers to distinguish among the levels of support. Opponents of Prime Minister Indira Gandhi (personnel and policies) were jailed: not because they opposed the prime minister but because such nonsupport was perceived by the Government as opposition to the constitutional order or to the community. The decision-makers simply can see no distinction between themselves and the structures and/or community. One last example of this confusion between the individual and the nation, an example which requires little elaboration, can be seen in the statement by one of Mr. Nixon's daughters immediately after she voted in the 1972 presidential election: when asked by a reporter whether she voted for her father, Julie Nixon Eisenhower said, "No, I did not vote for my father, I voted for *America*."[28]

Demands and supports are influenced by both the intra- and extrasocietal environments and these demands and supports are fed toward the decision-makers as inputs to the political decision-making process. All political systems, whether a large nation or the individual family, exhibit these inputs. Their content, volume, and frequency differ, of course, depending upon the particular system under examination but they are an integral part of a political system.

The Interest Aggregators

The column of small boxes in Figure 2.1 represents those institutions or processes which receive many of the raw unstructured demands and supports, combine and filter them, and then convert them into one or two policy alternatives which are then fed into the area where the decision-makers live. This process is termed "interest aggregation" and thus the boxes are "interest aggregators." These intervening variables, intervening in the sense that they come between the population and the decision-makers, exist in most but not all political systems. Only in the most unstructured and undifferentiated primitive or traditional societies (the Tasadays, Iks, Aborigines) are the raw demands/supports fed directly into the decision-makers. These unstructured and undifferentiated societies do not require interest aggregators because the capability or the efficiency rating of the decision-making unit is equal to or surpasses the volume of demands and supports generated by the population and inputed to the system. These intervening variables are usually found in technologically and industrially advanced countries and are the society's interest groups, lobbies, professional societies, or political parties. These groups receive the raw demands/supports of their adherents, combine them, and then present them as one single consolidated demand/support. Some examples would be the American Medical Association, the National Rifle Association, the AFL-CIO, the Bishop's Conference: all are interest aggregators which filter the demands and supports of the system. Political parties are very important and influential interest aggregators in democratic societies for a party platform can be regarded as the combination of, say, forty million individual demands.

These intervening variables can have a eufunctional (beneficial to the maintenance or continuity of the system) effect in political systems. They can help prevent the decision-makers from becoming overwhelmed by the amount/frequency of demands voiced by the population. One statement from the (now defunct) Committee of One Million to Keep Red China Out of the United Nations was much more beneficial for the efficient operation of the political system than one million individual statements to the same effect. These aggregators are important factors in the study of why some systems are able to adapt to the changing environment and why other systems have been less fortunate in dealing with the requirements of change. An analogy of the eufunctional or beneficial role of these groups would be the electric-power grid system of the United States. Megawatts and megawatts of electrical power (or millions and millions of raw demands/supports) are produced by the generating companies (population) but at each stage of the physical translation of this power to the individual user (decision-maker), there are "reducing" stations (aggregators) which decrease the wattage until it is small enough to be used in the home without a blackout. Without these "reducing" stations, a thousand-watt toaster plugged into an outlet with a hundred thousand or so watts on the other side would probably cause more than a blackout—the whole house (system) would be destroyed. The interest aggregators frequently reduce the demands to a manageable size for the decision-makers to handle.

But these variables or processes can also have dysfunctional (not beneficial to the continuity of the system) effects if they serve as barriers rather than as conduits/pipelines between the population and the decision-makers. An analogy here would be a gigantic dam with the sluice gates closed. As the water (demands/supports) piled up behind the dam (the aggregators), the decision-makers would be operating in a vacuum until the water eventually spilled over the top of the dam, or collapsed it, and then destroyed everything in its path (a revolution). It is entirely reasonable to approach the French and Russian revolutions in this way. The analogies may not be that direct but they do make a point: depending upon the way in which these intervening variables or structures perform, the political system will either have a greater likelihood to adapt and thus survive in a changing environment or the system will fall under the avalanche of water or be blacked out, as the case may be.

The Decision-Makers

These are the people who actually perform or decide what values are to be allocated. These are the people who receive the demands/supports (either as raw unstructured material direct from the population or as filtered and refined material from the aggregators, most often a combination of the two) and, based upon their individual society and resources and goals, decide the policies or outputs of the political system. This decision-making process can be achieved by a variety of methods: one-man/one-vote, by consensus, by fiat, by appeal to God, fate, or by astrology. What is important for this discussion is not so much how the decisions are made, but, rather, that they are made at all.

It is here again that the utility of Easton's framework is evident in the study of different systems. One can now focus on, say, the decision-makers in two or three different societies and begin to see who they are, what structures are employed, how the decisions are made (the U.S. Supreme Court makes decisions in an entirely different manner than the pope). The decision-makers may be presidents with congresses, prime ministers with parliaments, a strong monarch with yes-people, a tsar, a village council of elders, a university president, or the head of a family. But whatever the particular make-up and operating procedures, the function is the same: the decision-makers take the inputs and convert them into outputs and those outputs are the authoritative allocation of values for that society or for that parapolitical society.

Outputs

This refers to the actual values (decisions) which are authoritatively allocated by the decision-makers of the system. In other words, this is what is put out, produced, manufactured by the political system. As stated above, the *content* of this output varies widely from one culture to another (where to fish in the Eskimo society, or who receives the fat government contract in the United States) but the *nature* of the output is the same for all systems: it is the authoritative allocation of value. Easton identifies four categories or types of output for all political systems. These categories usually overlap (the same output can belong in two or more categories) but there are examples of specific output which do fall into only one general type. These categories are: (1) extractive, (2) regulative, (3) distributive, and (4) symbolic.

Extractive output is output which does exactly what it says—it extracts goods, time, resources, attitudes, money, lives, etc. from the population. Although the actual content of, say, the United States Internal Revenue Code and an Eskimo stipulation that one-tenth of the seal catch must be given to the society at large differs considerably, they are analytically and conceptually the same. Both extract something from the population. All political systems extract from the population: some may do it efficiently, others may do it haphazardly; some may do it peacefully, others may do it in a brutal fashion but these differences are not relevant to this discussion.

Regulative output is output which regulates the behavior of the system's members. Stop signs, no-parking signs, no-cutting-of-classes notices, no ———— (fill in at pleasure) are all examples of regulative output. Also illustrative of regulative output would be, in Easton's parapolitical systems, the parents' rules to the children, the pope's pronouncements on birth control, a fraternal club's prohibiting open membership. This category of regulation, of course, overlaps with extraction for regulative output, in a sense, extracts a certain behavior pattern from the individual. The categories are only broad general types and are not intended to be neat divisions or discrete categories.

Distributive output is output which in a sense extracts from one individual or group and gives to another individual or group. This can in some areas be distinguished from regulation and extraction for in these two someone else may not receive that which is being regulated or extracted. The Social Security system in the United States is an excellent example of distributive output: those who pay are being extracted from, those who receive are the beneficiaries. Revenue sharing and all other governmental spending programs are also distributive for *someone* has to receive the money, whether it is in the form of a welfare check, a business subsidy, an illegal kickback, or salaries for government workers. All systems perform this, whether that which is being distributed is government offices to the faithful and loyal party workers, or the results of the day's hunting or fishing expedition.

Symbolic output is the only category of output which does not overlap with the other three types because symbolic output is created for the sole purpose of being fed back into the system via the feedback loop in order to create higher levels of support (on all three support levels) or to manage (increase/ decrease) the frequency of demands. *Symbolic* does not mean hollow or empty output because this type of output is concrete and it is not just a facade. This output does not regulate, distribute, or extract, and it is for this reason that Easton terms it *symbolic*. Examples of symbolic output in the United States would be the president throwing out the first ball to begin the baseball season, lighting the White House Christmas tree, laying a wreath on the Tomb of the Unknown Soldier, issuing a proclamation of a day of Thanksgiving, declaring a national day of mourning. These are designed to be fed back into the system and to help create new levels of support. In Great Britain and other constitutional monarchies, it is the activity of the constitutional monarch (king or queen) which are mostly "symbolic." The English queen cannot regulate, extract, or distribute much of anything: but Elizabeth II can and does create new levels of support for the English system (levels 1 and 2—political community and constitutional structure) with her symbolic activities.

Feedback

Easton writes that the process of feedback is crucial to the system as a self-regulative and adaptive continuing system. Feedback is that part of the output (all four types of output) which is re-inserted into the system to help create new levels and new natures of the demands and supports. The people can then respond to the decision-makers' policies and then the decision-makers can alter their policies in light of the people's response. The system can thus handle stress: the decision-makers would be aware that the sluice gates were closed or open, and the system could respond to the output. This does not mean democracy, e.g., mass voting every four years with the freedom of choice, for democracy is not required for a well-functioning feedback loop. All that is required is open lines of communication—the Eskimo culture as well as Nazi Germany has (had) feedback although one did not operate as well as the other.

When this loop of information-response is cut or shut off, when the decision-makers are operating in total isolation from other parts of the system and from the environments, the system will be overwhelmed by stress. Marie Antoinette's "let them eat cake" can serve as an example: the feedback loop was closed in France in 1789 for the decision-makers had no idea how the output was affecting the population and thus could not even respond to the increasing demands (assuming the king wanted to respond, a doubtful assumption). The alleged activities by Mr. Nixon's White House staff which isolated the president from the feedback loop were instrumental in the former president's inability to govern effectively. It has been alleged that, after the 1968 "excursion" into Cambodia, members of Mr. Nixon's staff themselves sent congratulatory and supportive telegrams to Mr. Nixon. A large segment of the American population did not support this particular policy but their demands were barred from entering the president's feedback loop. Feedback is essential if the system, whether a national political entity or the family, is to handle the ever-present stress and be able to adapt and remain stable in a changing environment.

Easton's perception of politics as an integrated system of behavior is different from the conceptions and approaches of Hobbes, Locke, Rousseau, and Marx. Easton's approach is not what ought to be, what the ethical goal should be, but, rather, it is an analysis of the system itself and how the system operates, its major characteristics, and what the system must do if it wishes to survive. This framework for political analysis is an excellent methodological tool because its very abstractness— it is not tied to any one particular time, place, or actual historical political society—allows it to be employed or superimposed over a wide variety of political systems. David Easton's input-output system analysis provides a conceptual tool with which one can define politics as well as begin to study politics.

Part 2
An Approach to the
Study of Politics:
The American
Behavorial Movement

Introduction

Part 1 was concerned with the presentation of various views
and conceptions of politics and political science and they included the statement of some ethical goal and the procedures
to attain this goal, the study of the national sovereign State
and its activities, as well as the view that sees politics as a power
relationship between or among individuals. Four representative
conceptions were also discussed: Hobbes and politics as conflict, Locke/Rousseau and politics as a contract, Marx and
politics as a search for the just society, and Easton and politics
as a system. All these approaches and views are distinct but
there *is* one thin strand of common agreement among these
conceptualizations. This strand of common agreement is that
political science is a "social" or "behavioral" science, dealing
with the individual and his beliefs and his behavior. The philosophical approach of the pre-Christian Greeks might have emphasized the attitudinal or belief aspect to the detriment of
actual behavior but, nevertheless, the philosophical approach
does examine and analyze the individual's thought patterns.
The nineteenth-century traditional view of politics seen as the
State also, in a sense, studies the individual and his activity, for
even the sovereign, national, territorial state is a collection of

individuals. But once the unit of analysis becomes the individual, either indirectly as with the philosophical and traditional approach or directly with the politics-as-power approach, and not some inanimate verb form or chemical reaction, the "social" aspect of political science becomes dominant and there will be conflicting views as to what actually constitutes or defines the nature of politics.

This author personally is of the opinion, however, that one is on the right track, pointed in the right direction (although the destination is still quite distant), if politics is viewed as a power relationship in David Easton's sense of the term: not all power relationships are political for the act of throwing a brick through a window is not "political" behavior but, rather, it is nasty antisocial behavior. It is for the sociologist, psychologist, and psychiatrist, not the political scientist, to study and analyze such behavior and attempt to find meaning in it. Political activity includes only some segment of these power relationships, Easton's authoritative allocation of values, and political science is the study of these activities and man's attitudes concerning these activities.

Part 2, "An Approach to the Study of Politics: The American Behavioral Movement," presents an analysis of one approach to the study of political science and is divided into three chapters. Chapter 3, "A Brief Description of the American Behavioral Movement," contains a discussion of the movement's intellectual origins (the behavioral psychologists such as Pavlov, Skinner, and Watson and nonnormative philosophy); the specific stimuli within the United States which aided and hastened the spread of the behavioral persuasion (these stimuli ranged from the influx of European refugee scholars in the 1930s to the largesse of American foundations in the 1950s); and a brief listing of the major tenets and characteristics of the behavioral approach (a new level of analysis, the distinction between facts and values, an orientation toward mathematical techniques, a large-scale and unabashed borrowing from other disciplines, and a new goal for political science).

Chapter 4, "Three Examples of Unity," contains a more extended discussion of one of the major characteristics of the behavioral movement—the belief in the unity of the social sciences and the borrowing of theoretical orientations and research techniques from other disciplines in addition to the social sciences. These three extended illustrations are:

1. economics and Anthony Downs—an economic model dealing with the physical location of business enterprises as applied to the analysis of voting behavior and political party activity;
2. mathematics and game theory—precepts developed primarily by mathematicians to describe human behavior in symbolic mathematical language as applied to the Cuban Missile Crisis of 1962 between the United States and the Soviet Union; and
3. engineering and simulation—simulation techniques (having the appearance of being real without actually being reality) as applied to the study of the events leading up to the outbreak of World War I.

Chapter 5, "Contemporary Challenges to Behavioralism and the Current State of Political Science," contains a discussion of three movements directed against the major assumptions, tenets, and operating procedures of political behavioralism. These three countermovements are:

1. the "postbehavioral" movement (scientific knowledge—of course, but for what ends?);
2. the caucus for a new political science (knowledge for immediate practical political ends); and
3. philosophical political science (only philosophy can provide knowledge and wisdom for man).

In order to keep in step with contemporary demands for self-disclosure from political candidates and judges as to their financial holdings and dealings, the political scientist should (an ethical *should*) disclose his or her academic direction and holdings. My own personal position and biases on this whole question place me firmly within the ranks of the "postbehavioralists." This category agrees with the behavioralists in the belief that the only meaningful information and knowledge is that gained through the scientific technique or process: observation, explanation, and prediction based upon observable, verifiable, and reproducible constructs and not upon some vague notion such as the id, soul, fate, or God's will. But the postbehavioralist differs from the behavioralist when the latter states that the political scientist as a scientist cannot make any judgments from the knowledge so gained. The postbehavioralist says, in effect, scientific knowledge for what? For what ends? This self-disclosure is offered to enable the reader to better interpret the remarks contained in Part 2 for it is difficult to overcome one's attitudes and biases, even if one is completely aware of all such internalized attitudes.

3
A Brief Description
of the American
Behavorial Movement

THE BEHAVIORAL APPROACH to the study of politics and the American behavioral movement began essentially as an academic protest movement in the 1930s against the then-dominant view of politics and political science seen as the State and the traditional analysis of State activity, just as the view of the State was a protest movement against the philosophical speculation approach which preceded it. It was not until the end of World War II and throughout the 1950s that the behavioral approach grew and thus encountered heavy opposition from the more tradition-oriented political science profession. Certain universities became famous (or infamous, depending upon one's viewpoint) as havens for one group or the other and symbolic signs to the effect that "traditionalists (or behavioralists) need not apply" were posted at some political science departments' doors.

But by the end of the 1950s and in the early 1960s, behavioralism became dominant within the profession. This was probably due less to any inherent righteousness of behavioralism or to wholesale conversion by the traditionalists. It was a result of the simple process of the rapid growth of the teaching profession during the 1950s with the large influx of new professors fresh out of graduate school, along with the normal attrition of the older (and more traditional) members of the teaching profession. This chapter discusses this behavioral approach to the study of politics: its intellectual origins, its specific American stimuli, and its major characteristics.

The Intellectual Origins of Behavioralism

The behavioral approach to political science can trace its intellectual origins to the fields of psychology (the stimulus-response model of behavioral psychology, associated with the Russian physiologist Ivan Pavlov and the American B. F. Skinner) and philosophy (the subarea of philosophy known as "non-normative" philosophy).[1] Pavlov, Skinner, and the nonnormative philosophers were, it must be emphasized, "nonpolitical" for they were not studying a political situation or political behavior. Each was concerned with his own particular area of interest and expertise but their conceptual framework and general approach greatly influenced other fields. The political scientist learned of these developments in psychology and philosophy and wondered if political science could also benefit.

The Stimulus-Response Model of Behavioral Psychology

The stimulus-response model [S → R] of behavioral psychology was developed primarily by Ivan Pavlov in his research with dogs and by B. F. Skinner with his rats. Very briefly, the S → R model says that the behavior of an organism is the result of or is the response to a prior stimulus and that this stimulus is known, observable, and measurable.

The classic experiments by Pavlov in the early part of the twentieth century concerned the dog's salivary process.[2] Pavlov employed several dogs whom he had raised from puppies and thus he knew all the prior stimuli the dogs had received. Pavlov noticed that each time food was placed in front of the dog, the animal would begin to salivate. This type of behavior is called an *unconditioned response* (salivating in front of food is a natural behavior pattern for the dog). Slowly, a bell was rung each time but just prior to the placing of the food near the dog (the dog had never heard a bell before). The bell was first called a *neutral stimulus* for it elicited no response from the dog. But the bell was always followed by the food and the dog would salivate. This sequence—bell/food/saliva—was continued for some time until, in Pavlov's interpretation, the dog associated the ringing of the bell with the coming of food and thus began to salivate upon hearing the bell without any food being given to him. The unconditioned natural response was transformed into a *conditioned response* for now saliva was the response to the bell, not to the food. This conditioned response would slowly fade away if the process were not reinforced with the presentation of food at specific intervals.

The dog's behavior, salivation, could now be explained as a response to a certain observable and measurable stimulus and not as a response to some vague and undefined physiological construct such as "hunger." The dog's future behavior could also be predicted with amazing accuracy: he would produce a certain amount of saliva within a certain time after the bell was rung.

B. F. Skinner's classic experiments dealt with the learning and motor abilities of a white rat.[3] A rat was placed in what is now termed a "Skinner's box"—a closed box with a food tray, water trough, lever, and a beam of light. By a long and involved process of eliciting a chain of responses, Skinner was able to have these rats, upon the beaming of the light into the box, raise themselves up, seize, press, and then release the lever, take the deposited food pellet out of the tray and then eat it. The particular response of the rat was seen as a conditioned response to observable stimuli.

This $S \rightarrow R$ model of behavior had several implications and ramifications, for, although developed with rats and dogs, its extension to humans was not a very difficult step. Most important, it was an alternative model that competed with the two current methods of explaining and predicting behavior. These methods were, and still are, (1) the idealist tradition which explained behavior by reference to souls, minds, or God's will; and (2) Freudian analysis which explains behavior in terms of the clash among the id, ego, and superego. As Don Bowen comments: both these approaches, minds/souls and the id, attempted to explain and predict behavior with *nonobservable constructs.* "Whether one works with souls or ids," Bowen remarks, "one thing is certain—nobody ever observed either one of them."[4] Now the explanation and prediction of behavior appeared to be scientific: people act the way they do because they were influenced by certain stimuli and these stimuli can be discovered, measured, compared, and, perhaps, employed again to elicit some specific behavior pattern in the future (ring the bell, the dog will salivate; shine the light, the rat will press the lever; say the right words, the individual will press the right lever in the voting booth).

The $S \rightarrow R$ model influenced political science in the sense that political science saw the methodological and intellectual benefits of employing something that could be observed to explain behavior rather than some vague notion such as the soul or id. But political science did not adopt the extreme $S \rightarrow R$ model argued for by another American psychologist, James Watson. Watson argued that *only* observable stimuli could be allowed as an explanatory concept. This is the behaviorist (not behavior*al*ist) view: the simple $S \rightarrow R$ model and its extreme empiricism (only that which could be seen, touched, tasted, or smelled could be used to explain behavior). But political science is behavior*al*ist and not behaviorist. Political science accepts the basic meaning of the $S \rightarrow R$ model but its view of life and the individual is much more complex than a simple $S \rightarrow R$. The behavioralist has revised the model by placing an intervening variable, the individual, between the S and the R. The model for the political behavioralist reads: $S \rightarrow$ the individual with his beliefs, attitudes, values, prejudices, ideas $\rightarrow R$. The political behavioralist thus places much greater emphasis upon nonobservable constructs to explain and predict behavior than the behaviorist $S \rightarrow R$ model.

Nonnormative Philosophy

The second major intellectual influence upon political science behavioralism can be found in what is usually termed "nonnormative" philosophy. The specific subareas of this branch of philosophy are philosophy of science, logic and linguistic analysis. The philosophy of science, sometimes taught through a science department rather than through the philosophy department, deals with the development of paradigms or conceptual frameworks in scientific thought. Logic, often taught through the math department, deals with the internal proof or disproof of certain statements and the relationship among these statements. Linguistic analysis, often taught through a modern language department, deals with the relationship of sounds and words to abstract concepts.

The philosophy of science is the study of the accumulation of scientific techniques and knowledge through history, the obstacles which slowed such accumulation, and the role that scientific "discoveries" play in the cultural norms of society.[5] People such as Galileo, Newton, Lavoisier, and Einstein not only advanced startling scientific theories but, and this point holds most interest for the philosophers of science, these people altered the basic manner in which people viewed themselves, the environment, and the relationship between the two.[6] For example, Galileo's defense of Copernicus—the earth is not the center of the universe but is only one of several planets in orbit around a stationary sun—ran into violent opposition from the Roman Catholic Church starting in 1616. Church doctrine held that the earth was the center of the universe. Galileo was tried by a special Vatican court in 1633 for refusing to abide by the pope's order not to "hold or defend" the Copernican theory. Galileo was found guilty, threatened with torture, put under house arrest, he was prohibited from publishing, and his book (*Dialogue on the Great World Systems*) was listed on the Roman Catholic Index for some 200 years. The philosophy of science would not emphasize the truthfulness or falseness of Galileo's views but, rather, it would emphasize the relationship between such theories and the society of its time.

Logic, as stated above, deals with the internal proof of propositions and the relationships among propositions. Logicians also make the claim that logic will aid in the development of "correct" reasoning in the sense that one would be aware of false inferences, unwarranted conclusions, as well as general fallacies in argumentation (e.g., if something has not yet been "proven" true, then it must be false). There is some common ground between philosophy of science and logic: neither area investigates the inherent truthfulness or falseness of the material. A recent logic textbook by Nicholas Rescher describes this fact-value distinction:

> When analyzing the information contained in the discourse, the question for the logician is not whether this information is true or whether it is false. Logic does not care about the factual truth of the discourse with which it works, but only with the internal interrelationships of the information (or misinformation) embodied in it. In studying an inference, the logician does not inquire into the truth of its premises, but into whether the purported conclusion follows from them.[7]

Linguistic analysis is also seen as a subfield of nonnormative philosophy, and linguistic analysis deals with the relationship of sounds and words to abstract concepts. The Tasaday society described in Chapter 2 is presenting a very interesting area of study for linguistic analysis. This particular society not only does not have words for such concepts as war, theft, revenge, hate; it does not even have the concepts in its thought processes! It is one thing for a culture to "invent" a word to describe an understandable concept—the *Académie Française* in Paris continually updates the French language so that it may include "French" words for concepts or things developed beyond France. The Israeli Government is also engaged in a massive modernization process of the 5,000-year-old Hebrew language: they are either borrowing foreign sounds or "inventing" Hebrew sounds to describe concepts or things which did not exist when Hebrew was first developed. This is a tedious but not an impossible process: the modern Israeli thought process easily comprehends "modern" things as Mirage jet planes and atomic bombs. But what does one do when a culture does not even understand the concept (the Tasadays and revenge, for example)? It is questions such as these that linguistic analysis attempts to answer.

The philosophy of science, logic, and linguistic analysis all have something in common and it is found in the term *non-normative*: nonnormative analysis does not deal with norms, values, ethics, or morality, but with what is. In other words, this branch of philosophy has stated the fact-value distinction: some statements are value statements ("it is hot outside") and other statements are factual propositions ("it is 95 degrees outside"). This fact-value distinction is discussed in greater detail later in this chapter.

These two developments, behavioral psychology and nonnormative philosophy, greatly influenced the political science discipline. Political science did not adopt the S → R model but behavioral psychology did demonstrate the benefits of employing observable constructs in the explanation of behavior. Political science did not begin to investigate scientific discoveries or the origin of language but nonnormative philosophy, with its fact-value distinction, did demonstrate the benefits of a value-free approach in a discipline which, after all, called itself political *science*. But the actual development of behavioralism in American political science needed more than just these intellectual currents. There were certain specific stimuli which aided the growth of behavioralism and these stimuli are discussed in the following section.

Some Specific American Stimuli

The above discussion of behavioral psychology and its reliance upon observable, verifiable, and reproducible constructs for explanation and prediction, and nonnormative philosophy with its fact-value distinction, was concerned with the intellectual origins of the American behavioral movement. In addition to these academic origins, some long-standing traditional American attitudes and cultural outlook had, in a sense, prepared the environment so that these academic movements would be accepted. The traditional American belief in the goodness and benefit of "science" and "progress" and the overriding reliance upon "pragmatism" are mentioned by Bernard Crick as aiding the acceptance of the behavioral outlook.[8] But these phenomena or attributes—psychology, philosophy, and the American culture—only prepared the soil as it were: something or someone else had to drop the seed into the ground and water the plant. Robert Dahl identifies and describes this planting and watering. Dahl mentions six specific and powerful stimuli or influences which, when their effects combined and multiplied, provided for the actual creation of and impetus to the movement and gave form to political science behavioralism.[9] These six specific American stimuli are seen by Dahl to have been the following:

The Chicago School

This refers to the department of political science at the University of Chicago from about 1925 to the Second World War. Charles F. Merriam was chairman of this department for some years, Harold Lasswell was a faculty member, and both men were at the forefront of examining new ideas and new approaches to politics and political science. The department also had many graduate students who later turned into first-rate pioneering researchers and academic scholars. These graduate students—Dahl mentions V. O. Key, Jr., David Truman, Herbert Simon, and Gabriel Almond—left Chicago and taught countless other students at other universities and the behavioral approach slowly widened. The prestige and influence of the "Chicago" school are emphasized when one notes that Merriam, Lasswell, Key, Truman, and Almond, all served a term as president of the American Political Science Association. Dahl writes that Chicago was not the only university where behavioral studies were being pursued but, rather, the Chicago school had more long-term influence than other universities.

The European Refuges of the 1930s

The decade of the 1930s also saw a large number of European scholars who immigrated to the United States in face of the rise of Nazism in Europe. Some of these people had an enormous influence on the then-current political science discipline and profession. Many of these European scholars, but especially the refugees from Germany, were themselves deeply influenced by Max Weber and brought with them to the United States a sociological approach to political science. This does not mean that all these migrant scholars were behavioralists. However, scholars such as Franz Neumann and Paul Lazarsfeld,

by occupying leading positions in American university departments of sociology and political science, made the American
political scientist more aware of, and more receptive to, the relevance and usefulness of sociological and psychological theories.

World War II

It was not the war itself which influenced or stimulated the
behavioral movement but, rather, it was the side effects of
having to fight a global war for four years. These side effects
altered the political scientist's conception of the discipline. Dahl
writes that a great many political scientists left their academic
university positions (positions which even today usually do not
have much contact with the real world) and entered active participation in the administration of numerous organizations, committees, and bureaus created by the national requirements. These
political scientists found that their theories and ideal states
taught in the classroom had very little relationship with the
day-to-day "political" realities in Washington: the "is" was
totally different from the "ought." This experience in actual
practical and applied politics within the government bureaucracy convinced many of these transplanted political scientists
that an entirely new approach had to be taken with political
science because their conventional theories, descriptions, and
approaches bore so little resemblance to actual behavior in the
real world.

The Social Science Research Council (SSRC)

The SSRC is a national organization designed to foster
and promote scholarly research in the social sciences. Dahl
writes that the SSRC in 1945, partly on its own initiative and
partly as a result of the first three factors mentioned above,
established a Committee on Political Behavior. This Committee (and the ones which followed the original 1945 one) helped
to coordinate and, as Dahl cites an SSRC Report, to

> ... explore the feasibility of developing a new approach
> to the study of political behavior. Focused on the behavior

of individuals in political situations, this approach calls
for examination of the political relationships of men—as
citizens, administrators, and legislators—by disciplines
which can throw light on the problems involved, with the
object of formulating and testing hypotheses, concerning
uniformities of behavior in different institutional settings.[10]

Dahl believes that the Social Science Research Council has been
an "active stimulant" to the behavioral movement in political
science, particularly since the time the SSRC has been able to
distribute grant money for research projects.

Growth of the "Survey Method" as a Methodological Tool

This is one among many "tools" employed to study political attitudes, choices, and voting behavior. The survey method
enables the researcher to deal at the level of the individual rather
than being forced to deal with aggregate data (data based upon
a large number of individuals). Dahl writes that as the methods
of survey research became more and more scientific and precise
(less open to error), the political science profession saw what
they thought to be their exclusive area of expertise—the collection and interpretation of *voting* behavior data—being "taken
over" by the more methodological sociologists and social psychologists. These interlopers or intruders from other fields developed and employed the survey method within their own particular areas of expertise and when they applied their methods
and techniques to the study of elections (especially presidential
elections), the analysis and interpretation of voting behavior
was, in Dahl's terms, immediately changed "from impressionistic
history or insightful journalism to a more impressive and con-
vincing empirical science."

The successes of these voting studies (many done by nonpolitical scientists) gave reason for hope to the political scientist: if only *we* could adopt the mathematical and statistical
techniques of other disciplines, *we* also would then be able to
move beyond generalities and begin to offer statements regard-

ing the actual behavior of individuals in a political situation and the explanation of these activities would be based upon observable, verifiable, and reproducible constructs. This stimulus of the mathematical and statistical techniques in the study of electoral behavior snowballed until the belief in the efficacy (or usefulness), if not the requirement, of these techniques became one of the major tenets and characteristics of the behavioral movement.

The Philanthropic Foundations (Carnegie, Rockefeller, Ford)

The single individual political science professor doing research in the library requires very little financial support for his research. He or she may have to purchase one or two books but, in the main, facilities and resources are provided without cost as part of the university's general possessions or the public largesse provides the required resources through public libraries and the ever-present services of interlibrary loan. This very textbook is an example of such writing: a few dollars for miscellaneous out-of-pocket expenses, but paper, typewriter, office space, heat, electricity, and books have all been provided by the university.

But a good deal of behavioral research is different for it is no longer a simple matter of one individual in the library. Behavioral research, in the example of the presidential voting studies, is quite expensive and the university will not always take it on as a cost. The presidential voting studies require an enormous number of people to set up the questionnaires, to walk the streets or use the telephone and talk with hundreds, or perhaps thousands, of people and then to organize this data mass into one coherent whole. Interviewers have to be paid for their time, the telephone company has to be paid, postage has to be paid if it is a mailed questionnaire, and to employ a computer to organize and analyze data is a *very* expensive proposition.

Much behavioral research is thus very expensive and the universities, the telephone company, the Postal Service, and IBM simply do not give their services away in the amount required by some vast project. It is at this point that the American philanthropic foundations entered the picture. Dahl writes that these philanthropic foundations were also changed by World War II and, after the war, they viewed behavioral and inter-disciplinary studies quite favorably. The foundations financed countless studies and projects and it was this money which aided the behavioral movement. There would have been very few behavioralists if it had been financially impossible to conduct behavioral research. The foundations provided the money and behavioralism grew and prospered—the hills did contain gold! Dahl writes that had the foundations been hostile to behavioral-ism and closed their checkbooks, behavioralism would have been an idea whose time had not yet come.

These were not the only factors which aided the develop-ment of the behavioral approach but these were the major in-fluences. The decade of the 1950s saw the behavioralist ap-proach change from being a protest movement of deviant views into the "Establishment" of the political science profession. It was an academic revolution which altered both the basic con-cept of political science and the approaches to the study of politics.

The Major Characteristics of Behavioralism

We have, up to this point, discussed only very briefly and in a roundabout fashion the central element—what is "be-havioralism" and what is the behavioral approach to political science? Its intellectual origins and some specific American stimuli were noted above and this section is concerned with the tenets and major characteristics of the behavioral orientation. Robert Dahl writes that the behavioral approach is an

> ... attempt to improve our understanding of politics by seeking to explain the empirical aspects of political life by means of methods, theories, and criteria of proof that are acceptable according to the canons, conventions, and as-sumptions of modern empirical science.[11]

Behavioralism is essentially a conceptual framework, an orientation to the entire field of political science and it is not a sub-field of political science as is international relations, urban politics, or comparative politics. Dahl cites a 1951 Social Science Research Council Report as containing a succinct description of the behavioral approach and it appears instructive to cite at length from this Report:

> Political behavior is not and should not be a specialty, for it represents rather an orientation or a point of view which aims at stating all the phenomena of government in terms of the observed and observable behavior of men.
>
> . . . .
>
> The developments underlying the current interest in political behavior imply two basic requirements for research. In the first place, research must be systematic. . . . This means that research must grow out of a precise statement of hypotheses and a rigorous ordering of evidence. . . . In the second place, research in political behavior must place primary emphasis upon empirical methods. . . . Crude empiricism, unguided by adequate theory, is almost certain to be sterile. Equally fruitless is speculation which is not or cannot be put to empirical test. . . . The ultimate goal of the student of political behavior is the development of a science of the political process. . . .[12]

This SSRC statement contains two statements which require some additional comments: (1) the level of analysis is now man and his behavior, and (2) speculation which cannot be tested is idle philosophizing. First of all, the central focus of the political science discipline is now centered on the individual and his behavior and attitudes, rather than upon what the Ideal Life ought to be or upon the State and its institutions. This entails a complete restructuring of the traditional approaches to political science because man served as a sort of necessary evil within the traditional approach. The ideal State and State activity were seen as reifications (ascribing a concrete material existence to an abstraction) and the individual and his behavior received very little attention. Behavioralism reverses this tendency or outlook and now the individual with his behavior, attitudes, emotions, unconscious drives and needs, and his relationship with other individuals is the central core of political science.

The second point, speculation is idle if it cannot be put to an empirical test, stems from the behavioral movement's reliance upon facts rather than feelings, intuition, or value judgments. Behavioralism is the study of what *is*, not what *ought* to be and, therefore, speculation as to the *ought* is not political science but political philosophy. This point also means that any explanation of an individual's behavior must be based upon observable, reproducible, and verifiable statements and not upon nonobservable or impossible-to-disprove constructs such as the soul, mind, id, fate, or God's will and that value propositions ("it is good that . . ." or "man ought to . . .") must be separated from factual propositions.

This as-to-now brief description of behavioralism is not limited just to the field of political science. Behavioralism is a conceptual framework and the approach is widespread in areas outside political science. But political science also has not been alone in providing opposition to behavioralism, for other disciplines have had their internal battles and controversies over general orientations to their own particular subject matter. History, for example, has its own split between "traditionalists" and "behavioralists." J. H. Hexter, a professor of history at Yale University, has in two recent books described as "heresy" the view that history ought to adopt some of the methods of the natural or social sciences in the writing of history.[13] Professor Hexter sees very little benefit from techniques such as computerized content analysis, statistics, or psychological analysis. There are, of course, many historians who strongly disagree with Hexter's conception.

David Easton has presented a checklist, he terms it a "Credo of Behavioralism," of the major characteristics of the behavioral approach to political science.[14] Easton's checklist has eight points: regularities, verification, techniques, quantification, values, systematization, pure science, and integration/interdisciplinary approach. The following discussion is based upon Easton's conception of the behavioral approach.

Regularities

The behavioral approach believes that there are recurring and uniform behavior patterns in political activity and that these uniformities and regularities can be observed and studied. Such regularities can then be expressed as generalizations or theories in order to explain present behavior and to attempt to predict future behavior of the individual. For example, say the first ninety-nine husband and wife couples interviewed all stated that they vote the same way (each individual couple votes for the same party, all ninety-nine couples do not have to vote the same way). The reason for this remarkable similarity of views was that each couple had enough problems at home without the additional burden of political differences entering the family squabbles. Thus, in order to provide for domestic tranquility, the husband and wife decided to vote for the same political party. The researcher could most certainly conclude that there is a uniform and regular behavior here—husbands and wives vote the same! This observed uniformity or regularity can then be employed to (hopefully) predict the voting behavior of the hundredth couple because there is a very high probability that this last couple will also support the same candidate. This regularity, if actually observed, could be employed to generalize to even more and more couples.

Verification

The validity or the usefulness of the generalizations made from these uniform behavior patterns must be tested by reference to observable constructs and behavior. In other words, to see if our generalization regarding the voting patterns of husbands and wives is valid—whether it could be used to explain present and predict future behavior—one has to observe the actual behavior and seek out the actual attitudes and reasons of the actors. One cannot verify hypotheses or theories by referring to God's will (God caused the people to vote the way they did) or, to use a current expression, one cannot say that "the Devil made them do it." These constructs (God, devil, soul, mind, id, fate) cannot be verified and cannot be disproven: whatever the outcome actually is only proves that it was God's will. Verification does *not* mean that the actual theory has to be proven "correct." Verification does mean, however, that there are ways to see whether it is valid or not. In other words, if we base our explanation of voting behavior on the desire to keep domestic peace it can at least be tested: all those couples who argue over domestic affairs will vote the same way whereas all those couples who live in domestic bliss may decide to part ways in the voting booth (this is only an imaginary example but at least the theory can be tested). But explanation based upon God's will cannot be tested: God's will is whatever the people do and if they do (x) or (y), it is still God's will. Explanations based upon nonobservable and nontestable constructs do not add to man's knowledge.

Techniques

Facts and data do not interpret themselves and statements such as "it is obvious that . . ." or "the facts speak for themselves" or "one picture is worth a thousand words" are not permitted by the behavioralist. Easton writes that the task of collecting and analyzing data cannot be taken for granted. One must be continually aware of the pitfalls and traps of research (faulty assumptions such as either Hobbes or Locke, an unrepresentative sample such as talking only to M.D.'s to find out American attitudes toward socialized medicine; questionnaires that could be interpreted in more than one way, conclusions that may just be a result or function of chance happenings rather than a regular occurrence) and the techniques employed must undergo constant revision and refinement so that more rigorous and sound means can be used for observing and analyzing data.

Quantification

Basic to the behavioral conception of politics is the belief that the substance of politics, the political behaviors and attitudes, can be measured, classified, quantified, and/or compared. The question is always "how much" or "how much more than . . ." rather than abstract or imprecise statements. In other words, the behavioralist seeks as precise amounts or degrees as possible when dealing with data and concepts. For example, it is not sufficient to state that the United States is a democracy; what has to be done is to offer some information on how much actual democracy the United States has compared to either (1) some finite maximum standard or (2) the amount other countries have of this attribute under study; e.g., the United States has eighty percent of its maximum potential of democratic performance, or the United States has "more" democracy than one hundred other countries, but "less" of this attribute than ten other countries.

This belief (some would say it was a fetish) that political data can and must be quantified has led to an increased dependence upon mathematical and statistical modes of analysis and explanation and a general weakening of purely verbal or linguistic modes of description. That is to say, the political behavioralist employs symbolic mathematical language to convey his findings and conclusions rather than to employ the English language. One of the reasons for this increased use of mathematics and statistics is the behavioralists' view that ordinary language, words, are too vague and too open to subjectivity and misintrepretation whereas numerical relationships are not subject to a variety of interpretations (the statement "it is seventy degrees Fahrenheit outside" is not open to interpretation as is the statement "it is quite pleasant outside"). The methods employed here in political science range from some unsophisticated scales (nominal, ordinal, ratio) through relatively sophisticated correlation analyses, index construction, attitude scale construction, and probability statistics to quite sophisticated techniques such as factor analysis.

Values

The fifth basic and definitional component to behavioralism is the fact-value distinction. Factual propositions are statements which people agree represent or describe reality: "you are now reading this page," "it is fifty degrees outside," "there are fifty states in the United States," "objects fall when dropped from high places." Factual statements or propositions can be verified or reproduced: everyone will agree that yes, it *is* fifty degrees outside, or yes, objects *do* fall when dropped from high places. Factual propositions are not concerned with truth or righteousness since they only describe what people agree upon (a certain animal may look like a "cat" but if everyone agrees to call it a "dog," it *is* a dog even though it may purr and climb trees). Value statements or propositions, on the other hand, describe the goodness or truth of some particular part of reality or describe how reality ought to be organized or structured.

Some value propositions would be "it is warm outside," "the United States system of government is the best system in the entire world," "people ought to vote," "it is good that you are reading this page" (good not in terms of utility in order to pass the course but "good" in the sense of some intrinsic ethical moral purpose). Most value statements contain the word "ought" or "should" with the connotation or meaning that this is the way reality, in the eyes of the beholder, should be arranged and these words do not carry the connotation of utility: "it is good that it is fifty degrees outside for now the crops can grow" is not a value statement.

Value propositions are not verifiable or reproducible for they refer to ethics and moral judgments. They are not reproducible in this sense: everyone would agree that the temperature reads fifty degrees but not everyone would agree that it is "warm." Someone from Aden would probably remark that it was quite chilly whereas an Eskimo would remark that it was quite hot. The political behavioralist, only as a political scientist but not as an individual, does not believe in the presence of universally valid moral judgments. What the Nazi considered as ethically and morally acceptable behavior, the Allied Powers considered to be totally hideous and reprehensible. What the pope finds to be ethically unacceptable behavior regarding birth control and abortion, other people in other cultures find totally moral. The point is that there are two types of propositions, factual and value, and the behavioral approach continually attempts to keep them apart and distinct from each other and not confuse one with the other.

An analogy of this fact-value distinction can be found in the chemist's laboratory. The chemist combines, in the right amounts and under the right conditions, certain quantities of sodium and chlorine and the result is salt. The factual statement is: "sodium and chlorine form salt" and this statement only describes reality and can be reproduced by anyone operating under the same conditions. But if the chemist were to rush out of his laboratory to claim that it was "ethically and morally unacceptable that salt should come from sodium and chlorine" (a value proposition), people would then be unable to verify or reproduce his statement (someone else may think it was ethically and morally correct that salt was created). Or, if one remarks that the American democracy is the "best" form of government, one is really offering a value proposition whose validity cannot be proven or disproven.

This insistence upon the separation of factual statements from value statements does not mean, however, that the political scientist cannot study value propositions. The political scientist as a political scientist cannot inquire into the truth of these value statements, it is for the philosophers to inquire after truth, but he can inquire as to the existence of these statements. That is to say, the political scientist can study the values held by the individual as part of the makeup of his attitudinal and ideological beliefs and then employ these values as part explanation of the individual's behavior. To say that an individual believes democracy is the best form of government is a factual statement and, as such, can be studied; but the political scientist cannot entertain questions as to the validity of the value judgment.

This demand to avoid ethics has been well stated by Heinz Eulau and his remarks follow:

> . . . to say that the scientific study of man in politics has man as its goal is not saying very much, for men disagree on the nature of man in politics. Which is the man in whose service the behavioral persuasion finds its reason for existence? Is he a democratic man? A just man? A power seeking man? Is he a man who must be controlled because he is brutish and nasty? Or is he a man who must be liberated from the shackles of oppression to live a dignified life? *These are philosophical questions better left to the philosophers.*[15]

But this refusal to entertain discussion about moral and ethical precepts, this insistence upon what *is* rather than upon what *ought* to be, has left the behavioralist open to a very serious and telling criticism. Christian Bay has remarked that in their quest to achieve science and leave the philosophizing to the philosophers, the political behavioralists have turned political science into ". . . a device, invented by university teachers, for avoiding that dangerous subject politics. . . ."[16]The political behavioralists have, at one time or another, been accused of being nonpolitical, moral eunuchs, apologists for any type of hideous activity, and as white mice scurrying about unable to see beyond the tip of their nose. The confirmed behavioralist would collect data on, say, fascism and present a well-ordered and well-documented study on some particular behavior pattern of fascism. He would then be asked a question along these lines: "Well, what do you think about it? Do you think that specific behavior pattern is (was) good and just or evil?" The behavioralist would not answer for this would be the equivalent of the chemist stating that salt was evil—he would not make any value judgments. The reaction to this amoral characteristic of behavioralism is discussed in greater detail below in Chapter 5, "Contemporary Challenges to Behavioralism."

Systematization

Easton writes that research ought (an ought of utility, not of ethics) to be systematic; that is, "theory and research are to be seen as closely intertwined parts of a coherent and orderly body of knowledge. Research untutored by theory may prove trivial, and theory unsupportable by data, futile." This point concerns the warning to behavioralists to refrain from grandiose theoretical conceptions that are totally unconnected to the real world behavior of the individual, as well as the plea to look beyond the actual nuts and bolts of specific behavior and attempt to order such facts into a coherent body of knowledge. The statement "theory unsupportable by data is futile" is equivalent to the SSRC Report cited above with its view that "speculation which cannot be put to empirical test is fruitless."

Pure Science

This is another element of behavioralism which has caused severe criticism and is also discussed below in Chapter 5. Easton writes that the behavioral approach attempts to transform the study of politics into a pure, laboratory-type science in which the knowledge so gained about political behavior is more important to the scientist than the process of using or applying this knowledge in order to solve some of society's problems. It is the simple distinction between pure and applied scientific research: pure research is research for its own sake; applied research is research aimed at the solution of some specific problem or at the attainment of some specific goal. By placing emphasis upon theoretical understanding and by paying very little attention to the uses of their knowledge, the behavioralists are accused of being "apolitical" and "conservative" (if one does not ask questions such as "what ought to be?" or "what will be?" one is essentially dealing with what is, the status quo, and this makes the behavioral approach conservative and a supporter of current American values).

Integration/Interdisciplinary Approach

Easton's final tenet of behavioralism concerns the approach's belief in the unity of social sciences and a borrowing of techniques and orientations from other disciplines. This is due to the generally held belief that all the social sciences are studying man and his behavior and what, for example, the economist does to study his "economic" person the political scientist may find useful to study his "political" person. Figure 3.1 presents a representation of this belief in integration and an interdisciplinary approach and Chapter 4 below contains an extended discussion of some of this borrowing by political science.

There are two additional tenets or characteristics of the behavioral movement not mentioned by Easton in his Credo of Behavioralism but which are admirably discussed by Don Bowen. These two additional characteristics are seen to be a new definition of politics and a new goal for political science.

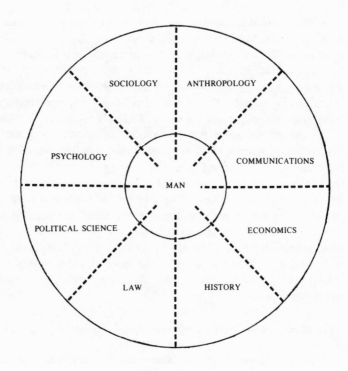

Figure 3.1
The Unity of the Social and Behavioral Sciences

A New Definition of Politics

This characteristic opens up once again the discussion in
Part 1: what actually is politics? The behavioralists reject the
Greek notion that it is the search for the ideal ethical society
and they also reject the nineteenth-century view that politics
is the State and the State's activities. We need not repeat the
arguments contained in Part 1 except to note or emphasize once
more that the behavioral approach to politics regards the ethical
approach as "idle speculation" which bears no relationship to the

real world, a view which does not endear the behavioralists to the philosophers, and that the institution was rejected as the defining element for it was too restrictive and did not study man's actual behavior. The behavioralist approaches the nature of politics from the perspective of man: some may ascribe to the concept of power, others to a conflict/consensus model, others to group theory, others to pluralism. But what is common to all these "definitions" is that they reject ethics and the institution as the level of analysis and, in their place, set up man with his behavior, emotions, attitudes, and unconscious needs and desires.

A New Goal for Political Science

The goal for the Greek conception of political science was to first prescribe the good life and then to describe the ways of attaining this goal; the goal of the nineteenth-century conception of political science was to analyze the State's origins, activities, and the best or ideal form of the State; the goal of the behavioralist conception of political science is to devise a *systematic empirical theory of politics*. A systematic empirical theory, in simplified terms, means a general statement based upon observable, verifiable, and reproducible evidence (empirical) which can explain as much if not all aspects of political behavior (systematic). The goal is to have a concise statement, preferably in mathematical terms, which can provide an explanation of past behavior and which can be employed to predict future behavior. Political behavioralists are thus seeking what other disciplines and other areas of study have claimed: a systematic theory to explain all the phenomena within their particular area of study. Some of these other theories have been empirical, others have not been, but all have claimed to be systematic.

Sigmund Freud believed he had discovered a systematic theory to explain and predict human behavior: it was the individual's sexual desires and the ability of the interactions among the id, ego, and superego to control or sublimate these internal drives. Whether Freud is "correct" or "incorrect" is not relevant for this discussion. What is relevant is that this can be seen as a "systematic" theory to explain all human behavior. Freud's theory was not empirical, however, for, as Bowen remarks, who has ever seen an id or a superego? The major criticism of Freud's theory is not with its nonobservable or nonempirical constructs, even the political behavioralists deal with attitudes and unconscious emotive feelings, but this particular theory cannot be disproven. Why did person A do act X? Because his id gained dominance over his ego. Why did person B do act Y? Because his ego controlled his id. These statements simply cannot be disproven, the researcher is always right, and thus Freud's contribution actually does not qualify as a systematic empirical theory (not that it is actually proven to be false but because it is impossible to undergo a proof).

Albert Einstein also had a systematic theory which, when first formulated, was not "empirical" but only theoretical; latter-day scientific technology has now changed $E = mc^2$ into a systematic empirical theory to both explain and predict the behavior of matter under certain circumstances (the energy [E] released by a specific mass [m] when subjected to a nuclear chain reaction equals the weight of the mass times the speed of light squared [c^2]). This is a systematic empirical theory in atomic physics. Charles Darwin believed he discovered a systematic empirical theory in biology with his statement on the survival of the fittest. But here, as with Freud, this cannot be disproven: who are the fittest? Those who survive. Who will survive? The fittest. And the exception to the theory only proves the point: to predict that animal x or plant y will survive, but it does not, does not disprove the theory—this particular animal or plant was not the fittest. Karl Marx also formulated what he believed to be a systematic empirical theory of societal behavior: his laws of history and dialectical materialism could (as the theory says) be employed to explain all past behavior and to predict future behavior (remember Marx said his stages of history were inevitable). Even the economists have offered their theory to explain and predict all economic behavior: buy low, sell high (or, in more academic terms, the maximization of profit).

Political science is seeking the same goal in regard to political behavior although the attainment of such a theory is about as far away today as it was when the behavioralists first started the quest. This is not to say that no progress has been made.

Several low-level theories dealing with voting behavior in particular have been formulated which appear to be valid. But voting behavior is only the very top of the exposed part of the iceberg and much additional work has to be done before political science can be said to have a systematic empirical theory of political behavior.

4
Three Examples of Unity

ONE OF THE above-mentioned major characteristics of the behavioral approach to politics and political science was the belief in the unity and integration of the social sciences. This belief leads to the widespread practice of borrowing orientations, conceptions, and techniques from all disciplines and not just from other social sciences. This belief is based upon the view that in all the social sciences the root is man—man and his attitudes and behavior in the real world is the central level of analysis and area of study. The individual plays certain roles in society and each of the various academic disciplines studies the same person as he performs a particular role: the economist studies man in his role as producer and consumer; the sociologist studies man in his role in interpersonal and intergroup relationships; the historian studies man and his past activities; the psychologist studies man's perceptions of himself and of others; and the political scientist studies man in his role of participant in the political process.

The separation of these disciplines or areas of study into distinct academic department is not seen as a formal separation by behavioralists. These divisions are regarded only as practical conveniences which enable one to specialize and make more efficient use of abilities and resources. In one sense, the behavioral approach is quite similar to the Greek conception of a "master science." All human phenomena are interrelated and there is a basic centrality to the social sciences, the natural sciences, and the humanities. The behavioral approach in all areas of study is thus characterized by the lack of hesitation to seek out other modes of analysis employed in fields beyond the behavioralist's immediate area of expertise. For example, ecomics may contain several interesting and productive theories regarding man and his behavior as a consumer; perhaps the political scientist can borrow these theories for his own research. This belief in the unity of the social sciences has also meant an invited intrusion by people outside the field of political science (an economist, a psychologist) to apply their particular views and methods directly to political science. The social sciences have been the major hunting grounds for political scientists although other areas outside the social sciences are providing useful theories and techniques with which to analyze political behavior. This chapter presents three examples of where political science has borrowed, or has invited entry, from other disciplines in its search to explain and predict behavior. These three examples are: (A) economics and Anthony Downs' economic theory of democracy; (B) mathematics and game theory; and (C) engineering and simulation.

Economics and Anthony Downs: An Economic Theory of Democracy

Anthony Downs, in his pioneering and ground-breaking book, *An Economic Theory of Democracy* (1957),[1] presents an analysis of political parties and voters in democratic countries and his analysis is based upon economic theories and methods. Downs presents an attempt to explain the behavior of both the parties and the electorate as well as an attempt to predict their future behavior. An economic model is applied to this "political" area and the results are a fascinating example of behavioralist borrowing and the linkage between different academic disciplines.

Downs' explanation of party/voter behavior stems from a *model* and a model is an attempt to represent reality without actually being reality. There are three types of models: physical, symbolic, and verbal. A physical model is one that has a specified mass and occupies physical space. A model airplane in a wind tunnel or a scaled architectural representation of a building are examples of physical models. A symbolic model is a mathematical representation of reality and it does not have mass or occupy space, except, of course, for the paper or blackboard on which it is pictured. A verbal model attempts to re-create reality with linguistic descriptions. Downs' model is a combination of the symbolic and verbal types. When one talks about the replication of reality with models, reality does not mean the totality of the entire real world. It would be impossible to construct a model (physical, symbolic, or verbal) which would accomplish the total re-creation of the real world. In models, reality refers to only that specific simplified portion or segment of the real world that the researcher wishes to re-create. A wind tunnel replicates wind conditions and one can study the effects of such wind on the plane; the wind tunnel does not re-create the hijacker with a bomb who blows up the plane. A plastic representation of a certain bridge may impart information on its capability for handling heavy loads; the plastic bridge does not re-create the earthquake which might demolish the bridge.

An essential element or characteristic to note about models is that they are not "true" or "false," "valid" or "invalid." They are only useful or less useful, depending upon the degree to which they actually do serve as a re-creation of the specific segment of reality under study. In other words, if a certain symbolic model represents 80 percent of reality (meaning that only 80 percent of the model's assumptions are "correct" or that these assumptions are "correct" only 80 percent of the time), then this particular model will have approximately an 80 percent probability of explaining and predicting real-life behavior. This 80 percent is better than a model with only a 10 percent probability of explanation and prediction. Many models aim at 100 percent predictive power: people just do not like to fly in planes where, attached to the window, is a notice to the effect that the aircraft has only an 80 percent chance of the wings staying attached to the fuselage or, when crossing a high bridge, receiving a notice from the tollbooth to the effect that the bridge has only an 80 percent chance of staying in one piece in a high wind. A model that does give 80 percent prediction is not invalid or false, it is more useful than a 70 percent model. Models in the social sciences and political science have much less predictive power than those in engineering or aeronautics but this does not detract from their usefulness in explaining and predicting segments of behavior.

Downs employs two models: the economic model is first and the political model is derived from the economic one. There is a common assumption which underlies both models. This common assumption states that the individual is a rational actor. In other words, Downs employs the rational actor model. The rational actor model, in its *general* sense, refers to an individual who behaves as follows: (1) the individual actor or decision-maker can always make a decision when faced with several competing choices; (2) the actor ranks these choices in order of preference so that each choice is seen to be preferable to, equal to, or inferior to the other choices; (3) the highest ranking alternative is always chosen; and (4) the individual would always choose the same alternative in subsequent identical situations.[2]

The rational actor model, in general, thus refers to the most coherent and efficient means of achieving a goal. The model refers to behavior, to actions, to the means, and *not* to the content of the actual goal held by the actor. For example, if my goal were to fall into bankruptcy, it then would be perfectly logical and rational to throw all my money away; if my predetermined goal were to lose at poker, it would then be logical and rational to discard high cards. The goal itself, bankruptcy or losing the game, may be irrational in and of itself but this point is not relevant to the rational actor model.

Downs superimposes some predetermined goals in the economic and political models. In the economic model, business firms are out to maximize their profits and the consumers are out to minimize their costs. Rational behavior in the economic model, then, is behavior which is consistent with the achievement of these predetermined goals. Whether business firms *should* maximize profits or whether consumers *should* minimize

costs is not at issue. There are equivalent goals in the political
model: political parties are out to maximize vote totals and the
voter is out to cast his ballot for the political party closest to
his own ideology and attitudes. Rational behavior in the political
model is behavior directed at the attainment of these goals. Irrational behavior would occur if a political party chose an alternative which would *not* maximize its vote total or if an individual voter did *not* vote for the party closest to his ideology.
Whether a party *should* maximize its voters or whether an individual *should* vote this way is again not at issue in the rational
actor model. These goals underlie Downs' economic and political models.

The Economic Model: Location of Firms and Spatial Competition

The economic model concerns the decision as to the physical location of, say, a new department store. There are many
factors which must be taken into account whenever a business
enterprise decides to build a new retail outlet, be it a gasoline
station, a fast-service take-out food stand, or a large department
store. The income of the people in the proposed site has to be
ascertained—an expensive and posh jewelry store may not do
much selling in a poor neighborhood; the people's buying habits
also have to be known—a take-out restaurant specializing in
pork chops probably will not do much business in an orthodox
Jewish area; the climate of the area also has to be added in—
Miami and San Diego could not support a store selling snow
tires; the local taxation policies, ease of access or egress, zoning
regulations and sign limitations, Sunday or "blue law" enforcement policies all have to be taken into account; the actual location of the people has to be known—to build a store in Death
Valley is a nonpaying proposition; and, finally, the location of
previously built or proposed future competitors has to be noted—
one gasoline station at a busy intersection will do more business
than if there were three other such stations already in existence
or proposed. All these factors have to be considered whenever
a new enterprise is physically located.

Downs' economic model can be employed to explain and
predict (1) where firms will locate and (2) at which store the

consumer will shop. Downs' model is based upon a model developed by Harold Hotelling in 1929 and later revised in 1941 by Arthur Smithies.[3] When the model is applied to the explanation and prediction of department store and consumer behavior, its usefulness depends upon the degree to which it actually represents reality and the yardstick of "true-false" is not applicable. The economic model has four assumptions and these assumptions are critical to the model's usefulness: (1) everyone shops—people cannot stay at home and do without; (2) people shop at the store which is physically the closest to them—the store that is three miles away will do the business rather than the one four miles distant; (3) the actual physical location of the store can be identified—the people know where the store is; and (4) the actual physical location of the people can be identified—the department store's management know where the people reside.

It is the extent to which these assumptions "hold" in real life which determine the model's usefulness. If they "hold" 75 percent of the time, the model will then have a 75 percent level of prediction. If only three of the four assumptions hold 100 percent of the time and the fourth is totally unreflective of reality, the model will again have a 75 percent level of prediction. Assumptions (3) and (4), knowledge as to the store's location and people's residence, are probably reflective of reality (the consumer *does* know where the store is and heads for it; he does not wander aimlessly until he bumps into the front door). But assumptions (1) and (2), everyone shops at the closest store, do not hold all the time. Downs, in effect, is controlling for or holding constant all variables except distance between the consumer and the store. Variables such as price, service, quality, parking, trading stamps, and other variables which are probably more salient than distance in the decision to choose store A over store B are *purposely* excluded from the model.

One of the assumptions of the economic model states that the people can be geographically located. This means that the number of people living in the different areas of the community is known and can be graphed. One hypothetical example of this geographical distribution is shown in Figure 4.1. Figure 4.1 is an example of a unimodal frequency distribution and, in this case, it is also an example of a bell-shaped curve. It is a uni-

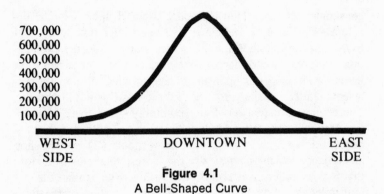

Figure 4.1
A Bell-Shaped Curve

modal curve for there is only one peak or mode to the distribution curve: most of the people live downtown in our city, and the further away one drives from downtown, the fewer people there are. A bell-shaped curve is a symmetrical unimodal distribution, wherein the *mean* (the average), the *mode* (the score or the location appearing with the greatest frequency), and the *median* (the score or location at which 50 percent of the people live to the west of downtown and 50 percent of the people live to the east of downtown) are all at the identical point. All bell-shaped curves are unimodal curves but all unimodal curves are not bell-shaped. It is entirely possible and reasonable to have a city's residence curve graphed differently than a bell-shape. In Figure 4.2, all distribution frequencies are unimodal but not bell-shaped. In Figure 4.2-A, most of the people live downtown and on the west side; in 4.2-B, most of the people live downtown and on the east side; and in 4.2-C, 99 percent of the people live in one huge apartment right in the center of downtown.

There are also bimodal (two peaks of modes) frequency distributions. In Figure 4.3-A, the people are evenly split between the east and west sides and very few people live downtown; in 4.3-B, there are still very few people in the central city but it is a different distribution than that in 4.3-A. There is still another example of a bimodal curve in Figure 4.3-C. Frequency distributions can also be multimodal (three or more modes or peaks). Figure 4.4-A has one-third of the population living in each of the three areas; 4.4-B has 90 percent of the people downtown and 5 percent in each of the other two areas; and

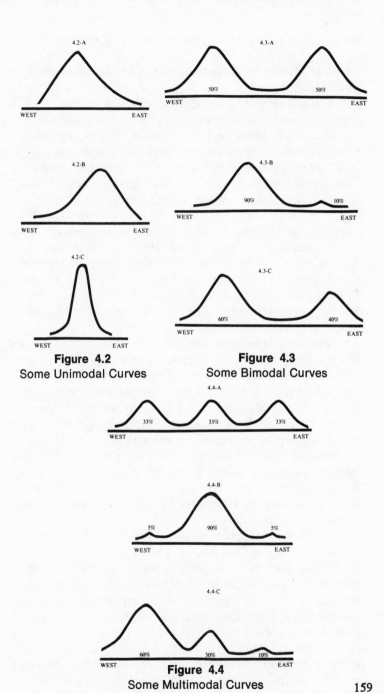

Figure 4.2
Some Unimodal Curves

Figure 4.3
Some Bimodal Curves

Figure 4.4
Some Multimodal Curves

159

4.4-C has 60 percent in the west, 30 percent downtown, and 10 percent in the east.

The bell-shaped symmetrical distribution (Figure 4.1) is employed as the distribution frequency of the population's residence in the following application of the economic model. Assuming this bell-shaped curve, where does department store A build? (The political applications of the economic model become evident when "voters" are substituted for "shoppers," "parties" for "stores," "voting" for "shopping," and "party platform" for "site location.") Given the four assumptions of the economic model, Store A can locate *any place* along the curve and be assured of receiving 100 percent of the shopping dollars. Store A is the only store and since people *have* to shop at the closest store, Store A does the business. One cannot predict where the store will locate in this example, there are an infinite number of points on the curve, but one can predict how many people will shop at the store (100 percent!).

The same example can be employed in a political setting: in a one-party (one store) system, the party can place its platform *any place* along the ideological spectrum and be assured of maximizing its vote total. As was the case with the economic model, one cannot predict where the party will be but one can predict its vote totals (100 percent!). Downs' models can help explain why the actual content or ideology of one-party systems can have extreme diversity. One-party (one department store) systems can be located from the far left (western suburbs) such as the People's Republic of China to the far right (eastern suburbs) such as Nazi Germany and still be assured of maximizing its vote totals.

But Downs' models emphasize competition (his book is an economic theory of *democracy*) and there is more than one department store/political party operating in the community. Now, as Chairman of the Board of Store A, where do you build, knowing full well that as soon as the concrete foundation is poured, Store B will then begin to construct its store? In the political model, this reads: being head of Party A, what do you put in the party platform, knowing full well that Party B will set up its platform immediately after you finish? It is thus very crucial in politics which party holds its convention first (or who pours the concrete foundation first). It is to the party's advantage to be the last to establish the location of its party (store) for once Party/Store A is locked in, Party/Store B has several options not available to Party/Store A.

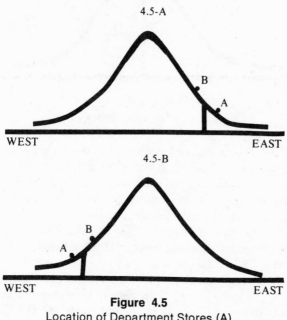

Figure 4.5
Location of Department Stores (A)

To return to the original question as revised in light of competition: where does Store A build knowing full well that Store B is right behind? There are several options, of course, but there is only one *rational* site, given the assumptions of the model and the bell-shaped geographical distribution of the population. Figure 4.5 shows *two irrational* locations for Store A. Figure 4.5-A shows that if Store A built in the east, Store B would build just to the west of A and thus B would receive most of the business. Figure 4.5-B shows the identical result except A built the store in the west. By choosing these two extreme positions when most of the people live downtown, Store A will receive very little business (by choosing to place its party platform at the left or right extremes of the political spectrum in a democracy when most people are middle-of-the-road will have Party A receive very few votes).

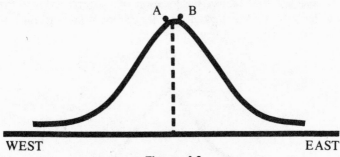

Figure 4.6
Location of Department Stores (B)

There is only one *rational* site for Store A: right at the tip of the peak or mode as illustrated in Figure 4.6. If this is done, B will then take the rational decision and build either directly to the east or west of A. Now Store A and B each has approximately 45 percent of the shoppers and competes for the 10 percent who live equidistant from both stores. Sales are offered, trading stamps are given out, free parking is offered; all are lures directed not at the people who live to the west of Store A or to the east of Store B (these people will shop at the respective stores under any circumstances), but, rather, lures directed at those shoppers living between Store A and Store B. The political model would substitute, in place of trading stamps, special pleas to blocs of voters in the middle who could swing to either party. This helps to explain, in part, why, before the coming of suburbia and mass automobile transportation (pre-World War II), the major department stores *were* physically next to each other in a downtown location. The model can predict where the stores will build (with a bell-shaped geographical distribution frequency, they will build downtown) and it can also predict how many shoppers will patronize each store (how many voters will vote for each party).

The economic model can be manipulated at will and one can insert a third or fourth store (a multiparty system) as well as alter the type of frequency distribution to a bimodal or multimodal curve. There is not space here to present all the possible variations but the reader is encouraged to devise a multimodal, multistore model and determine the location of the stores and the shoppers' behavior, according to the assumptions of the ecoomic model and according to the predetermined goals of the actors (maximization of shoppers and the minimization of distance traveled to the store).

The Political Model: Location of Party Ideologies and Voter Choice

The principles and techniques described above with the economic model's department stores can be directly applied to the political model's voter behavior and political parties. The political model can be employed to explain and predict the behavior of both the voter and the parties. One can begin to see this application when "voter" is substituted for "shopper," "vote" for "shop," "political party" for "department store," "attitudes of the voter" for "geographical location," and, finally, "party platform/ideology" for "location of stores." The assumptions, however, are changed from those in the economic to a new set in the political model. These are:

Economic Model	Political Model
Everyone shops, people cannot stay home;	Everyone votes, people cannot stay home on election day;
People shop at the closest store;	People vote for the party closest to their ideology/attitudes (rational actor);
People's geographical residence can be located; and	The attitudes of the people can be located along a left-right frequency distribution;
The stores can be physically located.	The parties' ideology/platform can be located along a left-right continuum; and
	Elections are carried out along a unidimensional curve (single-issue elections).

These assumptions, if "holding" 100 percent of the time in real life, would allow the model to explain and predict with conciseness but, as always when dealing with man, the assumptions do not "hold" 100 percent of the time as if he were a wind tunnel. Thus the political model is only as useful (it is not true or false) to the extent to which these assumptions actually do hold.

But, as stated above, the political model's assumptions do not hold 100 percent of the time. Assumption (1) says all people vote, that people do not stay home on election day. People in real-life situations do, however, stay home in vast numbers on election day in the United States. The following is only a brief list of reasons why people do not vote: failure to meet residence requirements, inability to secure an absentee ballot, illness, apathy, ignorance, satisfaction with the system to such an extent that any possible alternative is acceptable, dissatisfaction to such an extent that no alternative is acceptable, very little party competition, people on the West Coast know who won the national elections from television reporting of the eastern returns, a flat tire on the way to the polls. People just do not vote in high numbers in the United States and some reports on the 1972 presidential election state that only 40 percent (40!) of the 18-21 year olds actually voted, a dismally low figure. Downs' model may be more applicable to a system such as the Netherlands where voter registration lists are kept up by the government, not by the individual and the process of voting is compulsory with the threat of a fine for nonvoting.

Assumption (2), the rational actor statement (people vote for the party closest to the individual's attitudes/ideology) also does not hold to a very high degree. People do not vote "rationally"; wives vote the same way as the husbands in order to preserve domestic tranquility (this of course may be very rational action but not for the meaning given to rationality in this discussion); voters get tired at the end of the ballot and check off the first line; people vote "against" a party or candidate by casting a vote for another party which may or may not be reflective of his ideology. The classic example of "irrational" voting occurred in the 1960 presidential election between John Kennedy and Richard Nixon. 1960 was the year of the famous televised debates between the candidates and many observers believe these debates cost Nixon the election (or won the election for Kennedy, depending upon one's viewpoint). Tens of thousands of voters decided to vote for Kennedy after the debates but not from a rational decision (i.e., that Kennedy was closest to their ideology). The decision was based upon the "irrational" perception of Nixon during the debates: Nixon had the misfortune (misfortune only from the Republican viewpoint) of having a not-so-competent make-up man. Nixon appeared on television, to millions of voters, as tired, haggled, drawn, even sinister, with dark shadows under his eyes. The candidate gave a much better

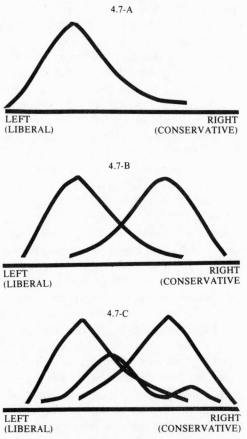

Figure 4.7
Some Hypothetical Attitude Distributions

appearance for the remaining three debates but the damage had been done for he could not now overcome the voters' (irrational) decision. This is not the only example of irrational voting but it is perhaps the best-known and most decisive.[4]

Assumption (3), the attitudes of the people can be located along a left-right distribution frequency, also does not hold 100 percent of the time. There are always a substantial number of "don't knows" and "no opinion." Related to this problem is assumption (5)—elections are contested only on a single issue. The model works with one-issue elections for it is very difficult to locate the individual and the parties along two or three dozen attitude curves. The model can work when, as in Figure 4.7-A, the election concerns only one issue, say the war in Vietnam. But superimposed on this curve is the attitude distribution on "law and order" at home and Figure 4.7-B illustrates this curve. But there are also the welfare issue, government spending, the Space program, revision of the Internal Revenue Code, state aid to education, penalties for smoking marijuana, abortion, overtures to the Chinese—*this* list is certainly endless. As shown in Figure 4.7-C, all the issues and the resulting attitude frequency distributions are superimposed over one another and the individual (or party) who is "left" on one issue may be "right" on the other. Elections are not carried out along a single issue or unidimensionally and thus it is very difficult to exactly locate where the people and parties "live" according to all the issues.

There are also some issues salient and important to elections which simply *cannot* be graphed along a left-right continuum. One of the major and overriding issues of the 1952 presidential election between General Eisenhower and Adlai Stevenson was "corruption in government." The Republicans were accusing the Democrats of allowing corruption to run wild during Truman's administration and Stevenson continually had to deny that (1) Truman's administration was corrupt and (2) even if it were, *his* administration would not support corruption. But the point is that the people's attitudes could not be graphed along a left-right continuum for this salient issue. It would be preposterous to say that such an issue would result in a bell-shaped (Fig. 4.8-A) or multimodal (Fig. 4.8-B) distribution. The left of the curves represents "a lot of corruption is desir-

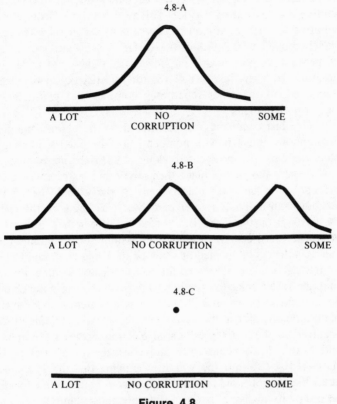

Figure 4.8
Hypothetical Attitudes on Corruption

able," the right is "some but not too much corruption is desirable," and the center represents "no corruption whatsover." As stated above, Figures 4.8-A and 4.8-B are preposterous: Figure 4.8-A says that although most people do not want corruption, there is still a large number who want either a little or a lot and Figure 4.8-B says that one-third of the population wants some corruption in government, one-third wants a lot, and one-third wants none. The actual attitude distribution frequency is shown in Figure 4.8-C and, in truth, the attitude distribution is nonexistent. All people are clustered at the same point, all people live in the same apartment (no corruption) and in place of a unidimensional curve we, if able, would draw a straight line coming directly out of the dot. This represents the attitude distribution toward corruption in government rather than the ones sketched in Figures 4.8-A or 4.8-B. Other such attitudes would be peace (everyone wants it), lower taxes, law and order, no inflation, equality, justice (who is for injustice?), dignity, freedom, and all the other repetitious homilies and platitudes of electoral campaigns.

One last comment is to be offered on the political model's assumptions and it is with number (4)—the parties' ideology/platform can also be located along a left-right continuum. It is not where the parties place themselves, but, rather, where the perception of the voter places them. A party could be on the left but if an individual voter perceives it as being on the right, the party *is* on the right. But regardless of whether the parties are on the left, center, or right, the assumption maintains they can nonetheless be located at some point of the continuum (just as the department stores could be physically located by the shopper). This helps to explain why party platforms in the United States tend to be vague milksops: it is an attempt to be every place along the line at the same time. The classic example of this occurred in the 1968 presidential election between Humphrey and Nixon. Nixon constantly and consistently referred to his SECRET PLAN to end the war in Vietnam. But the PLAN was never made public and thus the Republicans could not be located according to this issue. It was a flittering ghost: here, then there, now back over there, now down, now up—this SECRET PLAN was a successful attempt to avoid being located (e.g., build the department store on wheels instead of on a concrete foundation so one could move it around to chase the shoppers).

But let us grant the political assumptions. The political model discussed below thus has the following characteristics: (1) everyone votes, (2) everyone votes for the closest party, (3) and (4) the people's and parties' ideologies can be graphed along a left-right continuum, and (5) there are only single-issue elections. What uses does the model have beside explaining past elections and predicting future elections? Downs sets out five propositions which can be "proven" by the model:

1. A two-party democracy cannot provide stable and effective government unless there is a large measure of ideological consensus among its citizens.
2. Parties in a two-party system deliberately change their platforms so that they resemble one another; whereas parties in a multi-party system try to remain as ideologically distinct from each other as possible.
3. If the distribution of ideologies in a society's citizenry remains constant, its political system will move toward a position of equilibrium in which the number of parties and their ideological positions are stable over time.
4. New parties can be most successfully launched immediately after some significant change in the distribution of ideological views among eligible voters.
5. In a two-party system, it is rational for each party to encourage voters to be irrational by making its platform vague and ambiguous.[5]

The validity of these propositions becomes evident with the discussion below of past elections using this model as an explanatory tool. The elections analyzed are the 1964, 1968, and 1972 U.S. presidential elections and the 1971 mayoralty election in Cleveland.

The 1964 Presidential Election: Johnson vs. Goldwater and the Vietnamese War

We have forced ourselves into a single-issue election (assumption 5) and thus the most salient issue of the 1964 election is seen to be the scope and extent of U.S. involvement in the Vietnamese civil war. One may remember that Johnson categorically precluded any increase in American involvement, particularly the use of American combat troops and the bombing of the North. Goldwater took just the opposite stance—send in ground troops and bomb the North into submission (Goldwater might have lost the election but he at least won over Johnson and his coterie to his view). The attitudes of the people in 1964 concerning our salient war issue were decidedly left-of-center: no deployment of U.S. ground troops or bombing the North.

Figure 4.9-A is probably a fair representation of the 1964 attitude frequency distribution. Johnson was an astute politician and was able to precisely discern and pinpoint to ±1 percent

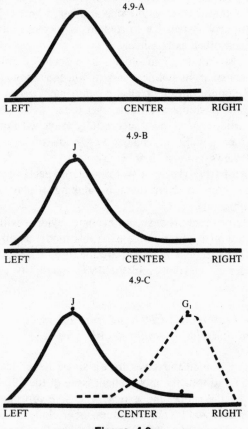

Figure 4.9
The 1964 Presidential Election (A)

the exact frequencies and he then placed his platform at the top of the peak or mode (position J in Figure 4.9-B). Goldwater, in the meantime, either from a genuine misreading of the attitudes (position G_1 in Figure 4.9-C) or from a desire to pull the attitudes further to the right (position G_2), placed his platform out to the right. Whatever the reason for Goldwater's location, he, *the son of a department store owner,* built his political store where there were very few customers (he appealed to a non-existent group of voters). Figure 4.10 illustrates how Johnson received the votes from those people living to the left of the vertical line (approximately 62 percent—the highest percentage of any candidate for the office), whereas Goldwater received the votes from the people living to the right of the vertical line.

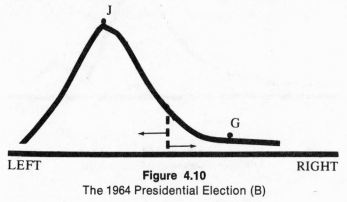

Figure 4.10
The 1964 Presidential Election (B)

The 1968 Presidential Election: Humphrey vs. Nixon vs. Wallace and "Law and Order"

This election is doubly interesting to analyze for it has a bimodal attitude frequency distribution *and* a multi-party system. With situations like this, there are several additional considerations that the parties must take into account which are not present in a simplified unimodal, two-party example. The war in Vietnam was not the most salient issue in 1968: Nixon's SECRET PLAN prevented the Republicans from being located on that issue and Air Force General [retired] Curtis Lemay's recommendations (Lemay was Wallace's vice-presidential running mate) on how to solve the war—increased bombing—was not much different from what the Democratic nominee Humphrey had been supporting over the past four years in his role as Johnson's vice-president. The most salient issue in 1968 was probably "law and order" and "crime in the streets." But, of course, this is another example of where certain attitudes cannot be

graphed along a right-left continuum: how many people were
for crime in the streets? But since the model forces a distribution, Figure 4.11 represents the imputed attitudes on "law and
order."

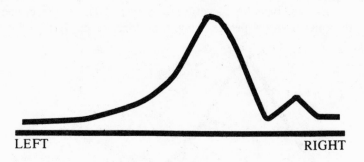

Figure 4.11
The 1968 Presidential Election (A)

Now the question is at hand: where do the parties place
their ideology/platform, knowing full well the nature of the
frequency distribution (they are not mistaken as Goldwater
possibly was in 1964) and knowing that there are three parties?
One of the crucial elements is now which party holds its nomi-
nating convention first (or, which department store pours its
concrete foundation first). The other two parties will then know
the location of the first and can thus plan accordingly. The
Democrats and Humphrey placed their platform at the left of
the peak (H is for Humphrey in Figure 4.12-A). Wallace and
the American Independent Party placed its platform and appeal
on the top of the second and smaller mode on the right (W_1 is for
Wallace in Figure 4.12-A). The Republicans with Nixon were
faced with what appeared to be an impossible dilemma: if Nixon
(N is for Nixon in Figure 4.12-A) placed his platform just to
the right of H, the rational obvious outcome would be that the
Republicans would have lost the election by receiving only 5
percent of the vote. This is so for Wallace (in position W_1), once
seeing that N was adjacent to H, would then move his party to
the left and stop one block to the right of N (position W_2 in

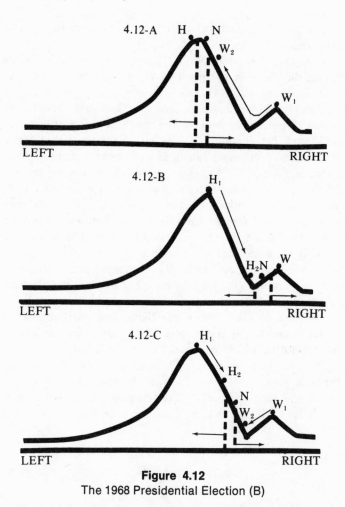

Figure 4.12
The 1968 Presidential Election (B)

Figure 4.12-A). This is possible with the model because the parties are not immobile concrete structures. They can move left or right provided they do not hop over another party (they can move up to but not beyond a party already located on the curve). Thus, if N placed his party just to the right of H, W_1 would move to W_2 and N would be squeezed down to only 5 to 10 percent of the vote while H and W shared the rest of the vote. To have placed N adjacent to H would be totally irra-

tional behavior for such behavior would not serve the goal of
maximization of votes.

But what, then, does N do? There is another option: place
N just to the left of W (Figure 4.12-B). But this would not have
solved the problem for H_1 would now move toward the right
(position H_2). If this had happened, the Democrats would have
received 80 percent of the vote and the other two parties would
have shared the remaining 20 percent. It appeared that Nixon
and the Republicans were caught in a pincer movement between
the Democrats and the American Independents. Even if the Republicans placed their platform at a position equidistant from
both H_1 and W_1 (position N in Figure 4.12-C), H_1 would then
close in from the left to position H_2 and W_1 would close in from
the right to position W_2 and the Democrats would have been the
victors. It appeared that the middle party (N and the Republicans, in this case) was about to be squeezed out, wherever it
placed its platform (the model says it has to place the platform
between H and W).

But it is at this point where Nixon and the Republicans
completely and totally confounded the model. Nixon performed
a master stroke which the model does not allow—he built a
branch store! In other words, *Nixon split the Republican platform so it could be in two places at the same time!* This split
location was accomplished by having Spiro Agnew as the vice-
presidential candidate. Agnew (position A in Figure 4.13) was

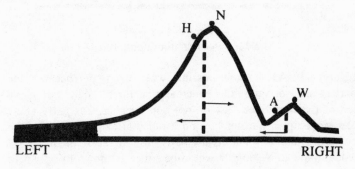

Figure 4.13
The 1968 Presidential Election (C)

sent scurrying down to the right to block any attempt by Wallace to move in (Agnew was joined by John Mitchell in this astonishing block) and Nixon with his liberal entourage of Robert Finch and John Lindsay set up position (N in Figure 4.13) just to the right of H and thus Humphrey was unable to move to the right to gain voters.

This was a perfectly logical and rational use of Spiro Agnew. Wallace tried to move in from the right to pick up more votes but Agnew would not budge from his position. Humphrey desperately attempted to push Nixon toward the right and almost succeeded. Many observers felt, Humphrey included, that if the campaign had lasted another week or two, he (H) would have been able to move far enough toward the right to win what turned out to be a very close election (the distance between N and A would have decreased).

But Humphrey and the Democrats were perhaps placing too much faith in the model of voter behavior and rational activity. The Democrats believed they were assured of their flank (the extreme left shaded area in Figure 4.13) for the model says people vote for the *closest* party. The extreme left would have to travel until they came to the first party, stop, and vote for that party. Since there were no viable parties to the left of H (at least there were none in our example), the Democrats thought that all they had to do was to move toward the right and then they would win the election. But the model's assumptions do not hold in real life! The extreme/flank saw H moving farther and farther away and they simply decided that *it was too far to travel to shop at that particular store.* These people stayed home and did not vote at all. The Democrats probably lost as many voters on the flank as they gained by moving to the right (this point is Smithies' addition to Hotelling's model: parties will not move that much out of fear of losing the voters who live in the far suburbs/flanks/or political extremes).

The moment the 1968 Republican convention selected Spiro Agnew to be on the ticket, the Democrats were doomed. It was simply impossible for the Democrats to overcome this splitting of the Republican department store. Not much is gained from discussions on "what might have been if . . ." but the two examples below (Figures 4.14-A and 4.14-B) show that the Republicans would have lost in 1968 if (a) they had picked a more liberal vice-presidential candidate, or (b) if, say, Barry Gold-

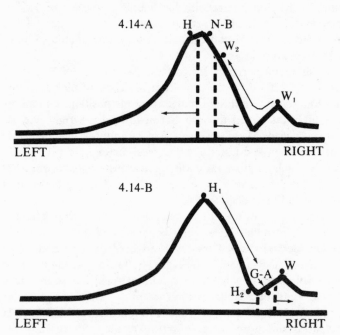

Figure 4.14
The 1968 Presidential Election (D)

water and Spiro Agnew made up the ticket. In Figure 4.14-A, assume the Republicans had picked Senator Edward Brooke of Massachusetts, a black, to run as vice president. Their location is shown as N-B in Figure 4.14-A. Nixon-Brooke would have been just to the right of Humphrey and George Wallace would have scurried in from position W_1 to W_2 and N-B would have been squeezed out. In Figure 4.14-B, assume the ticket was Goldwater-Agnew (position G-A). This platform would have been just to the left of Wallace and Humphrey would have moved from H_1 to H_2 and, once again, the Republicans would have been caught in the pincers. As stated above, the very moment Agnew was put on the ticket, the Democrats lost the

1968 election. It was a totally logical and rational use of Agnew in order to maximize the vote totals for the Republican Party.

The 1972 Presidential Election: McGovern vs. Nixon-Agnew vs. Schmitz and the State of the Economy/Foreign Policy

The 1972 election was almost a mirror image of the 1964 election between Johnson and Goldwater except for the bimodal attitude frequency distribution and a third party (American Independent Party) which were not present in 1964. The most salient issues of this election were probably the rate of inflation/unemployment and the then recent foreign policy initiatives toward the Soviet Union, China, and the beginnings of detente. The war in Vietnam was *not* a very salient issue in 1972 for, it is to be remembered, "peace" was declared one week prior to the election and this announcement effectively defused the war as an issue (who is against peace?). But, as also happened in 1964, election campaign statements and promises bore very little resemblance to reality: "peace" had not broken out and President Nixon, soon after the election, ordered the most devastating bombing of North Vietnam. If this bombing had taken place prior to the election, Vietnam would have been a salient issue but it was only after the election and Vietnam did not enter as a major issue.

Watergate was also *not* an issue during the 1972 election. McGovern of course attempted to link President Nixon with the break-in at the Watergate but there was no evidence in early November 1972 to connect the president with the break-in. It was also too soon for the cover-up to fall apart and very little was known at that time about the activities which later led to Nixon's resignation. As with the bombing of North Vietnam, if the Watergate scandal had unraveled prior to the election, it would have been a very salient issue. But the Watergate affair did not become known until long after the election and the people's attitude on this issue could not be graphed for the 1972 election.

Thus the salient 1972 issues are seen to be the economy

and detente policies and the attitude distribution is graphed in Figure 4.15. John Schmitz placed the American Independent Party at position S, occupying the building vacated in 1968 by

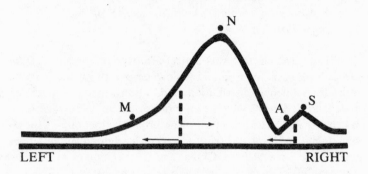

Figure 4.15
The 1972 Presidential Election

George Wallace. Spiro Agnew proved to be an excellent branch store manager and the Republicans again constructed two stores with President Nixon at position N. Position N is right at the peak of the larger attitude cluster and this position was congruent with the former president's claim that he was the president of "all the people." The Republicans' branch store was built at the old 1968 location with Spiro Agnew as manager. Position A in Figure 4.15 is just to the left of Schmitz and, by being so located, the Republicans prevented the AIP from moving to the left at the Republicans' expense.

The Democratic candidate, George McGovern, faced more problems than Hubert Humphrey did in 1968. Nixon's position at N effectively prevented McGovern from edging to the peak of the mode. But even if McGovern had been able to do this, the results would have been similar to 1968: Nixon would have stood fast at N and the distance between N and A contained enough votes to give the Republicans the election. But McGovern was unable to compromise his principles and he refused to locate just to the left of N. McGovern's campaign was quite similar to Goldwater's 1964 campaign: the losers did not follow Downs' dictum of attempting to gain as many votes as possible.

McGovern, through a comedy (or tragedy) of errors, misconceptions, misstatements, and outright gaffes, either placed his platform at M or was perceived by the population to be at M. McGovern's vice-presidential candidate, Sargent Shriver, was, *solely from the viewpoint of Downs' model,* a total disaster for the Democrats. Shriver did not represent a branch store for the Democrats as did Agnew for the Republicans. Shriver was located right at M along with McGovern and this left practically the whole field open to the Republicans.

As with the Republicans in 1964, McGovern and the Democrats were appealing to a nonexistent group of shoppers, the only place they lived was Massachusetts and the District of Columbia, and the Republicans won a massive victory in 1972. Spiro Agnew was the key element in both the 1968 and 1972 elections and once his usefulness was gone (the 1972 election won) the Republicans and the president had no desire or need to support him when accused of receiving kickback payments later in 1973. Agnew was no longer needed as the branch store manager and very few people rallied to his support.

The 1971 Mayoralty Election in Cleveland: Perk vs. Carney vs. Pinkney and the Black-White Issue Superimposed Over Strong Party Affiliation

The 1971 Cleveland mayoralty election is presented here but not for any inherent significance or importance to the American political process. This election does, however, provide an astonishing example of the usefulness of Downs' model as an *explanatory* tool for past elections. That Downs' model could be employed for *predicting* the results of this election was a fortuitous extra attraction; Downs' model is much less useful for predicting tomorrow's election than it is for explaining yesterday's election.

Unlike the presidential elections, the salient electoral issues did not have substance in the Cleveland election. The personalities of the candidates were much more important than any offered substantive issue and the black-white issue, a nonpolitical issue, does play a role in Cleveland politics. The salient issues around which the election was carried on involved this black-white issue superimposed over a very strong party affiliation. In other words, the issues for the voters were not the economy or foreign policy or law and order but "what color is the candidate?" and "to what party does the candidate belong?" There is a very strong tendency in Cleveland for white Democrats to give priority to a white Democrat over a black Democrat and then split approximately 50 percent for a black Democrat and 50 percent for a white Republican; black Democrats give priority to a black Democrat over a white Democrat, but, in contrast to the white Democrats, will support a white Democrat over a white Republican. Cleveland Republicans do not have this split: the fourth category of "black Republican" does not exist to any appreciable degree and thus these people can link color (white) with party affiliation (Republican).

The attitude frequency distribution graphed in Figure 4.16 is thus drawn to reflect the racial and party affiliation of the electorate: approximately 38 percent are white Republicans,

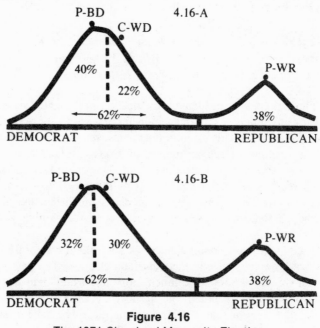

Figure 4.16
The 1971 Cleveland Mayoralty Election

40 percent are black Democrats, and 22 percent are white Democrats. The candidates were Ralph Perk, a white Republican; James Carney, a white establishment Democrat; and Arnold Pinkney, a black independent Democrat. The parties did not jockey back and forth for advantageous positions nor did they move toward one another. Each was solidified in position and each appealed to its particular group of shoppers: Pinkney to the blacks, Carney to the white Democrats, and Perk to the (white) Republicans.

A strict application of Downs' model and its assumptions to this election would have seen Arnold Pinkney winning with a 40 percent plurality. But this did not happen—Perk won the election—because the actual voting behavior was not *identical* to the black-white split within the Democrats. An astonishing development occurred here and Downs' model is very useful in the *ex post facto* explanation. The outgoing mayor, Carl Stokes (a black Democrat), played a very important role in this election. His activities probably led to Perk's election and it is a very instructive lesson in big-city politics to review Stokes' actions.

Carl Stokes obviously had aspirations to higher political office and it appeared that he was trying to use the mayoralty election as a stepping stone to the 1972 Democratic presidential nomination convention. This is not to say that Stokes seriously entertained thoughts about the presidency but perhaps the vice-presidency position, or, at least, a cabinet position in a Democratic administration might have been available. But Stokes had to have something to offer the Democrats in exchange for Carl Stokes because his race and Midwestern urban location were not of themselves sufficient. But being able to "deliver" the state of Ohio (via Cleveland and Cuyahoga County) to the Democratic candidate might have been sufficient and Stokes then embarked on a well-conceived plan to "control" the mayoralty election. The logic was that if Stokes could deliver the city of Cleveland to the Democrats, he would then be able to deliver Cuyahoga County and the rest of Ohio and its electoral votes.

But how does one "deliver" an election? Stokes' plan was well-conceived. There was, some months prior to the general election, a primary to determine which Democrat would face the Republican candidate. Arnold Pinkney did not run in this primary. The two major candidates were James Carney, a white Cleveland businessman, and Anthony Garofoli, a white politician who was at that time city council president. The relationship between Stokes and Garofoli left a lot to be desired and Stokes did not want Garofoli to win the formal endorsement of the Democratic Party. The black Democrats were not too involved at the beginning of the primary campaign: the white candidates did not particularly appeal to them and most might have stayed home or, of those who voted, might have split their vote between Carney and Garofoli. Stokes wished to knock Garofoli out and thus he embarked on a public relations campaign for Carney among the blacks.

Stokes and his staff campaigned competently and effectively for Carney among the black voters: letters, personal visits, telephone calls combined to convince many blacks that Carney was an able person and that a vote for Carney over Garofoli would further the electorate's goals. No evil was mentioned about Carney and he was portrayed as a very acceptable candidate. Also, no mention was made of Arnold Pinkney during the primary for Pinkney was not a candidate. Stokes' plan was a success: Carney defeated Garofoli with the help of black votes and he received the formal party endorsement. Carney was to be the establishment Democratic candidate against Perk in the general election.

The next stage in Carl Stokes' plan was to knock out James Carney in the general election and deliver the election to Pinkney. Pinkney entered the race after the primary as an independent Democrat. By appearing to control the electoral process, first defeating Garofoli with Carney and then defeating Carney *and* Perk with Pinkney, Stokes would have enjoyed a position of strength at the Democratic convention. Stokes duplicated his public relations campaign in the general election but this time it was directed *against* Carney: Stokes attempted to dissuade those voters who voted for Carney in the primary from remaining with Carney. This would have been an excellent example of backroom politics had it been successful.

Stokes' grand design was not successful for he apparently underestimated the intelligence of the black voters and he overestimated his own influence with this group. Approximately 8 percent of those early Carney supporters were not persuaded by Stokes that Carney all of a sudden was unacceptable. This 8 percent remained with Carney and, by so doing, ensured Ralph Perk's election as major. Figure 4.16-B represents this new distribution: in place of the 40 percent, approximately 32 percent supported Pinkney, the black independent Democrat (P-BD); 30 percent [the 22 percent white and 8 percent "defectors"] supported Carney (C-WD); and 38 percent still supported Perk, the white Republican (P-WR). The result of the election was predicted by several observers: P-BD and C-WD shared the 62 percent Democratic vote and P-WR won with a plurality of 38 percent.

The candidates were aware of the situation as graphed in Figure 4.16 and Ralph Perk was in the enviable position of having the opposition split. Perk did not have to move to the left (i.e., to pick up some white Democratic votes) for he was secure in appealing to the 38 percent who lived in his neighborhood. Pinkney and Carney soon realized that Stokes' plan was not working and if *either* of them had dropped out of the race (as each had invited the other to do on numerous occasions), it probably would have meant the defeat of P-WR. Most black Democrats would have voted for Carney if Pinkney were not a candidate or enough white Democrats would have voted for Pinkney if Carney were not a candidate to give either one a majority. But both P-BD and C-WD insisted on remaining and the result was that Cleveland, with an overwhelming majority of registered Democrats, elected a Republican mayor. The real loser in the entire affair was Carl Stokes. Stokes did not have viable bargaining chips at the convention and he rapidly faded from the political scene.

Figure 4.16 can also be employed to explain the 1970 senatorial race in New York between Goodell (Republican), Ottinger (Democrat-Liberal), and Buckley (Conservative). Goodell and Ottinger split the liberal vote, Goodell was the Republican candidate but incurred the wrath of the national Republican Party for his "too" liberal platform, and Buckley won with a plurality (39 percent). Had Goodell or Ottinger dropped out, as both constantly invited the other to do, Buckley

would have lost. But both Goodell and Ottinger were waiting
for the other to drop. Buckley remained stationary, no one
moved, and the result was equivalent to the Cleveland election.

An Application of the Model to a
Multimodal Attitude Frequency Distribution
and a Multi-Party System.

Downs' model can aid in explaining why, in a unimodal
attitude frequency distribution with two parties, the parties
become similar. This is because the parties gravitate toward
the peak of the mode in order to compete for the uncommitted
voters, the voters who are equidistant from each party, knowing that its flanks are assured. The model can also help to explain why, in a multi-party multimodal example, the various
parties attempt to remain as ideologically consistent as possible
and attempt to remain as far away as possible from neighboring
parties. As Downs is quoted above, it is rational for each party
in a two-party system to encourage voters to be irrational by
making its platform vague and ambiguous and such parties deliberately change their platforms so that they resemble one
another. But in a multimodal multi-party example, it is rational
for each party to have clear-cut platforms and attempt to keep
their distance from other parties. These parties are, in a sense,
"locked in" as if they *did* have a concrete foundation.

An instructive example of this situation can be seen in the
Fourth French Republic (1946-1958) as represented in Figure
4.17. There were five major and identifiable peaks or modes
(attitude distributions) on practically every issue and the major
political ideologies (parties or groupings of parties) can be assigned to the observed peaks. Each of the modes or attitude
groupings was more or less the same size, approximately 20
percent or so, and the application of Downs' model can help
to explain why (1) only the two extreme parties (Communist
or Conservative) would benefit by any shift of the "middle-of-
the-road" parties and (2) the extreme parties would themselves
lose votes if they moved too great a distance toward the center.
These two related points combine and "lock" the parties into
a concrete foundation.

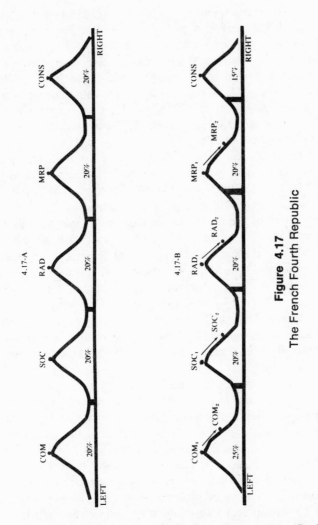

Figure 4.17
The French Fourth Republic

Any shift by one of the three inner parties (Socialist, Radical, Mouvement Républicain Populaire) in any direction would cost the wandering party approximately the same number of votes on the end opposite to that of the move and the only "winner" would be the extreme party on the end opposite to the direction of the move. Figure 4.17-B shows this relationship. Say the Radicals decide to move a bit to the right, hoping to pick up some votes and parliamentary seats from the MRP (position RAD_1 to RAD_2 in Figure 4.17-B). For every voter RAD picked up at the expense of the MRP, RAD would lose to the Socialists on their left because the Socialists, seeing that the Radicals moved to the right, would move from position SOC_1 to SOC_2. The Communists on the left extreme would then move (COM_2 from COM_1) and pick up approximately the same number of votes from the Socialists that the Socialists gained from the Radicals.

The MRP, losing votes on its left to the Radicals, is the party of decision: it can remain immobile or it can move to the right. To remain still is not rational, however. The MRP has lost, say, 25 percent of its vote to the Radicals on the left (the MRP's share of the total vote declined to 15 percent) but it is not the Radicals who have gained: from the MRP through the Radicals and through the Socialists the 5 percent accrues to the Communists who see their vote increase from 20 to 25 percent of the electorate. It is thus simply irrational for the MRP to remain still and, by so doing, give the Communists votes at their expense. That the Communists are going to gain is a foregone conclusion but the MRP is determined that it is to be at someone else's expense. Thus the MRP moves from position MRP_1 to MRP_2.

It is now the Conservatives who lose the 5 percent and these votes are transferred to the Communist Party via the three inner parties. Before this game of musical chairs, each party had approximately 20 percent of the vote; now the Communists have 25 percent, the Socialists, Radicals, and MRP still have 20 percent each, and the Conservatives now have 15 percent. The inner three parties knew this would happen; why do all this moving when we ourselves will not gain (these parties *still* have 20 percent each)? but any move will benefit the Communists (or Conservatives, depending upon the direction of the first move). Parties of the left or right extreme are the "winners" of the example represented in Figure 4.17-B and thus the three inner parties do not move. In a real sense, the three inner parties are "locked in" and cannot move. They are forced to remain ideologically distinct and are forced to keep a safe distance from their neighboring parties.

Point (2) above, the extreme parties cannot move too far into the center for fear of losing votes, can be explained by once again referring to Smithies' addition: parties will not move too distant from where most of its voters live. If the extreme parties were to move too far toward the center (the Communists just to the left of the Socialists or the Conservatives just to the right of the MRP), their voters would decide that the new location was too far and they would begin to look around for a smaller but closer store/party. There are countless minor and fringe parties in France and all are waiting to occupy a vacated prime location (the top of a mode). Figure 4.17-B illustrates a sort of dynamic immobilism: there is a tension exerted on all parties which encourages them to move but convinces them to remain still.

Contemporary French electoral politics no longer mirrors the example above because the 1958 change to the Fifth Republic began the downfall of the MRP and now the MRP no longer exists. The Communists and Socialists are, hesitantly, forming a Federation of the Left to jointly contest elections. The attitude distributions shown in Figures 4.17-A and 4.17-B are giving way to a distribution akin to Figure 4.3-A: two modes, approximately the same size, representing the Left and Right groupings. Figure 4.17-A can, however, be employed to analyze elections in solidified multi-party systems such as Finland, Italy, and Iceland.

Downs' economic model of democracy is extremely useful and beneficial when it is applied to an explanation of elections after they have taken place. It is less useful for predicting a future election for, not only do the assumptions not hold 100 percent of the time, the researcher is unable to even approximate the degree to which these assumptions actually will hold. People stay home, people do not vote rationally, parties have secret plans and build branch stores, some parties are not out to maximize their vote totals and some politicians are more concerned with principles than with appealing to a group of shoppers on the far side of town. But if the assumptions did hold, the model would be an excellent predictive tool. Anthony Downs' analysis is an original treatment of voting behavior and party behavior which, even though written in 1957, remains today as one of the best illustrations of the integration of, and borrowing from, other disciplines in the field of political science.

Mathematics, Game Theory, and the Cuban Missile Crisis

A second major area from which political science has borrowed is mathematics. Not only are basic mathematical and statistical manipulations performed on whatever data are being analyzed, as mentioned above in Chapter 3, but mathematical thought processes and frameworks have also been applied. One such example of this interdisciplinary approach is termed "game theory." Game theory was primarily developed by John von Neumann and Oskar Morgenstein with the publication in 1944 of their *Theory of Games and Economic Behavior*.[6] Jacob Bronowski in *The Ascent of Man* mentions that Neumann's work was a major intellectual achievement of the twentieth century and it appeared that most social situations involving conflict between or among the participants could be reduced to mathematical principles and notations. Stated very briefly and in simplified terms, game theory is a mathematical method, employing quite sophisticated and complicated mathematical notations, used to analyze the decision-making process in real-life conflict situations. This discussion purposely omits all but the most elementary mathematics but the interested reader is advised to supplement these notes with the writings on game theory by Brams, Rapoport, and Shubik[7] This section first presents the rudimentary concepts and principles of game theory and, second, applies these concepts to the explanation of a certain political event: the October 1962 Cuban Missile Crisis between the United States and the Soviet Union.

Concepts, Principles, and Terminology of Game Theory

A distinction must first be made between "game theory" and "gaming." John R. Raser writes that

> ... *game theory* is a set of mathematical tools for dealing with explicit types of conflict situations. It is used to bring

clarity to such social and political variables as information patterns, distribution of power and resources, goals, feasibility of various strategies, the different effects of moves made openly or secretly, and coalition formation. *Games and simulations* ... are attempts ... to construct operating models of complex social and physical systems.[8]

In other words, game theory can be used to analyze in mathematical terms a person's behavior and possible options when he is in an actual real-life conflict situation; political gaming and simulation, on the other hand, are attempts to re-create a real-life situation in order to discover what a person will (or should) do once he is in the real-life situation. Perhaps an example will illustrate the distinction more clearly: game theory techniques can be applied to the situation where an airplane pilot, upon being notified by a stewardess that the plane is being hijacked, mulls over the options open to him—appease the hijacker by flying to Cuba (and also inconvenience the passengers) or attempt to disarm the hijacker in order to continue with the normal flight plan (but run the risk of gunfire and death). Gaming and simulation techniques can be applied to the situation where the airplane pilot, in a mock-up cockpit on the ground in the company's training center, is informed that the landing gear will not lower for the (practice) landing—does the pilot attempt a forced landing with a high risk of a crash or does he circle the airport, hoping the landing gear will disengage before the fuel runs out? One is a real-life situation, the other is a re-creation of reality, and game theory applies to the former, gaming and simulation to the latter.

Game theory is a mathematical method, employing quite complicated mathematical notations, used to study the decision-making process in real-life conflict situations. Mathematically formulated principles can specify what is rational behavior in such situations. Rationality is used here in the same sense as did Downs: rational action does not mean intrinsic or inherent rationality; rational action means that the decision-maker is aware of his desired goal, the options open to him, the benefits and costs attached to each option, and that decision-maker will opt for that alternative which will enable him to best achieve his desired ends. The desired end may be "irrational" from one point of view: a father may want to lose a game of checkers with his daughter and thus he will choose those alternatives which best achieve his desired ends—he will not jump his opponent and thus play the game in order to lose. Rational behavior in game theory does not mean that the decision-maker can actually picture the matrix containing *all* the options of *all* the participants with their benefits/losses as if he had a game theorist sitting next to him; the rational actor model in game theory says, in effect, that this method of explanation and analysis of people's actions can be applied as *if* the participants had some goal.

There are some important characteristics of the type of conflict situations to which game theory is applicable. First, the participants (players, decision-makers) do not have complete control over the other participants in the situation and, in some situations, all the participants together do not completely control the entire situation itself—one's calculations as to what moves to make must take "chance" into account. Second, not every participant's desires, interests, or goals can be satisfied or achieved in the same amount all the time and some of these goals may not be attained at all. Third, each participant places his own self-conceived "value" or worth upon the outcome of the game, as well as upon each of the possible moves within the game, and these assigned values or utilities to the game's payoffs are thus frequently different for each player. Some examples of these points follow: the actions of the Israelis and the Egyptians may be dependent upon what the other side does but neither side can determine what alternatives the other will choose; goals and interests cannot be satisfied all the time for all participants because if the situation is one akin to the Fischer-Spassky chess match, one of the participants had to lose; the assigned utilities are often different because Nelson Rockefeller would not assign the same "value" to a game which had a $10 bill as the payoff as would this author, for example.

This lack of complete control and the presence of participants with different and competing strategies and objectives, but whose final result or standing in the game depends almost as much upon the other players' moves as upon his own, leads in some types of games to what is termed the "cross-purposes optimization problem." The individual player seeks to attain as much as possible, while at the same time seeks to keep his losses at a minimum. These winnings and losings can be anything the game concerns: the psychological satisfaction of winning a chess match, a large sum of money for winning a chess match, votes, high grades in place of low grades, prestige, honor, military capabilities, the list is almost endless. But the individual player cannot in some types of games (the different types of games are discussed below) pursue this strategy of maximizing winnings and minimizing losses in isolation: player A, while aiming to achieve as much as possible and to lose as little as possible, must plug into his calculations the fact that there are other players who may or may not have the identical goal in mind (the example above of wanting to lose a game of checkers is not widespread, especially in real-life conflict situations). It is quite possible that A's maximum winnings may represent B's maximum losings and B will thus play the game so that, under no circumstances, would B permit A to achieve his maximum. The cross-purposes optimization problem thus makes the rational player pursue a course of action that not only includes his own goals and abilities, but one that also reflects his assessment of the other players' goals and abilities. In other words, the question is (and we shall state it in verbal terms rather than employing mathematical notations): "What strategy will give me the highest possible winnings but will at the same time give B the minimal amount of losses as well as assuring me of minimum losses?"

The mathematical formulations and expressions, some of which are very complicated and involved (especially in what is termed n-person non-0-sum games) and thus not presented in this brief introduction, enter game theory through each participant's calculations of the values that each possible outcome or payoff has (these values can be positive or negative) along with the calculation of the probabilities of the actual occurrence of each possible outcome. And since the players cannot completely control each other, a move by one may totally upset all the calculations and the probabilities must then be recalculated. The players, in a sense, attempt to maximize the sum of the assigned payoff values and the probabilities and then follow this rational strategy.

Game Theory Terminology

Players. The player is described as the individual decision-maker in the game. It may be a person, an informal group, a political party, a country, an alliance, a business corporation, or a coalition. The player, whatever its composition, has certain objectives to gain from the game and he operates under his own control in the game. This last point means the players are autonomous but not independent—the activities of players A and B affect C's possible options. There must be at least two players (a two-person game) but there is no upper limit to the number of autonomous participants (an n-person game).

Resources. Each player has certain material with which to play the game and each person's resources may or may not be equal or available for inspection by the other players. These resources vary according to the content of the game: Bobby Fischer had his chessmen and his wits as resources against Boris Spassky in the now-famous Icelandic Chess Match; the professor has grades to assign; the politician has power to parcel out; a country has bombs to drop; the poker player has chips and cards; the general has soldiers.

Rules. The rules are the ways the resources may be employed or, in other words, the rules are the limiting conditions under which the game is played. All the rules are known to the players before the game begins in some situations: football, chess, Russian roulette, poker. However, in other games, the rules are not passed around before the game begins and one player knows more (less) than the other player: most political conflict situations do not have all participants aware of all the limiting conditions to the other players' behavior. There are two types of rules or two factors which limit the ways the resource may be employed: rules can be artificial or technological/environmental/physical. Artificial rules are those limiting conditions usually agreed to in advance of the game and known to the participants: hockey players cannot throw the puck into the net, a pawn cannot move backwards, a red cross on a roof signals "hospital—no bombing," and tacit agreements such as the non-use of gas during the Second World War. Artificial rules can be altered or disregarded at will but noncompliance of artificial rules usually upsets the strategies of all participants. Technological rules are not artificial for they cannot be altered at will although all participants may not have perfect information as to the technological limitations to their opponents, and even their own resources. Examples of technological/environmental/physical rules are: planes can travel only so far before fuel runs out, missile target capability may vary with range, a participant's physical endurance may limit his options, or a political party or candidate may not have enough funds for a saturated television appeal.

Strategy. Strategy refers to the plan of action (the "game plan" is a doubly apt term), not to the actual moves themselves (the tactics), which each player determines to be most rational and possible to achieve his predetermined objectives. There are two different types of strategy: pure and mixed. A "pure strategy" refers to a game in which the players follow their predetermined game plan regardless of what the other players do; a "mixed strategy" refers to a game where the players have to change or alter their original game plan in light of their opponents' moves in order to maintain the maximum payoff values. Chess is most certainly a mixed strategy game: to "attack" regardless of your opponent's moves is fatal. The term *optimum strategy* (optimum strategy can be either pure or mixed) refers to that planned set of moves that A can follow and be protected from *anything* the other player might possibly do. An optimum strategy, if available, can guarantee a player a predetermined payoff value. For example, assume the goal of Hockey Team A is *not to lose* the game with Team B. A's optimum strategy would be a pure strategy of placing all six men in front of A's net so Team B could not score a goal (this assumes, of course, that the rules permit this behavior and that Team B could not squeeze the puck past the six men). That Team A would not score either in this game is immaterial—A did not want to lose and a 0-0 tie is not a loss.

Another example of an optimum strategy can be seen in the classroom. The professor has a policy of giving, at random unannounced intervals, surprise quizzes to the students. These quizzes have, in past years, ranged from one to five in number over the semester. The quizzes may be a surprise but they are not unfair: the questions are such that all one has to do is study and a passing grade is assured. However, if the student does not study, a failing grade is assured. The student's optimum strategy—optimum because the student will be protected from *anything* the professor might do—is obvious: the student, if rational, should study. There are four possible alternatives here: (1) a quiz is given and the student studied; (2) a quiz is given and the student did not study; (3) no quiz and the student studied; and (4) no quiz and the student did not study. The student's payoffs for each of the four possible alteratives are (1) an A on the quiz; (2) an F on the quiz; (3) no payoff; (4) no payoff. Since the choice to study protects the student from whatever the professor decides this would be an optimum strategy.

Payoff/Utilities. This term refers to the values (plus or minus) that each player assigns to each pair of moves in the game as well as to the final outcome of the game. These values are partly determined by the probability of the certain outcome actually happening as well as by the individual player's own assessment of the game's worth or value. A player may opt for or at least try to achieve outcome Z—a $100 prize with a 40 percent chance of actually occurring—in place of opting for outcome W—a $1,000 prize with only a one percent chance of occurrence.

There are several important points to be noted with payoff values and utilities. First is that the different players frequently assign different values to the identical outcome. The example above of the card game between Nelson Rockefeller and this author for $10 illustrates this point. Second, an outcome which gives a player less than he thought he was going to win can be seen as a loss for the player. For example, a student may be convinced at some point in the game that he will receive an A for the course but he receives a C. The student can, and frequently does, regard the payoff as a loss—he "lost" two grades!—even though the same payoff from a different perspective would be seen as a win (the student *did* pass the course and receive credit).

The third point is just the opposite of the preceding remark: an outcome which does not give the player as large a loss as he thought he was going to lose can be seen as a win. This may be just semantical acrobatics but consider the following situation: you left your notebook with all your notes and a $10 bill clipped to a page in the classroom. Your "loss" is not discovered until that evening and you are totally despondent over the missing notes and the $10. The professor, however, found the missing items and returns the notebook (*less the $10* —the professor says he did not see any money) to you the next day. From one point of view, this outcome certainly represents a loss ($10) but for our purposes, it can be seen as a "win": you were convinced that your losses were the notebook and the money, the final outcome was less painful. You lost less than you thought you were going to lose and this can frequently be seen as a win.

The fourth point to be noted with payoff values and utilities is that the winnings of one player do not necessarily have to equal the losings of the other player(s). In other words, the pluses (+) do not have to equal the minuses (−). As with the example above with the lost notebook and money: both the student and the professor can legitimately claim and believe to have won something in the game. The professor "won" $10 from the student (say a value of + 10), the student "lost" the $10 to the professor (a value of −10) but the student also "won" the notebook (a value of +20). This example has both sides winning and thus the winnings do not have to equal the losings.

Payoff Matrix: A payoff matrix refers to a boxlike listing of all the possible strategies, the probabilities of their actual occurrence, and the values assigned to the outcome of each pair of strategies by each decision-maker. Figure 4.18 represents a very simplified payoff matrix of the utilities assigned to the student in the example above of whether to study or not to study for a possible quiz. Figure 4.18 is a very simplified matrix for only the utilities for the student are listed and no probabilities are assigned to the possible alternatives. But the matrix lists the possible alternatives and their payoffs to the student: +10 for the grade of A if the student studies and the quiz were given, −10 for the F if the student did not study and the quiz were given; −1 for lost sleep if the student studied and there were no quiz, and 0 for no studying and no quiz.

Figure 4.18
A Simplified Payoff Matrix: To Study or Not to Study?

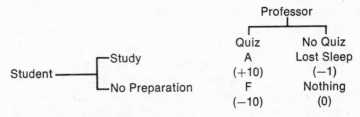

One can hopefully begin to see the mathematics involved if it is a game with three or four players, each having two or three strategies (depending upon what the other players do), and each assigning a payoff value to all the possible outcomes. Figure 4.19 is a more complex payoff matrix in our game of quizzes and studying, for now we have the additional variable of payoff values to the professor. The first entry in the cells refers to the student's payoff; the second value is the professor's.

Figure 4.19
A More Complex Payoff Matrix:
To Study or Not to Study?/To Quiz or Not to Quiz?

		Options for Professor	
		Quiz	No Quiz
Options for Student	Study	+10, −10	−1, 0
	No Preparation	−10, −5	0, 0

Once we assign the payoff values for the professor (the minus values represent the time and effort to write the quiz, grade 100 essays, and then listen to the inevitable complaints): however, the student's option is not as clear cut as it was previously. The obvious option for the student *not knowing the payoffs to the professor* would be to study. But once this matrix is known and assuming each player wants to maximize the pluses and minimize the minuses, the obvious option for the student is *not* to study and for the professor, the obvious option is not to give a quiz. This assumes that the professor has no desire to double-cross the students into believing that there would be no quiz (and thus the students would not study) but then giving the quiz. Many such situations do, however, contain deception, bluffing, and double-crosses but these situations are discussed below.

The payoff matrices presented in Figures 4.18 and 4.19 are not very sophisticated for, once again, the probabilities are not included and they are simple 2 x 2 matrices with four cells. Each cell in a payoff matrix contains the values for each player with the value for player 1 coming first, followed by the value to player 2. Thus in Figure 4.19, the southwest cell reads -10, -5 for the combination of giving the quiz without the students preparing for it. The student's payoff is -10 (the value of an F) and the professor's payoff is -5 (the cost of preparing the exam but there are no other costs—the exam books will be blank because the students opted not to study and thus there is no time expended on reading the answers).

Some Types and Examples of Games. There are three basic types of games: (1) a two-person, 0-sum game; (2) a two-person, non-0-sum game; and (3) an n-person, non-0-sum game (the non-0-sum games are also called nonconstant sum games).

Two-Person, 0-Sum Game. This type of game is defined as one in which there are two players (two decision-making units) *and* in which the winnings of Player A are identical to the losing of Player B. In other words, whatever gains are made by A are at the direct expense of B—whatever A "wins" B loses—and the winnings equal the losings. Thus the term "0-sum": the sum of all possible payoff values (the pluses and minuses) equals 0. This type of game is always one of pure unadulterated Hobbesian conflict without any crosspurposes, optimization, bargaining, cooperation, or coordination. The player should always assume the worst in these games and plan his options accordingly (one's opponent is always out to maximize his gains at your expense). Some "nonpolitical" 2-person 0-sum games, to cite just a few, would be Russian roulette, a duel, most sporting events (those which do not permit a tie), chess is usually an 0-sum game but there is always the possibility of a stalemate.

Two-Person, Non-O-Sum Game. This type of game is defined as having two decision-making units *but* the winnings of A do not necessarily equal the losings of B. In other words, the sum of the game is not 0: both players can win the same amount $(+,+)$ or one can win more than the other $(++,+)$, both players can lose the same amount $(-,-)$ or one can lose more than the other $(-,--)$, or one can win more than the other loses $(++,-)$. In any case, in a two-person, non-0-sum game, there is at least one (and frequently more) possible outcomes with a payoff value described above.

An important point to note here is that each decision-maker can assign different values to identical outcomes although the assigned values are frequently identical. Also, as mentioned above, if a player loses less than he thought he was going to lose, this can be seen as a win; if a player wins less than he thought he was going to win, this can be seen as a loss. For example, my attitude and expectations, if I were to play Bobby Fischer in chess, would be that I would be checkmated in four moves. But assume I held Fischer to a stalemate: *I* would most certainly regard the outcome of the game as a "win" (I lost less than I thought I was going to lose). If my opponent regards the stalemate as a "win" (it allows him to maintain his title and the prize money), the game would be non-0-sum: we both won! Fischer keeps his title and $250,000; I win psychological satisfaction and international recognition.

Since there is a strong possibility of both players winning (or minimizing losses) and that such gains are not necessarily at the other's expense in two-person, non-0-sum games, this particular type of game frequently necessitates bargaining, co-operation, and coordination. Each player must choose a strategy and moves that will (1) give himself the maximum value attainable and (2) allow his opponent to choose the moves that will accomplish the same results. In other words, each player must anticipate his opponent's strategy and moves so that a mutually acceptable point or level can be reached. Moves must be coordinated in order to maximize winnings or minimize losings.

An example of coordinated moves can be seen with two people in a cellar and this is taken from Martin Shubik.[9] Assume two people are trapped in an airtight cellar with an open spigot slowly raising the water level. There is, however, a heavy trap-door built into the ceiling and it will open only if the two people push on it simultaneously. The trapdoor will not open if one person refuses to push. The people do not know each other nor is each much interested in saving the other person's life: the only thing that interests each is getting out of the cellar before drowning. Figure 4.20 presents the payoff matrix for this situation.

Figure 4.20
Payoff Matrix for Men Trapped in the Cellar

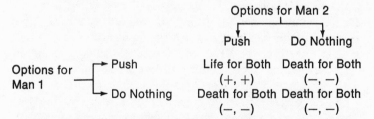

Source: Martin Shubik, "Game Theory and the Study of Social Behavior: An Introductory Exposition," in Martin Shubik, ed., *Game Theory and Related Approaches to Social Behavior* (New York: John Wiley and Sons, 1964), p. 32. Reprinted by permission.

Since each player prefers life to death, the only rational move for *both* players is to push—this move will give both of them a win (life) whereas any of the remaining three options would result in certain death. This is not a difficult game to conceptualize: the rational activity was obvious to both and since they were both in the cellar together, they could physically communicate and coordinate their moves to the benefit of each, even though each cared nothing about the other person. The process of achieving a mutually advantageous outcome, life, in the cellar was relatively simple. The two men could directly communicate with each other and their moves could be easily coordinated to achieve common interests. But how does each side achieve common interests in a non-0-sum situation (both can win, both can lose) when overt and physical face-to-face communication is not possible? This leads to tacit coordination in such situations for, especially in times of war, the participants, even though they may have common interests, simply cannot sit around a table and plan the next set of moves. Thomas Schelling has written an extremely interesting and readable essay on the study of tacit bargaining in non-0-sum situations— bargaining in which the communication process is totally shut off or incomplete—and the following remarks are based on Schelling's essay.[10]

Schelling presents some interesting situations in which the participants have common interests and thus must coordinate their actions but in absence of any overt communication:

1. Name "heads" or "tails." If you and your partner name the same, you both win a prize.
2. Name an amount of money. If you all name the same amount, you can have as much as you named.
3. You are to divide $100 into two piles, labeled A and B. Your partner is to divide another $100 into two piles labeled A and B. If you allot the same amounts to A and B, respectively, that your partner does, each of you gets $100; if your amounts differ, neither of you gets anything.[11]

These examples show that people can coordinate their behavior with others if each knows that the other is also trying to coordinate and if each knows that the other knows. The examples above, in Schelling's words, contain a focal point "for each person's expectation of what the other expects him to expect to be expected to do." But all these examples have common interests—both can win a prize, all can have some money—and the participants *do* attempt to find the "equitable" or "logical" focal point. Schelling extends his analysis to situations where, again, there is no communication but there are divergent interests. These problems also require coordination for common gains although one participant would "win" more than the other:

1. A and B are to choose "heads" or "tails" without communicating. If both choose "heads," A gets $3 and B gets $2; if both choose "tails," A gets $2 and B gets $3. If they choose differently, neither gets anything. You are A (or B); which do you choose? (Note that if both choose at random, there is only a 50-50 chance of successful coincidence and an expected value of $1.25 apiece—less than either $3 or $2.)

2. You and your two partners (or rivals) each have one of the letters A, B, and C. Each of you is to write these three letters, A, B, and C, in any order. If the order is the same on all three of your lists, you get prizes totaling $6, of which $3 goes to the one whose letter is first on all three lists, $2 to the one whose letter is second, and $1 to the person whose letter is third. If the letters are not in identical order on all three lists, none of you gets anything. Your letter is A (or B, or C); write here the three letters in the order you choose:

   ———, ———, ———.[12]

These examples demonstrate that the conflict sometimes contains within itself the solution ("heads," "ABC") and even the disadvantaged player (person C in example 2) conforms to the unstated message in order to maximize winnings, even though the other player(s) would "win" more.

Schelling also discusses situations in which there is imperfect or one-way communication: A is able to send messages to B but B cannot send messages to A and A knows this and B knows this and each knows that the other knows. In these situations, A has an enormous advantage because the focal point is not what "equity" or "logic" presents but, rather, the focal point is what A communicates to B:

1. You and your partner are each to pick one of the five letters, K, G, W, L, or R. If you pick the same letter, you get prizes; if you pick different letters, you get nothing. The

prizes you get depend on the letter you both pick; but the
prizes are not the same for each of you, and the letter that
would yield you the highest prize may or may not be the
most profitable letter. For you the prizes would be as follows: K = $4, G = $3, W = $1, L = $2, R = $5. You have
no idea what his schedule of prizes looks like. You begin by
proposing to him the letter R, that being your best letter.
Before he can reply, the master-of-ceremonies intervenes
to say that you were not supposed to be allowed to communicate and that any further communication will dis-
qualify you both. You must simply write down one of the
letters, hoping that the other chooses the same letter. Which
letter do you choose?[13]

Schelling concludes his discussion by presenting some political situations of tacit negotiations in a limited war. The very
fact of having a "limited" war—Korea, Vietnam, the Middle
East—implies that such tacit bargaining has taken place and
that there *are* focal points or solutions to the problem which are
agreed upon by the participants in the absence of communication or with imperfect communication. Schelling employs Korea
as an example: the geographical configuration of Korea provided geographical limits to the conflict. Korea's northern
border is a river and the rest of the area is surrounded by water.
These physical boundaries provided a focal point: the U.S. did
not cross the Yalu River and bomb targets in China; the U.S.
supply bases in Japan were not bombed. This was a tacit agreement, e.g., an agreement *not* reached by face-to-face communication and coordination.

The wars in the Middle East between Israel and the Arab
States have not been extended to the populated cities (Cairo,
Damascus, Tel Aviv). It may not be simply that each side does
not wish to attack these cities but, rather, it appears that each
side has common interests in this conflict situation (spare the
cities) and in order to achieve one's interests, moves have to
be coordinated with the other side. There has been a tacit
agreement and the agreement is as valid as if a written agreement had been signed. This assumes, of course, that each side
refrains from choosing moves which might appear to upset the
agreement. In 1967, the Israelis stopped at the Suez Canal and

the Egyptians could continue in Cairo; if the Israelis crossed the Canal (a move which could easily be perceived as a march toward Cairo), the Egyptians' expectations of Israeli behavior would have been upset (even though the Israelis had planned to stop one mile west of the Canal) and the agreement might have broken down.

The point with Schelling is that, even in conflict situations, there exists the possibility of common interests (non-0-sum) and the participants can attempt to choose that alternative which would give them the best possible payoff while at the same time choosing an alternative which would allow the other side to achieve the best possible payoffs. The possibility of deceit was not present with the situations presented by Schelling because deception would have resulted in minimal or no winnings for the participants. When opportunities for deceit and deception are present, however, a non-0-sum game takes on an entirely different character than those presented above. One example of such a situation is termed "Prisoner's Dilemma" and the variant presented here is also taken from Martin Shubik.[14]

"Prisoner's Dilemma" is a two-person, non-0-sum game with the lines of communication shut but with the opportunity for chicanery and deceit. The scenario is as follows: Two acquaintances are arrested by the police, separated into different cells (they cannot communicate as did the men in the leaky cellar), and accused of perpetrating some crime. These two people had never discussed prior to their arrest what they would do if arrested; neither has much loyalty or feeling for the other person; each would not hesitate to double-cross the other if it meant an advantage to the one doing the double-crossing; and, most important, each knows that the other knows that the other knows that there is no loyalty and each would deceive the other.

Enter the interrogation officer. The interrogator questions each one separately and tells each prisoner: (1) if you confess to this crime and the other person remains silent, you will be set free for turning state's evidence and the other person will be given a ten-year sentence; and (2) if you both confess, each will receive an eight-year sentence. Both prisoners know from past experience, however, that if they both remain silent, the most that can happen to them would be a one-year sentence for vagrancy. Figure 4.21 presents the payoff matrix for this situation.

Figure 4.21
Payoff Matrix for "Prisoner's Dilemma"

Options for Prisoner 2

	Silence	Confession
Options for Prisoner 1 — Silence	−1, −1	−10, 0
— Confession	0, −10	−8, −8

Source: Martin Shubik, "Game Theory and the Study of Social Behavior: An Introductory Exposition," in Martin Shubik, ed., *Game Theory and Related Approaches to Social Behavior* (New York: John Wiley and Sons, 1964), p. 38. Reprinted by permission.

As Shubik comments, if each prisoner selects the move that is best for himself without any consideration for the other, the selected moves would be disastrous for each. A confession is the best move for each individual but a confession would free the individual only if the other remained silent; when both confess, each receives eight years in jail.

The payoff matrix in Figure 4.21 is approached from prisoner 1's viewpoint. If he remains silent, his payoff would be one year in jail (if the other is also silent) or ten years (if the other confesses). But, on the other hand, if prisoner 1 does confess, he will get a payoff of 0 years (if the other remains silent) or eight years in jail (if the other also confesses). It is therefore more rational for prisoner 1 to confess: if he confesses, his payoff will be either 0 years or 8 years (depending upon what the other did) and this set (0, −8) is preferable to the other set resulting from silence (one year or ten years). In other words, 0 years in jail is preferable to one year, eight years is better than ten years. The same logic holds for prisoner 2: a confession would minimize his "losings." But by confessing, each would be worse off than if they had both remained silent (one year for each with silence, eight years for each with the confession).

It is at this point that the absence of loyalty enters. It is not so much a problem of the absence of communication or even imperfect communication. It is the opportunity for the double cross which will lead each prisoner to the confession. If these prisoners apply individual rationality without any regard for the other player, the payoffs would not be the most preferable in this two-person, non-0-sum game. The prisoners should anticipate what the other would do and both, in order to receive the lightest possible punishment, should remain silent. But we have added disloyalty and deceit. Each prisoner knows, and knows that the other knows, that silence is best *only* if both remain silent: silence is the worst if the other confesses. Both prisoners will have the payoff matrix before them and zero in on silence—silence is a coordination of interests to minimize losses.

But each will also know that the other is doing the idéntical calculations and each will decide to double-cross the other: "he thinks I will be silent but I will confess in order to be set free." However, each know that the other is doing the same, and each knows that the other knows, and each knows . . . so they then face a true dilemma. This situation would be totally different if the motive for deceit were not present but it is a true dilemma when the motive exists. Even if these prisoners could communicate their intentions—either face-to-face or through the interrogator—each might not believe the other (it would be a perfect set-up for A to lure B into believing A would be silent) and the interrogator's messages (A has confessed—you had better confess also) may not be believed. The dilemma exists because what appears to be rational action is irrational and what is irrational (confess) becomes rational. The reader is invited to reproduce the Prisoner's Dilemma situation and note the results.[15]

Some possible political examples of two-person, non-0-sum games would be the settlement in Vietnam. Limiting the decision-making units to the United States and North Vietnam (the situation would be an n-person game if South Vietnam and the Viet Cong were included), one sees that both sides "won" (or "lost" less than they could have lost): North Vietnam had its territory and population devastated by the American bombardments but it "won" South Vietnam; the United States "lost" South Vietnam but, in turn, "won" back domestic unity. Another example of a two-person, non-0-sum game would be Richard Nixon's unsuccessful attempts to appoint Clement Haynesworth and G. Harold Carswell to the U.S. Supreme Court. Limiting the decision-making units to the president and the Senate, it is plausible to argue that both sides "won": the president for appealing to the Southern vote (it was not *his* fault the Senate rejected his nominees) and the Senate for rejecting nominees perceived to be unqualified.

N-Person, Non-0-Sum Game. This type of game is defined as a situation in which there are three or more decision-making units and in which there is a nonconstant sum (the winnings do not equal the losings). N-person, non-0-sum games often involve the use of coalition theory—who will join up with whom? for how long? against whom? how will the coalition share the payoffs?—and coalition theory is as mathematical as game theory and thus is not discussed in these introductory comments. Those interested in n-person games should read Anatol Rapoport's *N-Person Game Theory;* although Rapoport's book is not for the mathematically naive.

Rapoport does, however, present a verbal description of a most insidious n-person game termed "So Long Sucker" and this game will make the most ethical player turn against his friends.[16] Briefly, "So Long Sucker" is a pleasant after-dinner parlor game in which four people participate with cards and chips. There is only one winner—the person who still has chips left at the end of the game. The problem is, however, that in order to knock the first player out of the game, three people have to form a coalition and coordinate their moves; to knock the second player out, two people have to form a coalition; the third player is eliminated head-to-head. "So Long Sucker" probably gets its lovely name from the practice of luring a trusting player into believing he is part of a winning coalition when, in fact, he is the object of a double cross. "So Long Sucker" needs very little material to play and it is a most vicious, deceitful, and delightful evening's activity.

*Concepts and Principles of Game Theory Applied
to the Cuban Missile Crisis of October 1962*

The above discussion presented the rudimentary principles of game theory and this section is concerned with the analysis and explanation of a specific political event—the confrontation between the United States and the Soviet Union in the fall of 1962 regarding the installation of offensive ballistic missiles in Cuba. This specific event is approached within the general game theory framework.[17] The actual historical events of that month, still vivid in the minds of people who even today can see John Kennedy on television one October day announcing a naval quarantine of Cuba and waiting for the Soviet response (run the blockade? submit to a search? sink the American ships?), can be briefly presented.

In April 1961, eighteen months before the crisis, a group of American-trained Cuban exiles landed at the Bay of Pigs in Cuba in an attempt to overthrow the Castro regime. The Bay of Pigs episode was a complete military and political fiasco for the United States. The civilian population did not greet the exile force as liberators but, rather, as enemies. The landing party was quickly rounded up by the Cuban military forces (the U.S. did not supply any air support although it is doubtful whether air support short of strategic bombing would have made any difference) and the Bay of Pigs episode served to increase an already very high level of tension between the United States and Cuba.

After the Bay of Pigs, Cuba with aid from the Soviet Union in the form of material and technicians, began to strengthen its armed forces and military capabilities. We are not attempting to impute motives at this point although Cuba probably believed that the United States would not be adverse to launching another attempt to overthrow the Castro regime. Around the end of August 1962, a reconnaissance overflight of Cuba by a U-2 secured photographic evidence that several SAM (surface-to-air missiles) sites had been installed by the Soviet Union in various parts of Cuba. This did not arouse much alarm at first because SAMs are obviously and patently *defensive* weapons to be fired, like antiaircraft batteries, at incoming attacking aircraft. These SAMs are, of course, more sophisticated and efficient than the antiaircraft batteries of World War II fame but their function is identical: SAMs cannot be targeted for Miami or Dallas and fired from Havana nor can they be leveled and fired at a fortified position.

But the Pentagon and the CIA had reason to believe that the SAM sites were intended for a strategic use other than repelling another invasion attempt by the United States. The U-2 overflights were continued throughout September and October and these reconnaissance flights were equipped with cameras so sophisticated that a newspaper headline would be legible from an altitude of ten miles! On October 14, the U-2 flight photographed a squarish-looking cleared area with a SAM site at each corner. The interior of this area contained missile erectors, launchers, transporters, and long cylindrical shapes covered with a canvas-like material. The interpretation of these photographs was obvious: the SAM sites had been installed not to repel any invasion attempt but, rather, as protection for short-range ballistic missile launching sites. These missiles had a range of approximately 1,000 miles, and therefore most of the heavily populated Eastern seaboard of the United States would be within easy reach.

The crisis came to a breaking point on October 22, 1962. Kennedy's televised speech was on October 22, and he described the facts as perceived by the United States and the American response. It was not until the president had confronted the Soviet ambassador with the photographs that the Soviet Union publicly admitted to have the missile sites in Cuba; several short-range missile sites (1,000 miles) were close to being completed and several intermediate range sites (2,000 miles) were in various preliminary stages. Long-range Soviet Ilyushin jet bombers were being uncrated and assembled in Cuba and the airfields to handle these long-range bombers were also being prepared. Kennedy announced that the United States regarded these developments as a direct threat to the entire Western Hemisphere—the 2,000-mile missiles could saturate an area from Canada to Peru—and that these missiles would have to be dismantled and removed.

The first option chosen by the United States was to set up a naval quarantine of Cuba with orders to the Navy to turn back any ship bound for Cuba containing a cargo of offensive weaponry. Other cargoes (nonoffensive weaponry) could pass through to Cuba and although the quarantine applied to any ship, it was obvious to all that it was directed at the Soviet Union. The Soviet response was predictable: it at first denied that any missiles were in Cuba and then it was reported that Khrushchev sent an indirect message to Kennedy warning the U.S. that, if any Soviet ships were stopped in international waters, Russian submarines would fire on the American ships!

The die was cast and one could only wait in agonizing suspense for what would transpire: would the Soviets attempt to sail the proscribed weaponry to Cuba? Would a Soviet ship allow the Americans to search it? Would the Americans fire on a Soviet ship? Would the Soviets retaliate and deploy their submarines? Most attention was directed toward the Soviet Union for the United States had made its first move with Kennedy's speech (demanding the dismantling of the missiles and announcing the establishment of the quarantine) and the entire crisis *appeared* to revolve around Khrushchev: would the Soviet Union back down and comply with Kennedy or would war result?

After more than a decade, it now appears that the preliminaries described above were more exciting than the actual outcome. There was a flurry of diplomatic activity between the United States and the Soviet Union for the rest of October and well into November. The hot line between Washington and Moscow permitted immediate communication and thus, at least with regard to the communication variable, the missile crisis was reflective of the two men locked in the leaky cellar and not akin to the Prisoner's Dilemma and the latter's absence of communication. The Soviet Union did not attempt to send offensive weaponry through to Cuba once the blockade/quarantine was announced nor did the U.S. board any ship or mount an air/ground strike against Cuba. Both sides knew that refusal to bargain or coordinate would result in a nuclear World War III; both sides would "lose" such a war; and each knew that the other knew that both sides had to cooperate. This situation is very analogous to the two men trapped in the cellar for each had to cooperate and each had to synchronize his activities with the other in order to be saved. If one of the men in the cellar had double-crossed the other (the Soviet Union firing the missiles or the United States bombing Moscow would be similar to one of the men refusing to push on the trapdoor), both would have died.

By October 28, a compromise solution was reached in this highly dangerous and volatile conflict situation. The crisis was "solved" through the bargaining process: the Soviet missiles in Cuba would be dismantled and removed, U.S. missiles in Turkey would be dismantled and removed, the Iluyshin jet bombers would be recrated and removed, and the United States would publicly pledge not to repeat an action like the Bay of Pigs (either supporting an invasion by Cuban exile forces or mounting a U.S. air strike/ground invasion). It was not until December 6 that the last Iluyshin bomber was crated and put aboard a Soviet ship. The crisis was terminated.

The crisis was over but why did it have the particular resolution described above? Why didn't the United States insist upon the removal of the missiles *without* giving the noninvasion pledge? Why didn't the Soviet Union insist that the missiles remain in Cuba and *threaten* their actual use unless the U.S. performed a specific act such as an allied withdrawal from West Berlin? An after-the-fact analysis of this crisis employing the concepts and principles of game theory will hopefully show some of the reasons for the actual events, rather than having to rely upon some vague explanatory construct such as "both sides wanted to avoid war" or "the Soviets were cowards when the chips were down."

The Cuban missile crisis is examined as a two-person (Castro and Cuba are not involved), non-0-sum game. As mentioned above, the winnings of one do not have to equal the losings of the other—both could win or both could lose—in non-0-sum situations. The specific type employed here is that both sides had a positive final payoff from the crisis: both sides won or both sides had "more" at the end of the crisis than they had at the onset. It is quite possible that the individual decision-makers in Washington and Moscow performed a similar cost-benefit accounting to the various options open to them as we are doing here. There are, however, three crucial points to keep in mind. First, the "game" begins for each player when he determines that it begins or when he starts to play—there is no starter's gun to signal an identical starting time for each side. Second, each player assigns or is capable of assigning different payoff values to the identical move or option. Signing the non-invasion pledge could have represented a different payoff value to the United States than it did to the Soviet Union (it most certainly had a different payoff value to the Cubans). Third, we assume each side was playing the same game (non-0-sum), both sides were willing to bargain, and each side knew that the other knew what type of game was in progress. If one side had approached this conflict situation as a 0-sum game (what is mine is mine and what is yours is negotiable) while the other side saw it as a non-0-sum game (everything is negotiable), the crisis probably would not have had the result as it actually had.

The reader can, of course, make the "game" come out any way he chooses simply by manipulating the payoff values we arbitrarily assign to each move. If one believes that the Soviet Union "lost" this particular game, the reader can alter the value and have the Soviet Union lose. But it is probably much closer to reality to describe the crisis as a two-person, non-0-sum game in which both sides "won" and this is the approach employed. Table 4.1 contains the assigned payoff values to each country for the various actual moves in the crisis. Table 4.1 is not a payoff matrix but, rather, only a simple listing of the moves actually pursued and the values for each move.

Table 4.1
Hypothetical Payoff Values in the Cuban Missile Crisis

		USA	USSR
1.	Missiles Installed in Cuba	−150	+150
2.	Missiles Removed from Cuba	+400	−250
3.	Missiles in Turkey	0	− 25
4.	Missiles Removed from Turkey	0	+ 75
5.	Ilyushin Bombers in Cuba	− 50	+ 50
6.	Ilyushin Bombers Removed from Cuba	+ 50	− 50
7.	Noninvasion Pledge	−50	+200
	Final Payoff	+200	+150

It is first necessary, however, to have some discussion as to the meaning of the numerical values assigned to the options as presented in Table 4.1. These numerical values represent an undefined total amount of the value each side perceives in each specific tactic or move. Part, but not all, of the components which make up this score are prestige, military capability, standing with other countries, respect, domestic support-discontent, and honor. These concepts are impossible to adequately define and measure given the nature of this presentation and thus the actual numbers in Table 4.1 signify or represent our arbitrary amount of the above qualities or characteristics. These values are symbolic analytical devices necessary to game theory and, while they can be compared internally (-150 for the United States is identical to -150 for the Soviet Union), they do not represent any absolute values which could be compared to some external maximum amount.

Missiles Installed in Cuba
(U.S.: -150; U.S.S.R.: $+150$)

The United States is assigned a loss (-150) for this particular act because the installation of the missiles in Cuba *did* represent a loss for the United States! There was an immediate and obvious loss in military defense capabilities: a weaker bargaining position vis-à-vis the Soviet Union and a loss in domestic support for the Kennedy administration (the Republican opposition constantly referred to offensive weapons only ninety miles from our shore). The Soviet Union is assigned the arbitrary value of $+150$ units: increased military capabilities, a very effective bargaining chip, and increased prestige in the eyes of client states (Cuba).

The reader should recall the discussion above in Chapter 1 on sanctions and threats: the Soviets might very well have missiles so that the United States would be aware of their existence. The Soviet Union made no attempt to camouflage the missile bases and, moreover, no attempt was made to shoot down any of the U-2s prior to the discovery and publicity about the missiles.[15] The Soviet Union certainly had the capability of tracking and hitting a U-2 for only a few years earlier, Gary

Francis Powers was shot down in his U-2 during a flight over the Soviet Union. A persuasive argument could be that the missiles were *never* intended to be used except as a bargaining ploy and this proof of their existence in Cuba had to be available to the United States. What use is a missle base in a bargaining situation if the other side doubts its reality? It would have been a totally irrational policy for the Soviet Union to install the missiles in complete secrecy and then attempt to force certain American behavior by threatening to use the missiles. The United States would not believe the threatened sanction and thus the Soviet goal (action *without* having to fire the missiles) would not be achieved. It is, of course, an entirely different question if the Soviets had simply wanted to fire off the missiles rather than employing them as a bargaining tool. But if this were the case, one has to wonder why the Soviets did not attempt to cloak the missiles in greater secrecy.

Missiles Removed from Cuba
(U.S.: +400: U.S.S.R.: −250)

The United States not only regained the 150 units it originally lost when the missiles were first installed, but also gained an additional 250 units for "standing up" to the Russians, for allowing the Soviets a graceful exit and thus preventing war, for choosing the relatively nonviolent naval quarantine in place of a ground invasion or airstrike, for increasing American prestige among its allies by showing the United States had the will to back up its statements and commitments. The Soviet Union is assigned −250 units for removing the missiles: the original 150 was lost and the additional loss of 100 units is for first appearing to be reckless (even the Chinese mentioned that the Soviets pushed the world to the brink of war) and then for capitulating or caving in to the American demands (would the Soviets keep *their* commitments to other countries now that they reneged on the deal with Castro?) But the U.S.S.R. did not lose more than our arbitrary −250 units because the very fact of "caving in" to the Americans made the U.S.S.R. appear as also wanting to avoid a nuclear war and for having the ability to recognize mistakes and back off from untenable positions.

Missiles in Turkey
(U.S.: 0; U.S.S.R.: −25)

The American Jupiter missiles in Turkey were installed by the United States prior to the Cuban missile crisis and thus did not immediately enter into the possible options. However, when the Soviet Union began to include these missiles in *its* calculations, the Turkish missile sites became relevant for the United States. We assign a value of 0 to the United States for having these missiles for, by 1962, they just did not represent a gain or positive position for the United States. The Jupiter missiles most certainly provided a positive payoff value when they were first installed but the Cuban "game" for the United States begins long after the original installation. Our analysis, however, says that the Russians took these missiles into their calculations from the beginning and, in a sense, we can say that the Soviets began the Cuban game when the Americans installed the missiles in Turkey.

The United States receives a value of 0 for having these missiles because they were obsolete by 1962. The earlier generation of missiles required a rather long time delay between the order to fire and the actual lift-off. By 1962, the Soviet Union had the capability to knock out these missiles long before they could be airborne. The actual military gain to the United States was quite small and one could, although we shall not do so here, argue that the presence of the missiles in Turkey represented a loss for the United States: the United States was spending millions of dollars to maintain obsolete missiles.

The Soviet Union receives a value of −25 units for the presence of the U.S. missiles in Turkey. The military defense capability was not compromised in 1962 but the same arguments employed above for the American perception of Soviet missiles in Cuba are relevant here. The Soviets could employ the identical "offensive weaponry only 90 miles from *our* border" and thus perceived their payoff as negative.

Missiles Removed from Turkey
(U.S.: 0; U.S.S.R.: +75)

Since the presence of the missiles in Turkey did not represent a gain for the United States, their removal is not seen as a loss. And if one accepts the argument above (that the missiles actually had a negative payoff), their removal would have represented a gain. The Soviet Union receives a $+75$ units for this move: 25 as compensation for the actual previous loss, and an extra 50 for increased domestic content (obsolete or not, there were no longer missiles ninety miles from the Soviet border) and for a slightly increased military capability (Soviet missiles that previously had to be targeted for the Jupiters could now be retargeted for more promising areas).

Ilyushin Bombers In/Out of Cuba
(U.S.: -50, $+50$; U.S.S.R.: $+50$, -50)

This set of transactions is regarded as a peripheral move without any inherent payoffs. This move was an internal standoff: each player valued the move in identical amounts and the total payoff value for the set equals 0 for both sides.

Noninvasion Pledge
(U.S.: -50; U.S.S.R.: $+200$)

The Bay of Pigs fiasco probably convinced the United States that Cuba was going to survive and that any subsequent invasion would meet stiff opposition from the military forces *and* from the civilian population. The majority of the Cuban people were simply not straining at the yoke of what the United States perceived to be totalitarianism and they would support the Castro regime from external invasion. With this interpretation, the United States, by signing the pledge not to support or mount another invasion, gave up very little. The United States, however, most certainly did "lose" something from this exchange because the pledge restricted American options. The pledge also increased domestic discontent and opposition to the Kennedy administration. The Republican opposition simply changed its charge from one of "offensive missiles ninety miles from our shore" to "a Communist regime only ninety miles from our shore." But the pledge did not substantially prevent the United States from pursuing previously decided policies toward Cuba such as the trade embargo, withholding diplomatic recognition, and maintaining Cuba's isolation and ostracism within the U.S.-dominated Organization of American States

(OAS). The value of -50 is assigned in order to symbolize the "loss" coming from the "soft on Communism" charge.

The Soviet Union, on the other hand, perceived receipt of the pledge in quite different terms than the U.S. had in giving it. The U.S.S.R. is assigned a payoff value of $+200$ because Castro's existence and survival was assured and the United States would put an (official) end to the constant harassment raids by the Cuban exiles. It is entirely possible that this goal, Cuba's survival as a Soviet client state, was the actual overriding Russian objective from the beginning: employing the missiles to force the United States to "recognize" the Castro regime.

Total Winnings/Losings
(U.S.: $+200$; U.S.S.R.: $+150$)

As stated above, the assigned utilities are arbitrary (but logical) and the values are open to question. But the crisis should be approached as a non-0-sum game and not as a 0-sum game. The United States, if playing a 0-sum, would have demanded the removal of the missiles without themselves removing the Jupiter missiles or signing the pledge. The Soviet Union, if playing a 0-sum, would have demanded the removal of the Jupiters and the signing of the pledge without themselves removing the missiles in Cuba. Both sides "won" the game and, in our example, the United States "won" more than the Soviet Union ($+200$ to $+150$). But it is very plausible to have the Soviet Union "winning" more than the United States—all one has to do is to interpret the missiles as a bargaining ploy to achieve the pledge. If this were the case, the Soviet Union would not have lost so much for withdrawing the missiles and would have gained more than they did for receipt of the pledge. The point is, in any case, each player had different goals and they were able to coordinate their moves in order to maximize their winnings.

What is necessary for a successful real-life game, successful such as the Cuban missile crisis where losses were minimized and both sides "won," is that both sides must have as precise and complete information as possible as to the utilities each player assigns to the various options. To the extent that this information is available, game theory can be applied to situations such as the missile crisis where one side can reason that "if we do x, it will cost them 10 units but that is an acceptable loss for they will then do y for +20 units." But this information is not always available and game theory cannot be indiscriminately applied to all political conflict behaviors.

But game theory is an excellent methodological approach to analyze some real-life conflict situations and the reader is invited to assign some utilities, strategies, goals, and moves to, say, President Nixon's futile attempt to seat Clement Haynesworth and G. Harold Carswell on the U.S. Supreme Court, the disengagement agreements between Israel and Egypt, and, to be very complicated, a three-person situation between the United States, the U.S.S.R., and China. The mathematics involved, purposely omitted from this presentation, are quite complicated when it is an n-person, non-0-sum game with mixed strategies; the utilities and probabilities are in a constant state of flux and it is only through mathematical notation that all the possible outcomes and preferences can be expressed.

Engineering, Simulation, and World War I

A third area from which political science has borrowed conceptual frameworks and techniques is engineering and its methods of modeling and simulation. Political science is not the only discipline to have adapted simulation techniques to its own particular needs. History has made some use of simulation but business management, economics, psychology, and sociology have employed simulation on an extensive scale within their own areas. This section first presents some concepts and principles of simulation and then presents an example of the applicability of simulation techniques to political science with an attempt to re-create the outbreak of World War I.

Concepts, Principles, and Terminology of Simulation[19]

Simulation and modeling techniques originated in the field of aeronautical engineering although the techniques have a wide applicability. In aeronautical engineering, models of planes would be constructed and then placed in a wind tunnel in order to study, say, the effects of wind currents on various structural aspects of the proposed aircraft. Simulation is also employed in other areas: models of bridges are constructed and then subjected to water and wind currents in order to study the stability of the bridge; the major airline companies have extensive training facilities with model cockpits in which the pilot in training "learns" how to fly the plane; even the entertainment industry employs simulation with the coin-operated machines which recreate an automobile on a highway.

All simulations have something in common: they are various forms of a model and, in return to the discussion above with Anthony Downs, models have the appearance of reality without being real. The model or simulation is a representation of reality without its essence. The wind tunnel reproduces real air currents but it is not reality: a real plane is not flying in an actual wind at 35,000 feet with a live pilot. Many simulations contain the characteristic of deception: various plants and animals "simulate" their environment so that their enemies will not see them. Those students who watched the television program "Mission Impossible" should at once remember that the IMF team always attained their goal by deceiving the villain into thinking that the simulated situation was the real thing (e.g., what appeared to be a submarine stuck on the bottom of the Atlantic with its air supply running out was, in reality, a stage prop on a concrete parking lot someplace in New York City). Social science simulations, however, are not meant to deceive and there is very little deception in political science's use of simulation.

But this by no means implies that chicanery and deceit are totally absent in social and behavioral academic use of simulation. There is a danger with unethical simulations and one of the most flagrant abuses of individual rights recently came to light with the publication of Professor Stanley Milgram's book *Obedience to Authority*.[20] Milgram's experiments were conducted while he was a member of the psychology department at Yale University. There was a public announcement inserted in the local New Haven newspapers with the headlines "Persons needed for a study of memory" and "We will pay you $4.00

for one hour of your time." People did volunteer and more than a thousand people took part over the time span of the experiment. The participants *thought* they were assisting in a memory-learning process but they were, in fact, subject-victims.

The scenario of Milgram's study is as follows. The volunteers were brought into a laboratory containing the usual intimidating scientific equipment and introduced to another "volunteer" and the "experimenter." The unsuspecting volunteer believes that the second volunteer is a person like himself, a person who answered the ad, but this was the first hoax. The second "volunteer" was not what he appeared to be. This person was a member of Milgram's investigating team who knew what was about to happen. The real volunteer was selected to be the "teacher" in this "memory" experiment and the plant was chosen to be the learner.

The "experimenter" explained to the "teacher" and "learner" that the experiment was concerned with the effects of punishment on the learning process. The fake "learner" is strapped into a chair and an electrode is attached to his wrist. The real volunteer is then seated in front of an "impressive shock generator." This generator has thirty switches, ranging from 15 to 450 volts. These switches also have descriptions such as "SLIGHT SHOCK" and "DANGER—SEVERE SHOCK." Then the teacher is told to administer a learning test to the person strapped in the chair: if the learner answers correctly, the teacher goes to the next question. However, every time the learner misses a question, the teacher is to administer the electric shock. These shocks start at 15 volts and, each time an "error" is made, increases at 15 volt intervals until the thirtieth mistake when the full 450 volts is given.

The "teacher" thinks this is the real thing but in actuality it is a simulation, a deception. Not one of the "teachers" refused to participate and the questions were given. The fake learner was a superb actor: he missed enough questions in order to give the teacher the opportunity to apply the shocks. The "experiment" begins and "at 75 volts, the 'learner' grunts. At 120 volts he complains verbally; at 150 he demands to be released from the experiment. His protests continue as the shocks escalate, growing increasingly vehement and emotional. At 285 volts his response can only be described as an agonized scream."[21]

Milgram's hidden interest, obedience to authority, enters at this point. To what extent would the "teacher" obey the commands of the experimenter and administer the (fake) shocks to the learner? The actual results are simply frightening! Approximately two-thirds of the "teachers" obeyed commands and administered the full 450 volts. A modified form of the experiment had the "learner" with a "bad heart" and he would shout and scream about chest pains. But, again, approximately two-thirds of the volunteers continued to press the switches and administer the (simulated) shocks. This is not the place to discuss the import of Milgram's findings except to note that the behavior of the Nazis in the extermination camps during World War II might appear more understandable when a cross-section of New Haven citizens followed and obeyed the experimenter's commands to administer the full 450 volts. The reader is encouraged to read Milgram's book to fully appreciate the nature of his ugly and obscene findings.

What we are more interested in here, however, is the nature of the experiment and not the findings. The "teachers" totally and completely believed it was the real thing—real shocks and real pain—although it was an elaborate simulated hoax. There are dangers with such unethical simulations: Milgram did not take any precautions in protecting the volunteers from what might have been severe consequences of their behavior. The volunteers were in a conflict and stress environment and probably did not realize what [they thought] they were doing. What does Milgram do with the feeling of guilt, shame, remorse, and, perhaps, psychological dislocations in people who believed they acted similar to Adolf Eichmann?—the experiment itself came to be known in academic circles as the "Eichmann Experiment." Hoax, fraud, and deceit are very entertaining for the Mission Impossible devotees because it is only the archvillain who is roughed up; unsuspecting people who answer ads in New Haven are not to be similarly treated. Social science simulations can and have been severely misused and any simulation which involves human participants must have as first priority the protection of the participants.

A second inherent danger with simulations with human participants is perhaps as frightening as the deception described above: the participants may very well "forget" that whatever they are doing is only a representation of reality and behave as if it *were* the real thing. A favorite simulation of social service departments within the area of corrections involves the re-creation of a prison situation. Some of the students portray the guards and others portray the prisoners. This type of simulation, when done properly, is an excellent teaching tool, and gives insight into the problems of penal administration and correction techniques. But, and this has happened, the "guards" and "prisoners" drift away from the re-creation of reality and enter reality itself. The "guards" behave as if they were real guards in a real prison and engage in all sorts of nasty behavior, particularly toward the prisoners; the prisoners also behave as if they were real prisoners and they, too, engage in nasty behavior, particularly toward the other prisoners. The experimenter or the researcher must pay close attention and if the subjects drift into reality, the simulation should be terminated.

Although simulations with human participants contain inherent dangers, they can be run without harm to the subjects if sufficient care is taken. Simulations—those with and without human subjects—*can* be employed to achieve honorable goals and those goals are *design, development of knowledge,* and *teaching/training.*

The first purpose of simulation is design: a simulation helps in the improvement of existing systems and can aid in the creation of new and better systems. A model airplane in a wind tunnel is perhaps the best example here. The model is studied in the wind tunnel and if any defects surface, these malfunctions can be remedied before the aircraft is put onto the assembly line. A second purpose of simulation is the development of a body of knowledge: theories and hypotheses can be tested over and over again with simulations and thus add to a specific body of knowledge. The third goal of simulation is teaching and training: pilots, drivers, and even the astronauts "learn" by simulating an event which has not yet happened but is expected to occur. Training simulations attempt to anticipate a real-life event and train the participants how to react or behave once the real-life situation occurs. Teaching simulations are an excellent pedagogical tool with which to convey information and understanding: a student who only reads about, say, the U.N. General Assembly would probably have less understanding of the U.N.'s deliberative process than a student who participated in one of the many model U.N. meetings conducted in the United States. These model U.N.'s have students portraying the various national delegates and it is an excellent teaching method.

But training simulations and, although to a lesser extent, teaching simulations have a major drawback and it is at this point that a very serious criticism of simulation enters. The participants *know* it is only a simulation, not a real-life situation, and thus quite often behave in a manner differently than they would in real life. For example, a Pentagon simulation of some crisis event (we could even say that the Cuban missile crisis is being imagined *before* it became a reality) would have the participants portraying various people: the U.S. president, the Soviet premier, their advisors, the military leaders. The simulation begins and the Americans "discover" missiles in Cuba. The scenario is played out except that the simulation did not anticipate real life: the Soviets sink a few American ships and nuclear war breaks out. What happens?—nothing! The participants in the simulation set off the missiles and bombs, notice that it is 5:00 P.M., turn off the lights, and head out the door for cocktails. "Let's go to war" is a very easy decision to make when one knows that at 5:00 P.M. everyone can go home; in real life this decision would be followed by real bombs and real explosions, particularly at the Pentagon.

This major problem is a defect with simulations employing human actors but the simulation cannot have it both ways. To have people act as if it were the real thing—hit the participants over the head with a club if they make the wrong decision, shoot the pilot in training if his plane "crashes," give the students electrical shocks if they are on the losing side or miscalculate— would move the situation out of simulation (re-creation of reality) and into real life. This is, in essence, what Milgram did for whatever guilt or psychic pain the "teachers" experienced after Milgram's experiment was the real thing and not simulated.

Such techniques—inflict real-life punishments on simulation participants—would indeed have the people act as if it were the real thing but such penalties cannot be applied even though the equivalent would occur in real life. Social science use of simulation with human participants is thus caught between two totally antagonistic poles: we would like to learn how people would act in a real-life situation and so we simulate but the simulation is not real life and our information may not be valid. But this is not to completely deny the usefulness or efficacy of social science simulations. Such simulations, when done properly, can provide useful information *and* remain only a re-creation of reality.

Simulations are thus employed for design, increased knowledge, and training/teaching. There are other ways to achieve these goals but simulation has four properties which render it particularly well-suited for these goals. These unique properties are *economy, visibility, reproducibility,* and *safety.* First is the issue of economy: it is most of the time simply less expensive to study some question or process through a simulation or model than to study it in its real form. It is, for example, cheaper to build a model plane than the real thing and savings in cost also enter if mistakes in design can be discovered and eliminated in the simulation rather than having to wait for the real thing. The engineers can place the model plane in the wind tunnel, turn on the wind, and see whether the wings stay on. If it works, fine; if not, all that is lost is a relatively inexpensive model and not the real thing.

The second advantage to simulation is visibility: one can abstract out certain segments of reality and make them more accessible to testing. For example, it is simply more accessible and visible to study the stress on a certain bolt in a plane's tail section in a wind tunnel than having to chase a real plane at 600 m.p.h.; it is more accessible to study the effects of zero gravity in a chamber on earth than having to transport men and material to the moon.

The third advantage to simulation is reproducibility: a simulation can be run over and over again whereas the real situation exists only for a fleeting moment in time. Separate variables can be added in or deleted in a predetermined order, something that may or may not occur in real life, and the variables themselves can be changed in the simulation. For example, assume the goal of a particular computer simulation is to estimate the number of people killed and the area destroyed in a large American city during a nuclear attack. The real-life situation could only be studied *once*—it would not be a simulation—and all the different variables which affect casualties and damage would be frozen in time. The simulation could be run over and over again and the variables could be changed at will.

Some of the variables relevant to our hypothetical nuclear attack simulation study on deaths and damage would be the time of day of the attack, day of week, the month, wind speed, wind direction, topological characteristics such as mountains, population density, building construction material (wood, brick, concrete), number and placement of fallout shelters, warning time, number of missiles launched, the size of the missiles' warheads, number of missiles shot down before reaching the city, distance that impact is from the target, and the number of missiles that actually detonate. A change in any one of these variables would affect the results and the simulation is able to run numerous studies, each with a different combination of values assigned to the variables.

The fourth advantage to simulation is safety: safety in the sense that people are not put into dangerous situations (the pilot in training in a mockup cockpit will not actually crash and die if the plane "crashes" during the simulation) and safety in the sense that dangerous situations can be studied without having to create the real thing (the example above with a nuclear attack). This safety advantage is, however, open to the criticism mentioned above: the participants know it is not the real thing and may behave differently in the simulation. This criticism is balanced out, though, by the very characteristic of safety: the participants *are* protected from dangerous situations and they very well might be better able to handle the real-life situation when and if it occurs.

There are certain terms and expressions in simulation and the following is a very brief listing of some of the more important terms. A *man-machine* simulation is a simulation in which human decision-makers and machines (usually computers although not necessarily) interact in the process of re-creation. Computers often serve as an integral part of the decision-making process in simulations and since they calculate faster than people, the simulation can re-create reality in less time than it would take the real situation to transpire. A *pure machine simulation* does not have any human decision-makers and the entire process is carried out by the machine (the computer in the nuclear attack example above, a model plane in a wind tunnel, a mock-up of a building on a vibrator to simulate an earthquake). A *pure man simulation* has no machines and the entire process is conducted by human decision-makers. *Real-time simulation* is when the simulated activity takes as long to conduct as its real-life counterpart. Real-time simulation can be contrasted to simulations where the time is either extended or compressed from what the real activity would normally require. Many simulations employ compressed time: to simulate a flight to Mars in real time is a waste of resources; to simulate the effects of wind and water erosion on a dike or breakwater would take centuries if run in real time. High tides would occur every ten seconds or so in the simulation rather than every twelve hours. The *Monte Carlo Method* is a particular process of simulation that includes probability distribution and chance happenings in the procedure.

The above section presented a very brief introduction to simulation. The following section presents an application of simulation techniques to the social sciences and political science. This particular simulation is pure man, compressed time, and the real-life event being analyzed is the outbreak of World War I.

An Attempt to Simulate the Outbreak of World War I

One of the most interesting uses of simulation techniques in political science is Charles F. and Margaret C. Hermann's attempt to simulate the outbreak of World War I.[22] Whereas many simulations attempt to peer into the future and anticipate an event (what will we do if they do . . . ?), this particular simulation employed an actual historical situation as a means to validate simulations. Validation in simulation refers to the process by which one can honestly describe the simulation as basically having the same characteristics of the real-life event: does one really know that a simulation is re-creating that small segment of reality that is undergoing study? The basic goal to the Hermanns' study, therefore, was to test or validate the very essence of simulation—does the simulation produce similar events to those which actually happened? If this is the goal, an anticipated future event cannot be employed for obvious reasons. With simulation validation, only past events, where a good deal of information is available, can be employed. But there were additional purposes to the Hermanns' study besides validation. The attempt to simulate the outbreak of World War I also studied the relationship between personality characteristics and political decisions, as well as providing an excellent teaching tool for the students to learn about the events immediately before World War I.

Procedure. Five nations were represented in the simulation "runs." These countries were England, France, Germany, Tsarist Russia, and Austria-Hungary. Each country had two decision-makers to represent it as well as a messenger to receive and deliver the diplomatic communications. The Hermanns attempted to use participants whose personality traits were as close as possible to the personality traits of the real-life decision-makers of 1914. This involved three steps: (1) a limited number of historical figures who participated in the real event had to be identified and selected; (2) these historical figures' personality traits had to be described; and (3) the participants in the simulation had to be selected who had similar or approximate personality traits.

The Hermanns' resources limited the number of participants to ten for each run (the simulation was run two times) and thus ten people per country had to be selected. The messengers were only information conduits and were not "participants." The Hermanns employed three criteria to select ten historical real-life decision-makers: these people had to dominate the foreign policy decisions of their country, had to receive and send the diplomatic cables, and the Hermanns had to have enough personal information available in order to construct the personality traits.[23] The following actual historical figures were selected: Austria-Hungary—Berchtold (Minister for Foreign Affairs) and Conrad (Chief of the General Staff); England—Grey (Secretary of State for Foreign Affairs) and Nicolson (Permanent Under-Secretary of State for Foreign Affairs); France—Poincaré (President of the Republic) and Berthelot (Acting Political Director of the Foreign Ministry); Germany—Wilhelm II (Kaiser) and Bethmann-Hollweg (Chancellor); and Tsarist Russian—Nicholas II (Tsar) and Sazonov (Minister for Foreign Affairs).

A content analysis was then performed on the personal letters, diaries, autobiographies, and biographies of these ten real people in order to discover some of their psychological traits. The Hermanns write that dominance, self-acceptance, and self-control were common to all ten. The subsequent stage involved "matching" the volunteer participants with a real-life personality. Approximately 100 high school students were given the California Psychological Inventory (CPI) and the psychological profile of each student generated by the CPI was compared to the profile of each of the ten historical figures. These students were not aware of the reason for the CPI but this was a very insignificant and totally nondamaging deception. The actual participants were "deceived" later on in the simulation but, as will be shown below, this deceit was legally, ethically, and academically acceptable.

Ten students, the ones who most closely matched the historical figures, were chosen, but only six could actually participate in the simulation. Five of these first choices participated in the morning run (M-run) and the sixth in the afternoon run (A-run). The remaining fourteen participants were second and third choices and since the major criterion of selection was similar personality traits, the participants' sex was not considered (there were four girls in the M-run and three in the A-run).

The students who were selected as participants were then introduced to the actual historical situation. The Hermanns write that a fundamental dilemma was faced with this attempt to provide the participants with historical information. Too much of the right kind of information would have enabled the observant and aware student participant to discover what the real event was and thus void the primary aim of the entire study. The participants were *not* supposed to know that they were simulating the outbreak of World War I because the study's goal was to see *if* they could re-create a situation like the one that existed in the summer of 1914. But if the content of the supplied information were drastically altered, or if vastly misleading or false information were supplied, the basic characteristics of the real event would have been so distorted that it would have been impossible to call the simulation a representation of reality. If such a simulation had any resemblance to reality it would be due more to chance than to any inherent characteristic of the simulation and similar results here could not be employed to validate simulations.

There is no one easy solution to this problem when the participants are expected to re-create an event but are not allowed to know what event is being simulated. This problem is not present in all simulations because many simulations require the total absence of false or misleading components in order to achieve its particular goal (a model plane in a wind tunnel, for example). The Hermanns' approach was that they "misled" the participants into thinking that a real event was not being re-created but, rather, that only some hypothetical future event was being analyzed.

This misleading was done in order to avoid the possibility that the high school participants would try to match their simulated event with a real-life situation and then act according to what actually happened in real life. The names of all individuals, countries, and alliance groupings were falsified: England was called Bega, France was Colo, Russia was Enuk, Serbia was Gior (Gior was not a represented country but was the focal point of the entire situation and had to be identified in messages), and the Triple Entente was the Tri-Agreement. Thus, in place of a real communication which might have stated that "England, France, and Russia formed the Triple Entente," the misleading message fed to the participants read "Bega, Colo, and Enuk formed a Tri-Agreement."

Deliberately misleading statements were also provided which tried to place the "imaginary" simulated event far more recent than the "real" event actually was. The Hermanns write that one example of a misleading statement was the deletion of the assassination of the Archduke (the actual event) and its replacement by a statement which led the participants into thinking that the event took place (or might have taken place) long after 1914. In the simulation, several officials from Austria-Hungary were killed by a strafing attack from a plane. The hope was that the participants would not focus on 1914 since strafing attacks were not a common characteristic of World War I. The Hermanns did not wish the participants' knoweldge of history to bias or influence their behavior and decisions once the simulation began.

Conducting the Simulation. Two separate runs were conducted (*M*orning and *A*fternoon), each with different participants. Each participant was placed in an individual cubicle and began to read the [misleading] information about the event as furnished by the Hermanns. The following information, altered as to names, dates, etc., was given to each participant: an annotated history of international affairs for some time before the summer of 1914; the domestic and foreign policies of the country each participant represented; a brief description of the personality makeup of the historical person each participant portrayed; and a relatively full set of (altered) messages and newspaper accounts for the interval between the assassination of the Archduke on June 28, 1914, and the Serbian reply to the ultimatum of July 25, 1914.[24] This information was given in the order of the actual 1914 occurrence and all participants did not have equal information (Enuk, for example, might not have known what Bega sent to Colo).

This preliminary segment of the simulation ended with what functions as the Austro-Hungarian ultimatum to Serbia on July 25, 1914. The participants were then told that they would have to continue the situation themselves for no additional information would be supplied—they had to handle the event as they saw fit. Each nation's participants were then placed together in a room (with an observer to prevent unauthorized discussion; e.g., discussion as to what they were actually doing) and a messenger was available to carry their messages to the other countries in the simulation. The simulation "began" and the five nations exchanged written communications.

Three 50-minute periods were conducted in sequence in both the M and A runs and each 50-minute period represented a twenty-four-hour day (July 26-27-28, 1914). However, the participants did not know that the simulation would last for only 150 minutes. They were deliberately misled into thinking a much longer time period would be simulated in order to force them into considering long-range factors and goals, something their real-life historical counterparts most certainly had to do. At the end of the 150 minutes, the participants were debriefed: they completed an extensive questionnaire and then described their reactions and activities. The messages generated by the students were also analyzed.

Results of the Simulation. The results of both simulation runs were tested for their validity on two different levels: (1) the actual macro event (war) and micro events (subsidiary happenings) of 1914 were used as standards in comparing the incidents generated in the simulations to real life; and (2) two general hypotheses, formulated independently of the simulation, were "tested" with data generated by the simulations.

The macro event used to validate the simulation was the outbreak of general war. In the real-life historical event, Austria-Hungary declared war on Serbia on July 28 (the last 50-minute period of the simulation represented July 28) and it was not until August 1 and soon thereafter (150 minutes of additional simulation time or three days of real time) that other declarations of war were issued. General war did not break out in either simulation run although the Hermanns write that "hostilities were imminent" in the M-run and that the equivalent of war would have been declared had the simulation lasted another one or two 50-minute periods (one or two real-time days).

The A-run had a completely different result on the macro level: hostilities were not at all imminent and the level of conflict and tension was lower at the end of the simulation than it had been at the start. The high school student representing the British Foreign Secretary Lord Grey—but it is to be noted that this student did not know he/she was portraying *Grey* of *England,* he/she was Mr. X of Bega—called for an international conference to discuss the crisis. It was with this point, the conference, that a significant difference occurred in the A-run as compared to the actual event: Austria-Hungary agreed to nego-tiate in the conference and withdrew its ultimatum to Serbia. The remainder of the A-run's time was then spent setting up and proceeding with this conference.

It was discovered in the postsimulation debriefing that the student portraying the Austro-Hungarian Chief of Staff, Conrad, was an internalized pacifist. These "pacifist tendencies" did not show up in this student's CPI profile. It is ironic that perhaps the most militaristic of the real historical figures, the Austro-Hungarian Chief of Staff, was portrayed by a pacifist. Conrad did not evidence any pacifist tendencies in *his* psychological-personality profile generated by the content analysis and it is certain that he would not have withdrawn the ultimatum to Serbia and agree to negotiate in 1914. This development prodded the Hermanns to comment that in simulations where validation is the main goal, there is a "need to match more closely the socio-political attitudes of the historical figures and the simulation participants."

The data generated by the simulation were also validated by comparing them to a whole series of smaller (micro) events which actually happened in 1914. There was practically no similarity between 1914 and the simulation in the A-run because of the problem mentioned above with the student portraying Conrad but the M-run's written messages were closely scruti-nized. By a process which need not be described here, the data generated by the M-run received 31 of 54 possible points when compared to the real historical events in timing, intent, and content. This score, 31 out of 54, cannot be judged high or low due to all the other factors and variables in the simulation which could have biased the results. It is interesting to note, however, that approximately 57 percent of the "events" generated by the high school students in the simulation also occurred in reality.

A second method employed to validate the simulation on the micro level was to use data generated by the simulation to test two hypotheses. These hypotheses were developed by other researchers independent of the Hermanns' study and these hy-potheses are based on the actual data of 1914. These two hy-potheses are: (1) the amount of communications sent *among* members of one bloc will be greater than the amount of com-

munication sent *between* blocs; and (2) the greater the threat
a country perceives, the less important its perception of capabilities becomes in a decision to go to war.[25] The M-run data
produced comparable results on these hypotheses as did the real
1914 data (the A-run did not) and thus can serve as another
test to validate the simulation.

Evaluation of the Simulation. The Hermanns write that
their attempts to disguise the actual event were not entirely successful. In the postsimulation debriefing, World War I was
identified by seven student participants to be either similar or
almost exact to the simulated crisis.[26] The problem is that to
disguise the actual event to such a degree that no one can
recognize it may, in fact, alter the situation so much that what
is being simulated is not the real event. Conversely, to furnish
detailed information about the real event may lead the participants to discover the actual situation and thus bias their responses. One way to solve this problem is to simulate an event
so obscure that perfect information can be given to the participants with very little chance of discovery. But obscure events
are obscure because there is very little available information
about them. It would have been impossible for the Hermanns
to construct a simulation with relevant messages and personality
studies of, say, a *coup d'état* in twelfth-century Afghanistan.

There is also the question whether a simulation participant
should play the role of the historical figure assigned to him or
her or should the participant be free to approach the decision-
making process in his own way. The Hermanns wanted the first
alternative but received the second with the quasi pacifist portraying Conrad. "Role playing" requires much more information
than self-structured activity but in studies such as the one described here, the more information available, the greater the
risk the real event will be discovered. This is not a problem in
all simulations involving human participants because all simulations do not attempt to keep the identity of the real situation a
secret. Many simulations, especially those which attempt to plan
for the future (war games, diplomatic scenarios), furnish complete information and the participants are expected to "role
play" and not carry out the simulation with self-structured
activity.

The attempt to simulate the outbreak of World War I is a fascinating use of simulation. This simulation made use of historical data and attempted to see whether a real event could be replicated (simulation validation). It is also an excellent teaching aid: the student participants in the M-run gained a much deeper understanding of the events immediately prior to the war than they would have gained only by textbook reading (the same cannot be said for the students in the A-run, however).

Simulation is an *excellent* teaching and explanatory tool in the social sciences; it is less useful for prediction in the social sciences because the participants *know* it is only a simulation and not a real-life situation. The participants do not suffer the same costs or punishments for their actions or misjudgments in the simulation that they would in a real-life situation and thus might take far greater risks than one would normally do. Simulation cannot be employed as a totally valid predictive tool in the social sciences until and unless the participants receive the same punishments for faulty judgment as they most certainly would in real life: an electric shock for the losers, a failing grade in the course. But participants *cannot* be given forty lashes or be clubbed over the head by the professor in a simulation (and participants should not have been exposed to psychic dislocations as in the Milgram study) and thus, at least in political science and other social science use of simulation for prediction, simulation will in all probability remain what it is: a replication of reality without having the essence of reality.

5

Contemporary Challenges to Behaviorialism and the Current State of Political Science

THE PRECEDING DISCUSSION of the American behavioral movement and the behavioral approach to the study of politics related to its status and characteristics from about the end of World War II to approximately the late 1960s and, at present, the behavioral approach is regarded as the dominant conceptual and methodological framework in political science today. There are, of course, numerous people who argue that behavioralism *is not* the dominant conception and there are also those who argue that behavioralism *should not* be the dominant approach. But a fair appraisal would be that the majority of political scientists today adhere to most of the major tenets of behavioralism, the most important of which is probably the more-or-less "scientific" study of politics: the gathering of information and the explanation of political behavior based upon observable, verifiable, and reproducible constructs rather than by divine inspiration, intuition, or other nonobservable constructs (the soul or id).

But the very success and acceptance of behavioralism as the dominant approach, its transformation from being a protest movement into the "Establishment," has brought behavioralism quite close to the fate the Greeks suffered at the hands of the institutional statists and the same fate the statists suffered at the hands of the behavioralists: the approach has been challenged as being unrepresentative of what politics actually is or should be about. This challenge can be seen along three broad fronts: (1) the "post-behavioralists" originate from within behavioralism itself and from those who at one time were the strongest and most vocal supporters of behavioralism but who are now becoming increasingly disenchanted with the approach; (2) the caucus for a new political science originated (it is no longer in existence as an organized group) from a varied group, both from within and outside behavioralism, who believed that the behavioral approach was only a device to avoid politics; and (3) the resistance from the political philosophers and institutional statists (this last challenge is not new—it is only gaining greater credence and more adherents). The three challenges were and are distinct and quite unfriendly to each other and it will be sufficient to give only one example of this unfriendliness. Professor Leo Strauss, until his death a leading exponent of the philosophical approach, comments:

> The crisis of liberal democracy has been concealed by a ritual which calls itself methodology or logic. This almost willful blindness to the crisis of liberal democracy is a part of that crisis. . . . Only a fool would call the new political science [behavioralism] diabolic: it has no attributes peculiar to fallen angels. It is not even Machiavellian, for Machiavelli's teaching was graceful, subtle, and colorful. Nor is it Neronian. Nevertheless, one may say of it that it fiddles while Rome burns. It is excused by two facts: it does not know that it fiddles and it does not know that Rome burns.[1]

But all three views—the philosophical/institutional, the new caucus, and the postbehavioralist—shared a common characteristic: all believed that the behavioral approach was sterile, amoral if not immoral, and irrelevant. All three are asking the same questions of behavioralism: what kind of knowledge? knowledge for what ends? A brief discussion of these challenges to behavioralism are presented below.

Postbehavioralism/Postpositivist Political Science

It is the same David Easton who helped to demolish the nineteenth-century institutional/statist approach with his espousal of behavioralism who is now seen to be the chief exbehavioral critic of behavioralism. Easton's description and defense of "postbehavioralism" was first aired in his presidential address to the 1969 meeting of the American Political Science Association[2] and the discussion of this challenge borrows heavily from Easton's remarks. Easton comments that the basic reason for the growing dissatisfaction with behavioralism is that the whole approach and conception were perceived as nonrelevant, amoral, and void of any human values, feelings, or emotions (what were seen as advantages to the approach in its protest against the traditional view are now seen as severe liabilities). Easton devised a "Credo of Relevance" or "Credo of Postbehavioralism" to describe what political scientists ought now be doing and it is instructive to note that it was Easton himself, only four years earlier, who presented the "Credo of Behavioralism" in his *A Framework for Political Analysis*.

Professor Easton lists the following seven points as the major components of this new "Credo of Postbehavioralism":
1. Substance must precede technique. If one *must* be sacrificed for the other . . . it is more important to be relevant and meaningful for contemporary urgent social problems than to be sophisticated in the tools of investigation.
2. Behavioral science conceals an ideology of empirical conservatism. To confine oneself exclusively to the description and analysis of facts is to hamper the understanding of these same facts in their broadest context. . . .
3. The task of postbehavioralism is to break the barriers of silence that behavioral language necessarily has created and to help political science reach out to the real needs of mankind in a time of crisis.
4. Research about and constructive development of values are inextinguishable parts of the study of politics. . . . [We] need to be aware of the value premises on which it stands and the alternatives for which this knowledge could be used.

5. Members of a learned discipline bear the responsibilities of all intellectuals. The intellectuals' historical role has been and must be to protect the humane values of civilization. . . .
6. To know is to bear the responsibility for acting and to act is to engage in reshaping society. The intellectual as scientist bears the special obligation to put his knowledge to work. . . .
7. If the intellectual has the obligation to implement his knowledge, those organizations composed of intellectuals—the professional associations—and the universities themselves, cannot stand apart from the struggles of the day. Politicization of the professions is inescapable as well as desirable.[3]

Easton's complaint against orthodox behavioralism can be summarized very briefly: political science behavioralism was too involved with techniques, too abstract, unconnected with reality, amoral, and nonparticipatory in the actual and real-life "political" crises of contemporary American society. A devastating example of this lack of social conscience among political science and political scientists is offered by Easton: in the ten-year period between 1958 and 1968, *the American Political Science Review* (the "official" and prestigious journal of the American Political Science Association) put out "only three articles on the urban crises; four on racial conflicts; one on poverty; two on civil disobedience; and two on violence in the United States."[4] In other words, out of an approximate total of four hundred scholarly articles published by the *American Political Science Review* in that ten-year period, only twelve dealt with relevant social concerns. It would have been quite difficult for anyone who restricted his reading to the *APSR* to have learned that there was a war in Vietnam. The behavioral political scientist was nonpolitical!

The postbehavioralists want more relevant research (applied science rather than pure science) and, by so doing, a full circle back to the Greeks has almost been drawn: postbehavioralism wants political scientists *as* political scientists, and not just as private individuals, to prescribe and then describe how to attain an improved Polis according to value systems and "humane criteria." But this does not mean a rejection of the

objectives of "science" or the scientific method. The postbehavioralists agree with the behavioralists that reliable knowledge
is gained only through reproducible techniques (both reject reliance upon nonobservable constructs) but the postbehavioralists go one step further. Whereas the behavioralist stops after
the accumulation of knowledge, as a "scientist" he cannot go
further, the postbehavioralist then employs this knowledge to
help solve the crises of society. But Easton believes that present
public policy questions and issues and social problem-solving
should not receive all the attention and emphasis. The academic
discipline as an intellectual endeavor itself has major problems
(concept formation and levels of political analysis) which
should not be abandoned in the name of social problem-solving.
In other words, the postbehavioralist approach conceives social
problem-solving and academic respectability as equally important. The behavioralist, on the other hand, views social problem-
solving as not within his area and concentrates on academic
respectability. The second but short-lived challenge to orthodox
behavioralism—the Caucus for a New Political Science—placed
less emphasis upon this academic respectability and directed
most of its energies to the immediate solution of contemporary
social problems.

The Caucus for a New Political Science

The Caucus for a New Political Science was (it is now
defunct as an organized group) critical of the behavioral outlook and conception for essentially the same reasons that Easton
notes above.[5] The Caucus, however, placed more emphasis upon
the immediate solution of society's problems (most of these
problems would be solved according to the tenets of the political Left) and demanded an increased politicization of the
American Political Science Association. The Association was to
be involved in the actual political questions and controversies
of the day: endorse specific candidates, use Association funds
to support various causes; in other words, involve the Political
Science Association in politics, something the Association had
not done in years. Some specific demands of the Caucus in-

cluded the termination of the Association's Congressional Internship Program (a certain number of political scientists and journalists are selected each year to work with members of Congress) and the immediate end of certain Association officials' links to and cooperation with the CIA. The Caucus opposed these "relevant" activities not because they involved participation in socio-political affairs but, rather, they involved participation with the "wrong" political overtones (cooperation with the CIA meant that the Association acquiesced in the CIA's activities).

The Caucus is no longer in existence as a formal group because the Association's "Establishment" recognized that the Caucus had revelant and serious criticism of both the discipline and the profession. The postbehavioral movement can be seen, at least in part, as a response to head off the Caucus. The Caucus had its period of activity from 1967 to about 1970[6] and Professor Hans Morgenthau, a distinguished political scientist, was the Caucus' nominee for Association president in 1970. Professor Morgenthau did much better than expected in the voting but was soundly beaten by the "Establishment" candidate. The Association then coopted most of the Caucus' demands and the Caucus slowly faded away. Some of the newly created committees of the Association reflect this greater awareness of pressing "political" problems and the necessity of the Association of being involved in relevant activities. A partial list of these committees (most included members of the Caucus) is: Constitutional Revision, Status of Blacks in the Political Science Profession, Journals, Status of Women in the Political Science Profession, Political Science in the Secondary Schools, Professional Ethics, and Undergraduate Instruction.

The Association, partly as a response to pressures from the Caucus and partly as a response to its own changing conceptions, is no longer as "apolitical" as it once was. The Caucus for a New Political Science was primarily an organized dissident group within the Association attempting to wrest control of the Association offices from the establishment. This failed and the Caucus slipped back into silent grumbling. But the Caucus also had substantial influence upon the discipline as well as upon the profession. The political science profession today is actually engaged in politics and not engaged just in the teaching of politics.

Political Philosophy/Institutional Statists

This challenge to behavioralism is not actually a challenge —it is the continuing resistance and opposition to the movement voiced from the very beginnings of the behavioral movement. The content and nature of this approach, but not its methods, have been vindicated for now its insistence upon what ought to be is being repeated by both the postbehavioralists and by the Caucus. One of the more outspoken, both in terms of opposition to other conceptions and in defense of philosophical political science, is Ellis Sandoz and the following discussion is essentially Sandoz' interpretation of the state of political science.[7]

Sandoz writes that American political science is in a position of flux and turbulence and all the challenges to the reigning orthodoxy of behavioralism are united in the demand for "relevance" and "social awareness." The communality of the challenges is pointed out by Sandoz and then he remarks that philosophical political science anticipated the Caucus' demands by more than thirty years:

> There is also to be noticed a substantial affinity between the efforts in the 1930's [the original resistance to behavioralism] and thereafter by those who have since sought the revival of a philosophical political science and the more recent men of the Left who clamor for relevance. . . . Both exoduses from received doctrine originated in an awareness of inadequacy gained under pressure of pragmatic crises in the social and political order: the former through the crisis of European and world politics of the Nazi period, the latter through urban turmoil, collapse of the universities and, more distantly, the contemporary threats of extinction by nuclear holocaust, surging demographic pressures, and a toxic environment.[8]

The philosophical science of politics approach rejects the distinction between facts and values, objective-subjective, and also rejects the behavioralist (all shades of behavioralism) and Caucus contention that philosophical political science downgrades "practical knowledge." But philosophical political science agrees with both Easton and the Caucus that something must be done to counteract the sterility of behavioralism. It is in this "what is to be done" and "how to do it" that the irreconcilable differences among the challenges are most apparent. Sandoz writes that common sense must be restored to political science as well as "knowledge" of what is "political reality." Whereas the New Left, as Sandoz calls it, would terminate the profession's ties with the Establishment (e.g., Congress and the Central Intelligence Agency), this philosophical approach would reject the methodology of the natural sciences and return to pure philosophy—the good life is determined not by partisan ideologies but by "wisdom"—and this wisdom can only be attained through philosophy. Sandoz comments:

> The most comprehensive knowledge of political activity is attained primarily through a *philosophical* investigation, not through one narrowly modeled on the supposed methodology of the natural sciences. This means that in contradistinction to the prevailing paradigm of American political science, there need be no preoccupation with phenomena, no naturalistic reduction, no restriction of "reason" to inferential reasoning, no juxtaposing of "traditional" and "behavioral" schools, no dogmatic postulation of assumptions of doctrine, no specious fact-value dichotomy, and no systems of political thought. . . .
>
> It is not man the animal . . . but man the political living being in the fullness of his *humanity* that science seeks to know and to assist toward a well-ordered and happy existence. No arbitrarily exclusive consideration of merely phenomenal reality can attain these objectives; and it is to philosophy that political science must ineluctably turn if it is to suffice as "relevant" to human needs.[9]

It should be immediately apparent that a half-circle has been drawn with political science. The original Greek view and conception, philosophical inquiry into wisdom with prescriptions on how to achieve the goal, was at first extensively revised by the nineteenth-century view and then totally ignored by the behavioralists. But this conception has re-entered political science: Sandoz and Strauss would say through the front door, Easton (and the Caucus) would say through the back door. But it is only a half-circle for the *methods* of philosophical political science are still regarded as being unproductive of verifiable knowledge. This short but turbulent period of behavioral political science is rapidly giving way—as did previous views, although only after much longer lives—to a different conceptual framework. Once again, this serves to illustrate the point offered above: politics and political science are concerned with people and their behavior and if the descriptions and conceptions of politics are hazy and vague, it is because we ourselves are non-rigorous, unpredictable, and impossible to categorize and compartmentalize as if we were inanimate objects.

Notes

CHAPTER 1—

1. Sir Ernest Barker, *The Political Thought of Plato and Aristotle* (New York: Dover, 1959), p. 1; Andrew Hacker, *Political Theory: Philosophy, Ideology, Science* (New York: MacMillan, 1961), p. 23.
2. Several readers may have had the extreme misfortune of seeing the film *One Million Years B.C.*, starring Racquel Welch. This film is a dramatization of what life could have been like in the caveperson society: no dialogue—the people only grunted and gestured at one another; people were eating the animals and vice versa; volcanoes erupted and the rains came; it was totally lacking as a form of art and even Ms. Welch couldn't save the plot. But as a commentary to the question at hand, *One Million Years B.C.* is very relevant. The cavepeople society generated leaders, had organizational structures, and decisions were made which affected the entire population. Ms. Welch and her friends certainly did engage in political behavior!
3. A most prestigious and distinguished scholar, H. G. Creel, has presented ample evidence that the ancient Chinese civilization predates that of Plato and Aristotle and that politics certainly did receive attention. Creel describes the Chou dynasty, founded in 1122 B.C., as a fully functioning political system. Even the

sage Confucius,, born in 551 B.C., predates the classical Greeks of Professors Barker and Hacker. See H. G. Creel, *Chinese Thought From Confucius to Mao Tse-tung* (New York: New American Library [a Mentor Book], 1953), especially Chapters 1, 2, and 3 (pp. 9-44).

4. A brief and concise description of Greek political institutions during this period can be found in Edward McNall Burns, *Western Civilizations,* 7th edition, Volume 1 (New York: W. W. Norton, 1969), especially Chapters 7 and 8, pp. 141-205. Short biographies of Plato and Aristotle can be found in Donald Kagan, *The Great Dialogue: History of Greek Political Thought from Homer to Polybius* (New York: Free Press, 1965), pp. 155ff. and 195ff.

5. Most of our contemporary terms of classifying political leadership organization is derived from the Greek: democracy is rule by the people, from the Greek *demos* (people); monarchy is rule by one from *mono* (one); oligarchy is rule by a few from *oli* (few); aristocracy is rule by a small select superior class from *aristo* (best); even the word *politics* is from the Greek *polis*.

6. Plato, cited in Kagan, *The Great Dialogue,* p. 157.

7. Herbert J. Spiro, *Politics as the Master Science: From Plato to Mao* (New York: Harper and Row, 1970), p. 3. Emphasis supplied.

8. For a concise edition of Plato's *Republic,* see the latest printing of *The Republic of Plato,* translated with an introduction and notes by Francis MacDonald Cornford (New York: Oxford University Press), especially Books V-VII, "The Philosopher-King."

9. It is unfortunate that the Platonic scholars refuse to address themselves to this quite relevant question. Spiro, *Politics as the Master Science* (p. 8), writes: "There is a book [T. L. Thomson, ed., *Plato: Totalitarian or Democratic?* (Englewood Cliffs, N.J.: Prentice-Hall, 1963)] in which some distinguished scholars have discussed whether Plato was a totalitarian or a democrat. This is a senseless question. . . . It is . . . a waste of time, except possibly for propaganda purposes, to ask whether Plato favored or contributed to the development of totalitarianism. . . ."

10. The discussion of Aristotle is based upon Sir Ernest Barker's *Political Thought of Plato and Aristotle,* pp. 237-292.

11. There are several editions of *The Prince.* One concise edition is edited and translated by Thomas G. Bergin in the Crofts Classic Series (New York: Appleton-Century-Crofts, 1947). D. Mackenzie Brown in *The White Umbrella: Indian Political Thought*

from Manu to Gandhi (Berkeley and Los Angeles: University of California Press, 1964), pp. 49-63 presents a discussion of Kautilya and his writings.

12. Bernard Crick, *The American Science of Politics: Its Origins and Conditions* (Berkeley and Los Angeles: University of California Press, 1960), p. 12.

13. Raymond G. Gettell, *Political Science,* revised edition (Boston: Ginn, 1949), preface.

14. Westel W. Willoughby, *The Fundamental Concepts of Public Law* (New York: MacMillan, 1924), p. 3.

15. Steven Leacock, *Elements of Political Science,* new and enlarged edition (Boston: Houghton-Mifflin, 1921), pp. 11-12.

16. Ibid., p. 13.

17. Gettel, *Political Science,* p. 21.

18. This is similar to the Italian Classicist Dante's writings with his three categories of places to go after death: Heaven—Purgatory—Hell. Dante had a real theological problem on where to put all those good souls who existed before Christ. Since Heaven was reserved for those who accepted Christ and since these people did not accept Christ (they were dead long before the coming of Christ), they could not be put into Heaven. But Dante could not put them in Hell, for these people were upright moral beings such as Plato and Aristotle. Dante thus created a special niche for these people between Heaven and Hell— the limbo called Purgatory. This insistence upon territory is similar to Dante's classification. All these nomadic and territory-less groups, even with authority, rule, leaders, and organization, just did not permanently reside in a fixed territory and thus whatever they did—and they did quite a lot!—was not "political" but something else. All these good people had to await the Coming of the State before they could be eligible for political behavior and thus be worthy of a political scientist's interest just as all the other good people had to await the Coming of Christ before they could be eligible to reside in Heaven.

19. Leacock, *Elements of Political Science,* p. 14.

20. David B. Truman, "Disillusion and Regeneration: The Quest for a Discipline," *American Political Science Review* 59, No. 4 (December 1965), p. 866.

21. Roy C. Macridis, "A Survey of the Field of Comparative Government," in Harry Eckstein and David E. Apter, eds., *Comparative Politics: A Reader* (New York: Free Press, 1963), pp. 47-48.

22. Alexander Passerin d'Entrèves, *The Notion of the State: An*

Introduction to Political Theory (Oxford: Clarendon Press, 1967).

23. David Easton, *A Framework for Political Analysis* (Englewood Cliffs, N.J.: Prentice-Hall, 1965), pp. 47-56.

24. The ramifications to this point are endless. Very few people would argue as does Harold Lasswell that all power relationships are political and thus worthy of study by the political scientist. But if the attitudes of the actors and the goals of the activity are also taken into account, then a seemingly non-political activity immediately becomes an activity that most people would call political: person (A) robs a bank and donates the proceeds to his favorite political party; person (B) hijacks a plane and demands the release of certain prisoners; person (C) mugs me on the street, steals my voter identification card, and then masquerades as me in order to vote. These examples may very well be "political" although they may not appear as such at first glance.

25. Hans J. Morgenthau, *Politics Among Nations: The Struggle for Power and Peace,* 4th edition (New York: Alfred A. Knopf, 1967), p. 26.

26. Karl W. Deutsch, *Politics and Government: How People Decide Their Fate* (Boston: Houghton-Mifflin, 1970), p. 24.

27. Maurice Duverger, *The Study of Politics,* translated by Robert Wagoner (New York: Thomas Y. Crowell Co., 1972), p. 16.

28. Harold D. Lasswell and Abraham Kaplan, *Power and Society* (New Haven: Yale University Press, 1950), pp. 75, 76.

29. L. S. Shapley and Martin Shubik, "A Method of Evaluating the Distribution of Power in a Committee System," *American Political Science Review* 48, No. 3 (September 1954), p. 787.

30. Robert Dahl, "The Concept of Power," *Behavioral Science* 2, No. 3 (July 1957), pp. 202-203.

31. Max Weber, *The Theory of Social and Economic Organization,* excerpts reprinted in *Power and Societies,* ed. by Marvin E. Olsen (New York: Macmillan, 1970), p. 36.

32. Ibid.

33. Eric Ambler, the master espionage novelist, has written on this very aspect in his *The Intercom Conspiracy* (New York: Bantam Books, 1969): let the other side see some of the cards you are holding through quasi-official leaks of information. Ambler complicates the story, however, by having the conduit mercilessly manipulated by both sides.

CHAPTER 2—

1. See the edition of *Leviathan* in the Library of Liberal Arts Series, edited with an introduction by Herbert Schneider (Indianapolis: Bobbs-Merrill, 1958).

2. There is a painting in the Louvre Museum in Paris by David titled "Studies for the Coronation of Napoleon." This painting has Napoleon seizing the emperor's crown from the pope and placing it upon his own head. Napoleon did not let the pope exercise authority on behalf of God. But "Studies" was not the official public painting of the coronation for Napoleon did not want to publicly display his lack of protocol. The "official" painting of the event, also by David, is "The Coronation of Napoleon" and this is also in the Louvre. "The Coronation" has Napoleon already crowned. See Walter Friedlaender, *David to Delacroix,* translated by Robert Goldwater (Cambridge: Harvard University Press, 1964), pp. 29-30.

3. See John Nance, *The Gentle Tasaday: A Stone Age People in the Philippine Rain Forest* (New York: Harcourt Brace Jovanovich, 1975). John Nance was for some time the Associated Press bureau chief in Manila and made several expeditions into the Tasadays' rain forest to gather first-hand information about the Tasadays.

4. This description implies that the Tasadays do not engage in politics if a strict adherence to the view of "politics as a power relationship" is followed. There seems to be no power or influence within the Tasaday society.

5. Colin M. Turnbull, *The Mountain People* (New York: Simon and Schuster, 1972).

6. Ibid., pp. 112, 136.

7. One should always make the distinction between "natural laws" and "laws of nature." Laws of nature are nonethical and only describe certain recurring physical phenomena in the real world, e.g., the earth spins, water freezes, objects fall at a certain speed. These "laws" are laws of nature and any comments as to their legality (it is illegal to have night follow day) or to their ethical goodness (it is morally evil that light travels at 186,000 miles/second) are totally inane and useless.

8. The Nuremberg Trials held in Germany at the close of World War II are an excellent example of this antagonism between man-made positive law and the assumed existence of a higher

natural law. A number of high-ranking German military personnel, civil servants, and politicians were tried by the Allied Powers (the United States, France, Great Britain, and the Soviet Union) for "war crimes" and for "crimes against humanity." The Germans employed the defense that they were only acting under the legal (man-made) laws of Germany and that they themselves would have been punished if they did not obey the positive law. This defense was not accepted by the Allied Powers for those sitting in judgment ruled that the defendants should have known that their acts were in violation of natural law and thus should have resisted positive law. The movie *Judgment at Nuremberg,* starring Spencer Tracy and Burt Lancaster, treats this very aspect.

9. This discussion of Hobbes as an authoritarian borrows heavily from William Ebenstein, *Great Political Thinkers: Plato to the Present,* 4th edition (New York: Holt, Rinehart and Winston, Inc., 1969), pp. 368-371.

10. The fascist glorification of war and violence undoubtedly stems from their social Darwinist conception of human existence. Social Darwinists accept Charles Darwin's biological findings—evolution of the species from simple to complex, life is a struggle of survival and the weak die out and the strong survive—and attempt to apply these findings to social situations. The view holds that man and the various races are in a constant struggle for existence and the only way the strong can survive, and prove thereby that they are strong, is to eliminate the weak. Hitler's *Mein Kampf* is illustrative of this but the classic statement can be found in Friedrich von Berhardi, *Germany and the Next War* (London: Edward Arnold Publishers, Ltd., 1914).

11. Zhores and Roy Medvedev, *A Question of Madness,* translated by Ellen de Kadt (New York: Alfred A. Knopf, 1971).

12. *Leviathan,* Schneider edition, p. 179.

13. See the edition of Locke's *Two Treatises of Government* edited by Peter Laslett (New York: New American Library, 1963).

14. Cited in Laslett, p. 311.

15. It is interesting to note that Jefferson substituted the "pursuit of happiness" for Locke's "property." Jefferson probably did not believe that the right to private property (e.g., a capitalist economic system) was a component of God's law.

16. Eric Fromm, *Marx's Concept of Man* (New York: Frederick Ungar Publishing Co., 1961), esp. pp. 1-7.

17. Ibid., pp. 4-5. There are those who do not accept this interpretation of Marx as a humanist. See especially Sidney Hook,

"Marx and Alienation," *The New Leader* (December 11, 1961), pp. 15-18; and Lewis Feuer, "What Is Alienation?" *New Politics* 1 (Spring 1962), pp. 116-134.

18. This problem of employing contemporary Soviet and Chinese practices as evidence of Marx's inhumanity and deceit is unfortunately quite prevalent in the West. Some examples of this writing genre can be found in *The Profile of Communism: A Fact-by-Fact Primer,* Moshe Dector, ed. (New York: Collier Books for the B'nai B'rith Anti-Defamation League, 1961) and J. Edgar Hoover (the late director of the F.B.I.), *Masters of Deceit* (New York: Henry Holt, 1958).

19. Two good acounts of Marx can be found in Isaiah Berlin, *Karl Marx: His Life and Environment* (New York: Oxford University Press, 1959, first published in 1939); and Edmund Wilson, *To The Finland Station* (Garden City, N.Y.: Doubleday, 1940).

20. Berlin, *Karl Marx: His Life and Environment,* p. 27.

21. Sidney Hook, *Marx and the Marxists: The Ambiguous Legacy* (Princeton, N.J.: D. Van Nostrand Co., 1955), p. 43.

22. These remarks describe Easton's basic outlook and approach in the 1950s and 1960s. He has since altered his orientation to political science: whereas his systems analysis is the study of what *is,* he is now an outspoken proponent of examining what *should* be. This attitude shift is discussed in greater detail below in Chapter 5.

23. David Easton, *A Framework for Political Analysis* (Englewood Cliffs, N.J.: Prentice-Hall, 1965), p. 50.

24. Ibid.

25. Ibid., p. 120.

26. Easton, "An Approach to the Analysis of Political Systems," *World Politics* 9, No. 3 (April 1967), p. 391.

27. Ibid., p. 392.

28. Cited in the *Cleveland Plain Dealer* (November 7, 1972), p. 1, emphasis supplied.

CHAPTER 3—

1. Don Bowen, *Political Behavior of the American Public* (Columbus, Ohio: Charles E. Merrill Publishing Co., 1968), Chapter 1, "The Origins of the Behavioral Movement," pp. 3-19, esp. pp. 4-7.

2. See Michael Kaplan, ed., *Essential Works of Pavlov* (New York: Bantam Books, 1966).

3. See B. F. Skinner, *The Behavior of Organisms: An Experimental Analysis* (New York: Appleton-Century-Crofts, 1938).

4. Bowen, *Political Behavior of the American Public*, p. 4.

5. Thomas S. Kuhn, *The Structure of Scientific Revolutions* (Chicago: The University of Chicago Press, 1962), contains an excellent discussion of the process whereby one scientific theory or paradigm replaces another paradigm in a society's view of the world.

6. Jacob Bronowski, *The Ascent of Man* (Boston: Little, Brown and Co., 1973) is perhaps the best work available on the history and philosophy of scientific ideas.

7. Nicholas Rescher, *Introduction to Logic* (New York: St. Martin's Press, 1964), p. 13.

8. Bernard Crick, *The American Science of Politics: Its Origins and Conditions* (Berkeley and Los Angeles: University of California Press, 1960).

9. Robert A. Dahl, "The Behavioral Approach in Political Science: Epitaph for a Monument to a Successful Protest," *American Political Science Review* 55, No. 4 (December 1961), pp. 763-772.

10. *Annual Report of the Social Science Research Council for 1944-1945*, cited by Dahl, "The Behavioral Approach," p. 764. Dahl's emphasis in the original has been deleted.

11. Robert Dahl, "The Behavioral Approach," p. 767.

12. Social Science Research Council, *Items* (December 1951), pp. 37-39; cited by Dahl, "The Behavioral Approach," p. 767.

13. J. H. Hexter, *The History Primer* (New York: Basic Books, 1971) and *Doing History* (Bloomington, Ind.: Indiana University Press, 1971).

14. David Easton, *A Framework for Political Analysis,* pp. 6-16, esp. p. 7 for the first eight points of the major characteristics of the behavioral movement.

15. Heinz Eulau, *The Behavioral Persuasion in Politics* (New York: Random House, 1963), p. 133, emphasis supplied.

16. Christian Bay, "Politics and Pseudopolitics," in Charles A. McCoy and John Playford, eds., *Apolitical Politics: A Critique of Behavioralism* (New York: Thomas Y. Crowell, 1967), p. 12.

CHAPTER 4—

1. The basic model is described in Anthony Downs, *An Economic Theory of Democracy* (New York: Harper and Row, 1957),

esp. Chapter 8, "The Statics and Dynamics of Party Ideologies," pp. 114-141.

2. Ibid., p. 6.

3. See Harold Hotelling, "Stability in Competition," *The Economic Journal* 39 (1929), pp. 41-57 and Arthur Smithies, "Optimum Location in Spatial Competition," *The Journal of Political Economy* 49 (1941), pp. 423-439.

4. Theodore C. Sorensen, *Kennedy* (New York: Harper and Row, 1965), pp. 195-206 has a detailed description of the debates. Sorenson comments: ". . . Nixon looked weak. Between the bleak gray walls and the bright floodlights of the television studio, his gray suit and heavily powdered jowls looked flabby and pallid beside Kennedy's dark suit and healthy tan." p. 199.

5. Downs, *An Economic Theory of Democracy,* pp. 114-115.

6. See John von Neumann and Oskar Morgenstein, *Theory of Games and Economic Behavior* (Princeton: Princeton University Press, 1944).

7. See Steven J. Brams, *Game Theory and Politics* (New York: The Free Press, 1975); Anatol Rapoport, *Two-Person Games Theory* and *N-Person Game Theory* (Ann Arbor: University of Michigan Press, 1966 and 1970, respectively); and Martin Shubik, ed., *Game Theory and Related Approaches to Social Behavior* (New York: John Wiley and Sons, 1964). These books contain extensive bibliographies.

8. John R. Raser, *Simulation and Society: An Exploration of Scientific Gaming* (Boston: Allyn and Bacon, 1969), p. x.

9. Martin Shubik, "Game Theory and the Study of Social Behavior: An Introductory Exposition," in Shubik, ed., *Game Theory and Related Approaches to Social Behavior* (New York: John Wiley and Sons, Inc., 1964), pp. 31-32.

10. See Thomas C. Schelling, "Bargaining, Communication, and Limited War," *The Journal of Conflict Resolution* 1, No. 1 (March 1957), pp. 19-36.

11. Ibid., p. 21. Schelling comments that in his sample, 36 of 42 people chose "heads"; 36 of 41 split the $100 in example 3 fifty-fifty. It was with example 2 (choose an amount of money) where coordination broke down: only 12 of 41 coordinated ($1,000,000).

12. Ibid., pp. 23-24. Schelling reports the behavior of his sample: in the first example, 16 out of 22 A's and 15 out of 22 B's chose heads. If each had tried to win $3, the payoff to everybody would have been 0. A "won" more than the disadvantaged

B but the participants coordinated moves in order to maximize winnings. In example 2, 9 out of 12 A's, 10 out of 12 B's, and 14 out of 16 C's coordinate on the order ABC.

13. Ibid., p. 24. Schelling comments that in his sample, the letter R won 5 out of 8 votes from those who had proposed it, and 8 out of 9 votes from those who were on the other side. An interesting variation of this example would be where B has knowledge of A's schedule of prizes but A does not have the equivalent knowledge about B and each knows what the other knows. This is an example where weakness (noninformation) is a source of strength for A: what letter would be offered in order to choose the identical letter? B is almost forced to choose R for B knows that A knows that B knows that R is best for A and B knows that A knows that B knows that A does not know what is best for B.

14. Shubik, "Game Theory and the Study of Social Behavior," pp. 37-38. There are numerous variations to the one presented here. These variations have different participants in different environments but they are all prisoners' dilemmas. For an extensive review of research done on Prisoner's Dilemma, see Anatol Rapoport and Albert M. Chammah, *Prisoner's Dilemma: A Study in Conflict and Cooperation* (Ann Arbor: University of Michigan Press, 1965).

15. This author has performed some Prisoner's Dilemma situations in the classroom, although the scenario had quizzes, cheating, confessions, and failing grades instead of jail terms and "crimes." The students invariably opt for confession.

16. See Anatol Rapoport, *N-Person Game Theory* (Ann Arbor: University of Michigan Press, 1970), pp. 271-283.

17. Much has been written on this confrontation and the book by Elie Abel, *The Missile Crisis* (New York: Bantam Books, 1966) contains a brief description of the day-to-day events. Other books on this confrontation include Graham T. Allison, *The Essence of Decision: Explaining the Cuban Missile Crisis* (Boston: Little, Brown and Co., 1971), Robert F. Kennedy, *Thirteen Days: A Memoir of the Cuban Missile Crisis* (New York: W. W. Norton, 1969), and Henry F. Pachter, *Collision Course: The Cuban Missile Crisis and Coexistence* (New York: Frederick A. Praeger, 1963).

18. A U-2 was shot down over Cuba by a Soviet SAM on October 27 but this appears, in retrospect, to have only been a parting shot at the Americans. The crisis had been defused by then

and on the very next day, October 28, Khrushchev announced that the missiles would be withdrawn from Cuba.

19. The first part of this section borrows heavily from Richard E. Dawson, "Simulation in the Social Sciences," in Harold Guetzkow, ed., *Simulation in Social Science: Readings* (Englewood Cliffs, N.J.: Prentice-Hall, 1962) pp. 1-15 and from John R. Raser, *Simulation and Society: An Exploration of Scientific Gaming* (Boston: Allyn and Bacon, Inc., 1969), esp. Chapter 1, "What and Why Is a Simulation?," pp. 3-19. These books contain extensive bibliographies and those desirous of a more involved discussion of simulation should read Goetzkow and Raser.

20. Stanley Milgram, *Obedience to Authority: An Experimental View* (New York: Harper and Row, 1974). See pp. 3-4 for the basic description of Milgram's experiment.

21. Ibid., p. 4.

22. This entire section is based upon Charles F. and Margaret C. Hermann, "An Attempt to Simulate the Outbreak of World War I," *American Political Science Review* 61, No. 2 (June 1967), pp. 400-416.

23. Ibid., p. 404.

24. Ibid., p. 402. The Hermanns also write that an effort was made to fit the programmed parameters and variables of the simulation to the national profiles of the countries involved. These parameters included (1) Basic Capability Units (human, natural, and industrial resources available); (2) Force Capability Units (the regular peacetime army and navy); (3) Validator Satisfaction (the degree to which a decision-maker's policies are acceptable to the country's elite); and (4) Decision Latitude (the degree to which the decision-maker's tenure in office depends upon validator satisfaction).

25. Ibid., p. 411. The first hypothesis was developed by Dina Zinnes, Robert C. North, and Howard Koch, "Capabilities, Threat and the Outbreak of War," in James A. Rosenau, ed., *International Politics and Foreign Policy* (New York: The Free Press, 1961), p. 470. The second hypothesis was developed by Dina Zinnes, "A Comparison of Hostile Behavior of Decision-Makers in Simulate and Historical Data," *World Politics* 18 (1966), p. 477.

26. The other situations viewed as similar, with the number of students so believing, were: Hitler's Ultimatum to Poland in 1939 (6), Berlin Crisis (6), Hitler's Ultimatum to the Sudeten-

land (6), Israeli-Arab Conflict (6), French-Algerian Conflict (5), Korean War (5), nineteenth-century Colonialism (5), Spanish-American War (4), Pearl Harbor (1), and World War II (1). The total responses are greater than 20 because the students could give multiple answers.

CHAPTER 5—

1. Leo Strauss, cited by Ellis Sandoz, "The Philosophical Science of Politics Beyond Behavioralism," in George J. Graham, Jr. and George W. Carey, eds., *The Post-Behavioral Era: Perspectives on Political Science* (New York: David McKay Company, 1972), p. 289.
2. Reproduced as "The New Revolution in Political Science," *American Political Science Review* 63, No. 4 (December 1969), pp. 1051-1061.
3. Ibid., p. 1052.
4. Ibid., p. 1057.
5. A description of this view, as well as a critique of behavioralism, can be found in Charles A. McCoy and John Playford, eds., *Apolitical Politics: A Critique of Behavioralism* (New York: Thomas Y. Crowell Co., 1967) and the article by Theodore J. Lowi, "The Politics of Higher Education: Political Science as a Case Study," in Graham and Carey, eds., *The Post-Behavioral Era*, pp. 11-36.
6. The 1968 Democratic Convention in Chicago provided the political scientists with an opportunity to practice some real-life social awareness. Initially outraged by the city's behavior during the convention, the American Political Science Association decided to remove Chicago as one of the cities where the Association holds its annual meeting. This outrage did not last very long, however, and political scientists are once again flocking to Chicago.
7. Ellis Sandoz, "The Philosophical Science," pp. 285-305. The problem with Sandoz' article is, however, that it is a nasty polemic against behavioralism, postbehavioralism, the Caucus, *and* the individuals themselves who adhere to these views.
8. Ibid., pp. 289-290.
9. Ibid., p. 296.

Selected Bibliography

Chapter 1 A Brief Historical Overview

Pre-Christian Greek Thought

Aristotle. *The Politics*. Translated and edited by Sir Ernest Barker. New York: Galaxy Books, 1962.

Barker, Sir Ernest. *The Political Thought of Plato and Aristotle*. New York: Dover Publications, Inc., 1959.

Burns, Edward McNall. *Western Civilizations*. Volume I. New York: W. W. Norton and Co., 1969.

Creel, H. G. *Chinese Thought from Confucius to Mao Tse-tung*. New York: The New American Library, 1953.

Hacker, Andrew. *Political Theory: Philosophy, Ideology, Science*. New York: The Macmillan Co., 1961.

Kagan, Donald. *The Great Dialogue: History of Greek Political Thought from Homer to Polybius*. New York: The Free Press, 1965.

Plato. *The Republic (of Plato)*. Translated with an introduction and notes by Francis MacDonald Cornford. New York: Oxford University Press, 1941.

Ritter, Constantin. *The Essence of Plato's Philosophy*. New York: Russell and Russell, 1968.

Spiro, Herbert J. *Politics as the Master Science*. New York: Harper and Row, 1970.

Stern, S. M. *Aristotle on the World State*. Columbia, S.C.; University of South Carolina Press, 1970.

Thomson, T. L., editor. *Plato: Totalitarian or Democrat?* Englewood Cliffs, N.J.: Prentice-Hall, 1963.

Veatch, Henry B. *Aristotle: A Contemporary Appreciation*. Bloomington, Ind.: Indiana University Press, 1974.

The State and Sovereignty

Bryce, James. *The American Commonwealth*. Newly edited, abridged, and introduction by Louis M. Hacker. New York: Putnam's, 1959 (first published in 1888).

Crick, Bernard. *The American Science of Politics: Its Origins and Conditions*. Berkeley and Los Angeles: University of California Press, 1960.

D'Entrèves, Alexander P. *The Notion of the State: An Introduction to Political Theory*. Oxford: Clarendon Press, 1967.

Gettell, Raymond G. *Political Science*. Revised edition. Boston: Ginn and Co., 1949. (First published in 1933.)

Leacock, Steven. *Elements of Political Science*. New and enlarged edition. Boston: Houghton-Mifflin, 1921. (First published in 1906.)

Machiavelli, N. *The Prince*. Edited and translated by Thomas G. Bergin. New York: Appleton-Century-Crofts, 1947. (First published in 1532.)

Macridis, Roy C. "A Survey of the Field of Comparative Government." In Harry Eckstein and David E. Apter, editors, *Comparative Politics: A Reader*. New York: Free Press, 1963, 43-52.

Truman, David B. "Disillusion and Regeneration: The Quest for a Discipline." *American Political Science Review* 59, No. 4 (December 1965), 865-873.

Willoughby, Westel W. *The Fundamental Concepts of Public Law*. New York: Macmillan, 1924.

Wilson, Woodrow. *Congressional Government*. Boston: Houghton-Mifflin, 1885.

Politics as a Power Relationship

Dahl, Robert. "The Concept of Power." *Behavioral Science* 2, No. 3 (July 1957), 201-215.

Deutsch, Karl W. *Politics and Government: How People Decide Their Fate*. Boston: Houghton-Mifflin, 1970.

Duverger, Maurice. *The Study of Politics.* Translated by Robert Wagoner. New York: Thomas Y. Crowell, 1972.

Lasswell, Harold D. and Kaplan, Abraham. *Power and Society.* New Haven: Yale University Press, 1950.

Morgenthau, Hans J. *Politics Among Nations: The Struggle for Power and Peace.* Fourth edition. New York: Alfred A. Knopf, 1967.

Olsen, Marvin E. *Power and Societies.* New York: Macmillan, 1970.

Schelling, Thomas, *Arms and Influence.* New Haven: Yale University Press, 1966.

—————. *The Strategy of Conflict.* New York: Oxford University Press, 1963.

Shapley, L. S. and Shubik, Martin. "A Method for Evaluating the Distribution of Power in a Committee System," *American Political Science Review* 48, No. 3 (September 1954), 787-792.

Chapter 2   Four Representative Conceptions

Thomas Hobbes, John Locke, Jean-Jacques Rousseau

Barker, Sir Ernest, editor. *Social Contract: Essays by Locke, Hume, and Rousseau.* New York: Oxford University Press, 1962.

Costa-Gravas, Costi. *The Confession.* Paramount Pictures, 1970.

Ebenstein, William. *Great Political Thinkers: Plato to the Present.* Fourth edition. New York: Holt, Rinehart and Winston, 1969.

Goldsmith, M. M. *Hobbes' Science of Politics.* New York: Columbia University Press, 1966.

Grimsley, Ronald. *The Philosophy of Rousseau.* New York: Oxford University Press, 1973.

Hobbes, Thomas. *Leviathan.* Edited with an introduction by Herbert Schneider. Indianapolis: Bobbs-Merrill, Inc., 1958. (First published in 1651.)

Locke, John. *Two Treatises of Government.* Edited by Peter Laslett. New York: New American Library, 1963. (First published in 1690.)

Masters, Roger D. *The Political Philosophy of Rousseau.* Princeton: Princeton University Press, 1968.

Medvedev, Zhores A. and Medvedev, Roy A. *A Question of Madness.* Translated by Ellen de Kadt. New York: Alfred A. Knopf, 1971.

Nance, John. *The Gentle Tasaday: A Stone Age People in the Philippine Rain Forest.* New York: Harcourt Brace Jovanovich, 1975.

Rousseau, Jean-Jacques. *The Social Contract.* Translated with an introduction by Willmoore Kendall. Chicago: Regnery, 1954. (First published in 1762.)

Turnbull, Colin M. *The Mountain People.* New York: Simon and Schuster, 1972.

Vaughan, C. E., editor. *The Political Writings of Jean-Jacques Rousseau.* Volumes I and II. New York: John Wiley and Sons, 1962.

Karl Marx

Berlin, Isaiah. *Karl Marx: His Life and Environment.* New York: Oxford University Press, 1959.

Feuer, Lewis S., editor. *Marx and Engels: Basic Writings on Politics and Philosophy.* Garden City, N.Y.: Doubleday, 1959.

Fromm, Eric. *Marx's Concept of Man.* New York: Frederick Ungar Publishing Co., 1961.

Marx, Karl. *Economic and Philosophic Manuscripts of 1844.* Edited with an introduction by Dirk J. Stvik. Translated by Martin Milligan. New York: International Publishers, 1964.

_____. *On Society and Social Change.* With selections by Friedrich Engels. Edited with an introduction by Neil J. Smelser. Chicago: University of Chicago Press, 1973.

_____ and Engels, Friedrich. *The Communist Manifesto.* Authorized English translation by Samuel Moore. Edited and annotated by Friedrich Engels. New York: Labor News Co., 1959. (First published in 1848.)

Shonfield, Andrew. *Modern Capitalism: The Changing Balance of Public and Private Power.* New York: Oxford University Press, 1965.

Tucker, Robert C., editor. *The Marx-Engels Reader.* New York: W. W. Norton, 1972.

Wilson, Edmund. *To the Finland Station.* Garden City, N.Y.: Doubleday, 1940.

David Easton

Easton, David. *The Political System: An Inquiry into the State of Political Science. New York:* Alfred A. Knopf, 1953.

_____. "An Approach to the Analysis of Political Systems," *World Politics* 9 (April 1957), 383-400.

_____. *A Framework for Political Analysis,* Englewood Cliffs, N.J.: Prentice-Hall, 1965.

_____. *A Systems Analysis of Political Life*. New York: John Wiley and Sons, 1965.

_____. *Varieties of Political Theory*. Englewood Cliffs, N.J.: Prentice-Hall, 1966.

_____ and Dennis, Jack. *Children in the Political System: Origins of Political Legitimacy*. New York: McGraw-Hill, 1969.

Chapter 3 The American Behavioral Movement

Bay, Christian. "Politics and Pseudopolitics." In Charles A. McCoy and John Playford, eds., *Apolitical Politics: A Critique of Behavioralism*. New York: Thomas Y. Crowell, 1967, pp. 12-37.

Bowen, Don. *Political Behavior of the American Public*. Columbus, Ohio: Charles E. Merrill, 1968.

Bronowski, Jacob. *The Ascent of Man*. Boston: Little, Brown and Co., 1973.

Crick, Bernard. *The American Science of Politics: Its Origins and Conditions*. Berkeley and Los Angeles: University of California Press, 1960.

Dahl, Robert. "The Behavioral Approach in Political Science: Epitaph for a Monument to a Successful Protest." *American Political Science Review* 55, No. 4 (December 1961), 763-772.

Easton, David. *A Framework for Political Analysis*. Englewood Cliffs, N.J.: Prentice-Hall, 1965.

Eulau, Heinz. *The Behavioral Persuasion in Politics*. New York: Random House, 1963.

Hexter, J. H. *Doing History*. Bloomington, Ind.: Indiana University Press, 1971.

_____. *The History Primer*. New York: Basic Books, 1971.

Kaplan, Michael, editor. *Essential Works of Pavlov*. New York: Bantam Books, 1966.

Kuhn, Thomas S. *The Structure of Scientific Revolutions*. Chicago: University of Chicago Press, 1962.

Rescher, Nicolas. *Introduction to Logic*. New York: St. Martin's Press, 1964.

Skinner, B. F. *The Behavior of Organisms: An Experimental Analysis*. New York: Appleton-Century-Crofts, 1938.

Chapter 4 Three Examples of Unity

Anthony Downs and Economics

Downs, Anthony. *An Economic Theory of Democracy*. New York: Harper and Row, 1957.

Hotelling, Harold. "Stability in Competition." *The Economic Journal* 39 (1929), 41-57.

Smithies, Arthur. "Optimum Location in Spatial Competition." *Journal of Political Economy* 49 (1941), 423-439.

Game Theory and the Cuban Missile Crisis

Abel, Elie. *The Missile Crisis.* New York: Bantam Books, 1966.

Allison, Graham T. *The Essence of Decision: Explaining the Cuban Missile Crisis.* Boston: Little, Brown and Co., 1971.

Brams, Steven J. *Game Theory and Politics.* New York: Free Press, 1975.

Davis, Morton D. *Game Theory: A Nontechnical Introduction.* New York: Basic Books, 1970.

Kennedy, Robert F. *Thirteen Days: A Memoir of the Cuban Missile Crisis.* New York: W. W. Norton, 1969.

Neumann, John von and Morgenstein, Oskar. *Theory of Games and Economic Behavior.* Princeton: Princeton University Press, 1944.

Pachter, Henry F. *Collision Course: The Cuban Missile Crisis and Coexistence.* New York: Frederick A. Praeger, 1963.

Rapoport, Anatol. *Fights, Games and Debates.* Ann Arbor, Mich.: University of Michigan Press, 1960.

————, editor. *Game Theory as a Theory of Conflict Resolution.* Dordrecht, Holland: D. Riedel Publishing Co., 1974.

————. *N-Person Game Theory: Concepts and Applications.* Ann Arbor, Mich.; University of Michigan Press, 1970.

————. *Two-Person Game Theory: The Essential Ideas.* Ann Arbor, Mich.: University of Michigan Press, 1966.

———— and Chammah, Albert M. *Prisoner's Dilemma: A Study in Conflict and Cooperation.* Ann Arbor, Mich.: University of Michigan Press, 1965.

Schelling, Thomas C. "Bargaining, Communication, and Limited War." *The Journal of Conflict Resolution* 1, No. 1 (March 1957), 19-36.

Shubik, Martin. "Game Theory and the Study of Social Behavior: An Introductory Exposition." In Martin Shubik, ed., *Game Theory and Related Approaches to Social Behavior.* New York: John Wiley and Sons, 1964, 3-77.

Simulation and World War I

Dawson, Richard E. "Simulation in the Social Sciences." In Harold Guetzkow, ed., *Simulation in Social Science: Readings*. Englewood Cliffs, N.J.: Prentice-Hall, 1962, 1-15.

Hermann, Charles F. and Hermann, Margaret C. "An Attempt to Simulate the Outbreak of World War I." *American Political Science Review* 61, No. 2 (June 1967), 400-416.

Milgram, Stanley. *Obedience to Authority: An Experimental View*. New York: Harper and Row, 1974.

Raser, John R. *Simulation and Society: An Exploration of Scientific Gaming*. Boston: Allyn and Bacon, 1969.

Chapter 5   Contemporary Challenges to Behavioralism

Easton, David. "The New Revolution in Political Science." *American Political Science Review* 62, No. 4 (December 1969), 1051-1061.

McCoy, Charles A. and Playford, John, editors. *Apolitical Politics: A Critique of Behavioralism*. New York: Thomas Y. Crowell Co., 1967.

Sandoz, Ellis. "The Philosophical Science of Politics Beyond Behavioralism." In George J. Graham, Jr. and George W. Carey, eds., *The Post-Behavioral Era: Perspectives on Political Science*. New York: David McKay Co., 1972, 285-305.

Index